This book is Dedicated to:

My Beloved Parents, With Love and Respect

Hansa (Mother), Mahendra (Father)

Catching Fish, while Riding on Tiger

The New Age Technology that makes Intraday Stock Trading so SIMPLE!

CA (Dr) Nikhil Zaveri

notionpress.com

INDIA • SINGAPORE • MALAYSIA

ISBN
Hardcase 979-8-89610-363-9
Paperback 979-8-89556-390-8

Contents

Preface

When the world shut down in 2020, life as we knew it came to a halt. Our days became a blur of sitting on sofas, pacing through our homes, and endlessly scrolling through our phones. The hustle of jobs and small businesses was replaced by a deafening silence. Yet, amidst the chaos, one group quietly thrived—small retail stock traders. The stock market was the lone beacon of normalcy, and those who had honed their trading skills over the years found themselves in a unique position to not just survive, but to prosper.

This stark contrast made me reflect deeply. After spending 30 years in education, I began to question the very foundation of our knowledge-driven system. Diplomas, degrees, and prestigious qualifications felt inadequate in a time when human existence, especially economic survival, was at stake. Who were the real earners during this crisis? Not those with flashy degrees, but those with practical skills—skills sharpened by experience and empowered by technology. Meanwhile, I was in my thoughts of doing something in this realm of stock trading world, there came my nephew Shobhan Marfatia, a Mumbai-based broker, who encouraged me to experiment with the technology in stock trading. He created immense interest in me for embracing the new technology in stock trading which furthered my interest turning into a passion.

This exposure and realization birthed a new mantra for me: "More Skills, Less Knowledge." I recognized that the post-COVID world would be even more challenging, with emerging demands that traditional education systems would be slow to meet. The future of our young students weighed heavily on my mind. Despite their talents and education, many bright young women, especially, find themselves sidelined after marriage, unable to fully contribute due to family obligations. But I've always known the immense potential within these young minds—their capacity to learn anything they set their hearts on.

And so, I found my inspiration in them—to introduce stock trading as a new skill, one that could empower young students and homemakers alike. This skill has the power to transform lives, offering a path to financial independence and self-worth in uncertain times.

Since 2020, I embarked on a journey to organize my thoughts and ideas for writing this book. While I was acquainted with few expert professionals in the field, I chose not to limit myself to their knowledge. Instead, I aimed to showcase a diverse range of skills practiced by traders of all experience levels—from novices to seasoned veterans.

Years ago, I had the chance to teach stock market courses, yet the element of "Technology in Stock Trading" was missing. This realization led me on an extraordinary adventure, delving into the world of trading technology, learning its applications, and connecting with traders who generously shared their experiences across various platforms. It was particularly inspiring to discover a few traders from India, like Dr. Vinay Prakash Tiwary from Varanasi, who were contributing their research through innovative tools like the LTP Calculator. Many young, Hindi-speaking traders were also sharing their experiences to help others, proving that a lack of English proficiency is not a barrier to mastering stock trading—technology itself becomes the universal language. This realization gave me the confidence that anyone, with dedication and practice, can acquire this skill.

As I dug deeper into my exploration, I discovered different philosophies in trading. Initially, I was introduced to the widely accepted notion that "Price is God," a belief held by all most all traders. However, my exploration revealed other profound dimensions. I found that "Data is God," as the data-driven approach, especially through Order Flow Analysis, is gaining prominence among traders who rely solely on data. I went even further and, to my surprise, uncovered that "Time is God"—a time-driven approach known as "financial astrology" is drawing attention for its remarkable accuracy.

With a clear framework in mind, I began writing this book in 2022 while on an extended holiday in the UK with my daughter's family. A simple, yet profound moment occurred when I introduced my four-year-young granddaughter, Aurora, to a candlestick chart. I taught her the fundamental concept: "Blue Candle - Buy" and "Red Candle - Sell." Just like learning to drive a car starts with understanding the brake and accelerator, mastering stock trading begins with these basics. To my delight, Aurora grasped the idea quickly and would excitedly say, "*Nana-papa* (Grand Pa), Blue candle – Buy, Red candle – Sell" whenever she saw a chart on my computer. Her enthusiasm became my first source of inspiration to continue writing this book.

I spent countless hours back-testing strategies and trade setups advocated by various traders. Through rigorous experimental research in live markets and drawing from my own experiences, I have compiled twelve trade setups that can be easily learned by anyone eager to acquire new skills. I found trading to be as straightforward as learning to drive a car—mastery comes with consistent practice.

During my experimental research, I found myself torn between two powerful emotions. On one side, there was the gut-wrenching anxiety of navigating a fiercely unpredictable market. It felt like I was riding a Tiger—an untamed, formidable force that was constantly on the move. Every volatile leap of the market mirrored the Tiger's wild erratic movements, forcing me to cling on for dear life, adjusting to its every twist and turn.

Yet, amid the chaos, there was an exhilarating joy in seizing profits. Each trade felt like the thrill of catching a prized fish—a moment of pure triumph pulled from the jaws of uncertainty. But the true challenge lay not just in making the catch, but in doing so while managing the Tiger's wild, unpredictable nature.

The secret to thriving in this duality was discipline—trading with strict rules and a sharp risk-reward system that allowed me to limit losses with expected reasonable profits. This is the essence of my journey: the art of enjoying the hunt while mastering the beast. And so, I titled my book, *Catching Fish, while Riding on Tiger.*

The book is designed to offer readers valuable insights into stock trading, focusing on the importance of practical skills over theoretical knowledge. Through the author's personal experiences during the challenging times of the COVID-19 pandemic, the book highlights the limitations of traditional education and the critical role of skill development, especially in unpredictable environments like the stock market.

Key Benefits for the Reader:

- **Practical Skill Development**: The book emphasizes the need for hands-on experience and practical skills in stock trading, rather than relying solely on academic qualifications. Readers will learn that success in trading is about mastering specific techniques, such as reading candlestick charts, and understanding market dynamics.
- **Adapting to Market Volatility**: The book uses the metaphor of "riding the Tiger" to illustrate the unpredictable nature of the stock market. Readers will gain strategies for managing risks and navigating the volatility of the market with confidence, ensuring that they can protect their investments while capitalizing on opportunities.
- **Psychological Insight**: Trading is as much about mindset as it is about technical knowledge. The book delves into the emotional aspects of trading, teaching readers how to handle the anxiety of market unpredictability while maintaining the discipline to follow a structured trading plan.
- **Comprehensive Learning**: By drawing from the experiences of various traders, the book offers a broad spectrum of trading strategies to beginners. Moreover, this approach ensures that readers at any stage of their trading journey can find value and improve their skills.
- **Inspiration and Empowerment**: The book is also a source of inspiration, particularly for those who feel stuck in their careers or are looking for new ways to contribute to their families. It encourages readers to take control of their financial futures by learning a skill that can be practiced from anywhere, at any time.

What Readers Can Expect to Gain:

- **A solid foundation in stock trading**: Starting with the basics like understanding candlestick charts, the book gradually builds up to more practicable and profitable strategies.
- **Confidence in navigating the stock market**: Readers will learn how to approach trading with a structured plan, reducing the risk of emotional decision-making. They will learn new technology that is simple, and useful.
- **The ability to generate income independently**: Whether it's as a full-time trader or a side hustle, the skills taught in this book can help readers earn money in any economic condition.
- **A new perspective on education and skill acquisition**: The book challenges the traditional notion of education, advocating for skill-based learning that is directly applicable to real-world scenarios.

The book is more than just a guide to stock trading; it is a roadmap for personal and financial empowerment in an uncertain world with a focus on "More Skills, Less Knowledge".

Readers will gain confidence in navigating the stock market, learning how to balance risk with reward, and applying disciplined strategies to achieve consistent success. They will also develop a resilient trading mindset, equipped to handle the emotional challenges that come with market volatility.

The journey through this book is not just about learning to trade; it's about understanding the deeper psychological aspects that drive successful trading. It empowers readers to harness both the technical and mental tools necessary to thrive in the world of stock trading, particularly in the unpredictable post-pandemic landscape.

At this precious moment, my heart swells with gratitude for my wife, Rajani, who has been the quiet force behind my journey, gracefully shouldering the mundane burdens of life so I could focus on my passion. Her unwavering support made this dream a reality.

To the wonderful couple, Sheel and Zankhna Dholakia, my deepest thanks. Zankhna, despite being new to this field, embraced my research with enthusiasm, exploring and experimenting trading strategies with me at her cost. Her feedback was a beacon of encouragement. Sheel, your constant reminders were not just nudges but affirmations that I was on the right path, filling me with confidence and joy. I am deeply grateful to my nephew, Parag Gandhi, an esteemed senior lawyer, who never failed to ask during each of our conversations, "*Mama* (uncle), how far along are you?" That has been a constant source of encouragement, keeping me focused and motivated to complete my book. I am grateful to Dr Suryanarayan Iyer, one of my favourite past students for his various suggestions from time to time for making the book more relevant and useful.

My daughter Radhika, all the way from the UK, your persistent "Where have you reached, Dad? Hurry up!" was the vigilant watch I needed to keep me on track. To my dear friends who have eagerly awaited this book, your interest has been a source of immense motivation. The pivotal moment in my journey of writing this book was when I discovered the TradingView platform. This incredible charting and analysis technology became more than just a tool; it was my companion in navigating the complex world of live markets. TradingView graciously provided me with complimentary access to their premium features, enabling me to explore countless tools and indicators, each one revealing new insights and deepening my understanding. I am deeply grateful to Mr. Abhishek Singh, the Growth Director (India), whose steadfast encouragement and support have been a guiding light throughout this year.

As William James once said, *"Act as if what you do, makes a difference. It does."* This book exists because of all of you.

I passionately encourage you to immerse yourself in this book, for within its pages lies the power to transform not just your financial future, but your entire life. In these challenging times, the ability to earn and thrive is not just a skill but a necessity. This book is a lifeline for students and homemakers alike, offering the wisdom of seasoned experts who have walked the path of success. It is crafted with simplicity, making it accessible to all, regardless of your prior knowledge.

Imagine the impact on your life if you could master stock trading, a skill that has the potential to unlock financial freedom. If even one student or one homemaker gains this mastery, the ripple effect could be profound. As Helen Keller once said, *"Alone we can do so little; together we can do so much."* This book is not just a guide; it's a beacon of hope and empowerment. Let it be the tool that helps you build a brighter future for yourself and your loved ones.

Nikhil Zaveri

CHAPTER – 01

So Easy to Learn Stock Trading.....

So easy to learn stock trading seems to be a loud statement for many, even an overconfident claim. However, the reality is that our perception of stock trading has been negatively influenced over the years, often being seen as a difficult, impossible, and deceptive endeavor, particularly by teachers and parents. Consequently, many individuals have refrained from attempting it altogether, while others have abandoned their efforts after facing losses, convinced by the warnings they received.

Nonetheless, I firmly assert that stock trading has become much more accessible and approachable, thanks to the revolutionary impact of technology, particularly the internet and online trading platforms. These advancements have transformed the landscape of stock trading, rendering it far more feasible for aspiring traders.

In the past, traditional teaching methods and societal attitudes propagated the notion that stock trading required specialized expertise, making it appear daunting and unattainable. However, the digital age has brought forth a wealth of resources, educational materials, and user-friendly tools that have democratised stock trading knowledge. As a result, the barriers to entry have significantly diminished, making it feasible for anyone with a willingness to learn.

The advent of online trading platforms has been a game-changer. These platforms offer intuitive interfaces and powerful charting tools that empower users to make informed decisions and execute trades with ease. With just a few clicks, individuals can access real-time market data, analyze stock trends, and execute trades from the comfort of their homes. The narrative that stock trading is an insurmountable challenge is now outdated. The introduction of technology has transformed the stock trading landscape, making it far more approachable and manageable for individuals from all walks of life, and more importantly, making it easy to learn as a skill. Knowledge creates confusion and complexity which hinders its application, but skill focuses on those aspects which require application only. So, trading stocks does not require all the knowledge about stocks market, trading, research, but requires only to learn those tools which help in making profits in the stock market. Due to techno-based trading, trading has become more of skills, and less of knowledge.

I will simply say that learning stock trading is nothing less than learning car driving.

Neuroplasticity: A New Dimension in Learning

The science is proving with new research one can learn new skills at any age. Throughout history, humans have displayed an incredible ability to adapt, learn, and master new skills. This remarkable capacity for learning is intricately tied to a process known as neuroplasticity. Neuroplasticity, also referred to as brain plasticity or neural plasticity, is the brain's remarkable ability to reorganize its structure and function in response to experiences, learning, and environmental changes, and plays a pivotal role in our ability to acquire and refine new skills.

Traditionally, the Scientists believed that the brain was thought to be a static and rigid organ, with fixed neural circuits that developed during early childhood and remained unchanged throughout adulthood. However, groundbreaking research in neuroscience has debunked this notion, revealing that the brain is anything but fixed. The brain is a dynamic and adaptable organ, continuously forging new connections and pruning old ones in response to learning experiences, environmental influences.

Neuroplasticity occurs at various levels in the brain, ranging from molecular changes within neurons to large-scale modifications in brain regions. There are two primary forms of neuroplasticity -

Structural Plasticity: This form of neuroplasticity involves physical changes in the brain's anatomy. It includes the growth of new dendrites and synapses, as well as changes in the density of neurons and the size of brain regions.

Functional Plasticity: Functional plasticity refers to changes in the brain's neural pathways and organization, allowing different brain regions to take over tasks or compensate for damaged areas.

Neuroplasticity is the driving force behind our ability to learn new skills and adapt to different challenges throughout life.

How neuroplasticity helps us acquire and refine new abilities -

Neural Rewiring: When we engage in learning a new skill, whether it's playing a musical instrument, learning a language, or mastering a sport, our brain creates new neural pathways. These pathways represent the connections between different regions of the brain that are involved in the execution of that particular skill. The more we practice and repeat the skill, the stronger these neural connections become, optimizing our performance over time.

Synaptic Plasticity: At the cellular level, synapses, the tiny gaps between neurons, are modified during the learning process. The repeated firing of neurons strengthens synaptic connections, leading to more efficient transmission of signals between brain cells. This enhanced communication facilitates smoother and quicker execution of the skill.

Skill Consolidation: Neuroplasticity plays a crucial role in the consolidation of newly acquired skills into long-term memory. As we learn and practice, our brain forms more robust and stable neural networks, allowing us to retain and retrieve the skill when needed, even after periods of rest or disuse.

Unlearning and Relearning: Neuroplasticity also enables us to unlearn outdated or incorrect skills and relearn new and improved ones. This is particularly relevant in areas where advancements occur rapidly, such as technology and medicine. The brain's flexibility allows us to adapt to changes in our environment and stay relevant.

Age is Just a Number: Contrary to the belief that learning becomes harder with age, neuroplasticity remains active throughout life. While the rate of plasticity may decline with age, the brain can still form new connections and learn well into adulthood and beyond. Engaging in challenging mental and physical activities can help maintain and boost neuroplasticity in older individuals.

Neuroplasticity is a captivating phenomenon that showcases the brain's astounding adaptability. Its role in learning new skills cannot be understated. From childhood to old age, the brain retains its capacity to rewire and reorganize itself in response to our experiences and actions. Embracing neuroplasticity empowers us to unlock our full potential and embark on a lifelong journey of continuous growth and self-improvement.

The purpose of discussion on Neuroplasticity is to instill confidence in all-across age-groups that stock trading is a skill, and can be learnt with systematic approach.

Take the example of learning car driving. Learning to drive a car is a rite of passage for many individuals, marking a significant step toward independence and freedom. However, for beginners, the process can be a daunting and fear-inducing experience. The fears of learning car driving are common and can vary from person to person, but understanding and addressing these apprehensions are essential to gaining confidence and becoming a skilled driver.

Similarly, learning stock trading as a beginner can be a daunting experience, but it's important to recognize that fear and uncertainty are normal in the process. By acknowledging these feelings and taking proactive measures to overcome them, novice traders can gain confidence and competence in the stock market. Just like driving, learning stock trading is a skill that improves with practice, patience, and a positive attitude. It's advisable to seek guidance from experienced professionals, consistently practice trading, and remember that even seasoned traders were once beginners. Embrace the learning journey and relish the sense of empowerment that comes with mastering stock trading.

Fears – Learning Car Driving vs. Learning Stock Trading

- **Fear of Losing Control vs. Fear of Losing Money**

One of the most common fears beginners experience is the fear of losing control of the vehicle. The thought of being in charge of a powerful machine can be overwhelming, leading to anxiety and hesitation. It is essential to remember that learning to drive is a gradual process, and with proper guidance and practice, control over the vehicle will improve over time. Taking professional driving lessons can help build a solid foundation and instill confidence in a beginner driver.

One of the most common fears beginners experience when learning stock trading is the fear of losing money. The thought of investing in the stock market and being responsible for their financial decisions can be overwhelming, leading to anxiety and hesitation. It is essential to remember that learning stock trading is a gradual process, and with proper guidance and practice, confidence in making investment decisions will improve over time. Taking advice from experienced traders or seeking professional guidance can help build a solid foundation and instill confidence in a beginner stock trader.

- **Fear of Making Mistakes vs. Fear of Committing Errors**

Learning any new skill involves making mistakes, and driving is no exception. The fear of making errors on the road can be paralyzing for beginners, but it is essential to understand that making mistakes is part of the learning process. It is crucial to stay patient with oneself and learn from the errors, rather than letting them discourage further progress. Practice in a safe and low-traffic environment initially to build confidence before venturing into busier areas.

Learning stock trading involves making errors, just like any other skill which can be bothering and crushing, but it is vital to recognize that making mistakes is a natural part of the learning journey. Instead of letting fear paralyze your progress, embrace it as an opportunity to grow. Patience is key in stock trading. Be patient with yourself and acknowledge that mistakes will happen. Every mistake presents a valuable lesson that can improve your trading abilities. Avoid letting mistakes discourage you; instead, use them as stepping stones towards improvement.

To gain confidence and experience, start by practicing in a safe and controlled environment. Utilize demo accounts or virtual trading platforms to test your strategies without risking real money. As you become more comfortable and capable, gradually move on to trading in low-pressure scenarios. This will help build your confidence before delving into more complex and volatile market conditions.

Remember, even experienced traders make mistakes. The key is to learn from them, adapt, and continually improve your skills. Over time, your fear of making mistakes will diminish as you become a more knowledgeable and confident stock trader."

- **Fear of Accidents vs. Fear of Misfortunes**

The fear of being involved in an accident is natural and can be a significant source of anxiety for beginner drivers. While accidents can happen, taking preventive measures, such as adhering to speed limits, maintaining a safe following distance, and staying focused on the road, can significantly reduce the risk. Always wear a seatbelt and ensure that passengers in the vehicle also buckle up for added safety.

Fear is a common emotion among beginner stock traders, and it can lead to significant anxiety and hesitation. This happens due to greed in making money which is a very tempting psychological condition of a human being. While losses can occur in stock trading, taking proactive steps to mitigate risks can alleviate these fears. Strategies such as learning to manage positions, setting stop-loss orders, and staying focused on market trends can significantly reduce the likelihood of substantial losses. Additionally, staying informed about market developments and using tools like trailing stops and limit orders can provide an extra layer of safety and protection for traders. Just like wearing a seatbelt in a car to ensure safety, implementing risk management techniques is essential to safeguarding your capital and building confidence in the stock market journey. If the goal is protecting the capital first instead of making huge money, can eliminate the fear of losing fortunes.

- **Fear of Other Drivers vs. Fear of Other Traders**

Navigating through traffic can be challenging for beginners, especially when dealing with aggressive or impatient drivers. It is essential to focus on one's driving skills and maintain a defensive driving mindset. Being aware of the surroundings, anticipating potential hazards, and remaining calm in challenging situations are crucial to staying safe on the road.

Learning the ins and outs of stock trading can be challenging for beginners, particularly when dealing with the aggressive or impatient behavior of other traders in the market. Their success or failure creates anxiety of own success or failure. Their mistakes create uncertainty and lack of confidence resulting into a fear of failure. It is essential to concentrate on honing one's trading skills and maintaining a disciplined and cautious mindset. Being aware of the market conditions, anticipating potential risks, and staying calm in challenging trading situations are vital to ensuring success and safety in the stock market.

- **Fear of Hitting Other Cars vs. Fear of Executing Trades**

Parallel parking is a dreaded maneuver for many novice drivers. The fear of hitting other cars or not performing the maneuver correctly can cause anxiety. Practice is the key to overcoming this fear. Find an empty parking lot or an uncrowded street and practice parallel parking regularly until it becomes second nature.

Trading in the stock market can be an intimidating endeavor for many inexperienced traders. The fear of executing trades in the initial stage for beginners can lead to anxiety. As a beginner, there is always a doubt whether the trade is being correctly taken or not. This results into losing profitable trades. Also, such a fear leads to taking trades late which results into losses, and losing confidence. However, like parallel parking, practice is crucial for overcoming this fear. Consider starting with a small investment or using a demo trading account to gain confidence. Regularly practice trading strategies and analyzing market trends until it becomes second nature to make informed and calculated decisions in the stock market.

- **Fear of Driving at Night or in Bad Weather vs. Fear of Trading in Volatile or Uncertain Market conditions**

Driving in adverse conditions, such as rain, snow, or at night, can be particularly nerve-wracking for beginners. Reduced visibility and slippery roads pose additional challenges. To combat this fear, practice driving in different weather and lighting conditions with an experienced driver or instructor by your side. Gradually increase exposure to such situations to build confidence.

Trading in the stock market during periods of high volatility or uncertain economic conditions can be particularly nerve-wracking for novice traders. Reduced market visibility and unpredictable price movements pose additional challenges. To overcome this fear, practice trading in various market conditions with the guidance of a mentor. Gradually increase exposure to such situations to build trading confidence and develop a better understanding of the market dynamics.

- **Missing out Take-Overs Vs. Fear of Missing Out Trades (FOMO)**

Missing out on take-overs in car driving is a dangerous situation that can lead to accidents on the road. Take-overs involve the process of safely maneuvering around other vehicles, changing lanes, or overtaking slow-moving traffic. When drivers fail to execute these take-overs effectively, they put themselves and others at risk. Common reasons for missing out on take-overs include indecision, lack of awareness, or mis-judging the speed and distance of other vehicles. This can result in sudden lane changes, cutting off other drivers, or attempting take-overs in unsafe conditions. To prevent accidents caused by missing out on take-overs, drivers must stay vigilant, maintain a safe following distance, and signal their intentions early to ensure smooth and safe maneuvering on the road. Defensive driving practices and attentive awareness of the surrounding traffic are essential to avoid such accidents and promote road safety for everyone.

The fear of missing out (FOMO) in stock trading is a common psychological phenomenon that can have significant consequences for novice traders. FOMO occurs when traders are driven by the fear of not capitalizing on potential profitable opportunities and are compelled to act hastily in response to market movements or others' success. This fear can lead to impulsive decision-making, causing traders to jump into trades without adequate analysis, ultimately risking their investments. Successful stock trading requires discipline, patience, and a well-thought-out strategy; succumbing to FOMO can disrupt this balance and lead to regrettable outcomes. The traders should learn the rule-based trading in order to avoid FOMO. (This Rule-based trading is discussed in detail in the later chapters).

Thus, both car driving and stock trading have learning curves that beginners must overcome to become proficient in their respective fields.

Followings are two most important elements of achieving success in stock trading.

- **Practice and Experience:** Trading skills improve with practice and experience. Regular practice is essential to build confidence and competence.
- **Risk Management:** While car driving involves safe driving practices to prevent accidents, stock trading requires risk assessment to minimize financial losses. The objective is to protect the capital first, then making profit. Such an approach will automatically lead to higher profits.

Recall your learning car driving experience, you will realize how foolish were you with the fears of learning at that time. Now, you are an expert, and drive flawlessly under all conditions. May be, you are in your own thoughts, but car runs on its own without realizing that you are driving.

The same experience you will undergo while learning stock trading, and over some time you will become an expert "driver" in the stock market. This is my confidence for you.

HISTORY OF STOCK MARKETS IN BRIEF

It is always interesting to know the historical aspects of any new area where we are venturing into. Learning the historical aspects of stock markets reveals the evolution of economic systems, investor behaviour, and financial regulations. It helps in understanding how financial crises were managed, the emergence of global markets, and the development of investment strategies. Moreover, it gives us an idea how trading was manual-driven as we look back, and how it has transformed into a technology-driven trading today which has made it possible for everyone to trade from home.

In the 12th century, in France, a group of people traded their debts, particularly, agricultural debt. The country came out with regulations for managing this activity. In 13th century, commodity traders started to meet in a house in the city of Antwerp in Belgium, and this idea spreaded in other neighbouring countries soon. In 14th century, in Italy, in the city of Venice, bankers started to trade in government securities, and thereafter, shares in the stock market.

In 1602, the world's first formal stock exchange was created, that was Amsterdam Stock Exchange, initially to promote the trading of securities issued by The Dutch East India Company. It was the first company to issue corporate bonds and stocks to the public. Different derivatives came into being thereafter. Short selling was started, but was banned in 1610.

The success of Amsterdam Stock Exchange led others to develop. But, it took almost a century to catch on elsewhere. In the late 17th century, King William III of England sought a way to help pay for the country's wars, and started issuing government bonds which led to the establishment of Bank of England. As people bought these bonds, this created interest in trading them. Private companies started issuing on their own shares to the public which also sparked interest in trading. The natural place for this stock trading activity was London at the Royal Exchange which, at the time, was the centre of commerce in the city over 100 years. Around that time, stock trading and stock brokers started to catch on in London, new regulations came in, to drive them out who ended up locating at a short distance away at Jonathan's Coffee House. Many other coffee houses in the area also took in stock brokers and their customers, and this area came to be known as Exchange Alley. These coffee houses posted securities trading prices on their boards, and customers would come to visit to trade in securities. After a century, in 1801, London Stock Exchange was formed. Around that time, the first securities were traded in US by the way of Buttonwood Agreement of 1792. Like London, coffee house was the first place of securities trading in US before New York Stock Exchange was established in 1817.

In India, the first stock buying/selling took place in Mumbai. Four Gujaratis and one Parsi used to meet under a banyan tree in front of Mumbai Townhall during 1850s. They used to trade informally in cotton. Their group grew in number and they formed the association called "The Native Share and Stock Brokers' Association", which was renamed as Bombay Stock Exchange in 1875. Thereafter, Ahmedabad Stock Exchange came up in 1894, which was focused on trading in shares of textile mills. Then came Calcutta Stock Exchange in 1908 trading in shares of plantations and jute mills. Later, in 1920 Madras Stock exchange came up.

In order to increase regulatory efficiency, there came in 1988 a statutory body known as Securities Exchange Board of India (SEBI). During this time the world was changing the method of trading from manual to electronic. Therefore, in India, National Stock Exchange was born in 1992 which became operational in 1994.That was the first stock exchange where trading took place electronically. In response to this, BSE introduced electronic trading system known as BSE On-line Trading (BOLT) in 1995. There are approx. 2300 companies listed on NSE, while 5300 companies are listed on BSE. (Year 2023).

It is interesting to note that USA is the largest stock market accounting for almost 60% of the world's equity market value, while the second one is Japan having 6.2%. India stands at 11th position having 1.5% of the value.

There are 60 major stock exchanges in the world, out of which 16 fall under "1 Trillion Dollar Club". NSE and BSE fall under them. There are about 30 countries which have no stock exchange like Afghanistan, North Korea, Cuba, etc.

Are Stock Markets Required ?

Stock markets play a pivotal role in the overall health and growth of any economy. These financial markets facilitate the buying and selling of company shares, making them a crucial mechanism for capital allocation, wealth creation, and economic development.

One of the primary functions of stock markets is to efficiently allocate capital. Companies can raise funds by issuing shares to the public, and investors can participate by buying those shares. This process enables businesses to access a diverse pool of investors, both institutional and individual, to raise large amounts of capital quickly.

Every economy's fundamental objective is to bolster its Gross Domestic Product (GDP). One effective approach to achieve this is by encouraging increased investment in the country's companies. A well-performing stock market not only attracts domestic investors but also foreign direct investment, contributing to economic growth. Several studies have explored the connection between stock markets and economic growth, consistently finding a positive relationship. The degree of regulation, transparency, and liquidity in the stock markets further amplifies economic growth. Stock markets play a vital role in stimulating capital formation, which ultimately drives economic growth. When companies raise funds through initial public offerings (IPOs) or subsequent equity offerings, they utilize these funds to invest in new projects, expand their operations, or improve productivity. This increased capital investment fuels economic growth and job creation. According to a study by McKinsey & Company conducted between 2010 and 2020, countries with robust and efficient stock markets generally experienced higher economic expansion. For instance, during this period, the Philippine economy, buoyed by its growing stock market, maintained a steady upward trajectory, with an average annual GDP growth rate of 5.2%. This outperformance was notable in comparison to many other Asian economies and highlighted the positive impact of a flourishing stock market on overall economic prosperity.

The efficient allocation of capital allows companies with growth potential and innovative ideas to secure the necessary funding for expansion and development. This, in turn, fosters entrepreneurship, promotes technological advancements, and stimulates economic growth. According to a study by the World Bank, countries with more developed stock markets experience higher levels of investment in research and development (R&D) as a percentage of GDP. For instance, South Korea, with a robust stock market, consistently invests more than 4% of its GDP in R&D, contributing to its impressive economic growth in recent years. The existence of stock markets demands transparency and accountability from listed companies. To attract investors, companies must adhere to stringent reporting and disclosure requirements. As a result, stock markets encourage better corporate governance practices. When companies have transparent reporting standards and strong corporate governance, investor confidence increases. This, in turn, leads to higher investments, lower costs of capital, and better overall market efficiency. A study conducted by the Organization for Economic Cooperation and Development (OECD) found that countries with well-developed stock markets tend to score higher in corporate governance assessments. For instance, Scandinavian countries such as Sweden and Denmark, known for their robust stock markets, consistently rank among the top countries with strong corporate governance. Stock markets enable investors to diversify their investments across various companies, sectors, and asset classes. By spreading their risk, investors are better protected from the adverse effects of individual company performance or economic fluctuations. This risk diversification encourages individuals to invest in the stock market, leading to a broader participation in wealth creation.

For companies requiring substantial funds, seeking public investment becomes essential, as an alternative to taking on debt to generate capital. By inviting the public to share ownership through equity, companies enable potential investors to share in the profits through dividends. However, to facilitate expansion over time, companies need continuous attractiveness to potential investors, and they typically have three main strategies:

- Offering higher dividends to shareholders, thereby sharing a greater portion of profits. This approach may lead to significant cash outflow and limited funds for reinvesting in business expansion.
- Issuing bonus shares instead of higher dividends, which saves substantial cash outflow while increasing the number of shares held by existing shareholders.
- Maintaining liquidity in the stock market, allowing original shareholders the freedom to exit at their discretion. To access significant funds, companies rely on stock markets to provide liquidity and generate good returns.

Stock markets not only offer companies a means to raise capital but also provide the general public with opportunities to invest and build personal wealth. In comparison to traditional banking or government investments, stock markets generally yield better returns, safeguarding individuals from inflation and preserving their purchasing power. Unlike earning a mere 6% interest while facing a 7% inflation rate, which erodes wealth over time, stock markets offer superior returns, enabling wealth growth and protection against inflation.

The presence or absence of stock markets can significantly impact a country's economic indicators and the overall well-being of its citizens. Stock markets enable wealth creation and distribution. As companies grow and thrive, their shareholders, including individuals and institutions, benefit from rising stock prices and dividends. This increased wealth percolates through the economy, leading to higher per capita income for the population. In economies without stock markets, the scope for wealth generation and distribution is limited. This can lead to disparities in income distribution, with only a few elite individuals or entities having access to significant capital, while the majority of the population may struggle to improve their standard of living. Stock market economies generally experience a higher standard of living due to increased investment, job creation, and access to financial instruments that can aid in wealth accumulation and financial security. The stock market's role in stimulating capital formation and economic growth also contributes to the development of infrastructure, education, and healthcare, all of which are essential components of a higher standard of living.

CHAPTER - 02

How Stock Markets Operate

A stock exchange, also known as a stock market, is a dynamic marketplace where buyers and sellers come together to trade financial instruments such as stocks, bonds, and other securities. It operates as an auction house, where participants negotiate and agree on the prices of these financial assets based on the principles of supply and demand.

The core participants in the stock exchange are buyers and sellers, with sellers being the fundamental element in the transaction process. Sellers represent the supply side and declare the price at which they are willing to sell their securities, known as the "Offer/Ask Price." On the other hand, buyers indicate the price they are willing to pay to purchase the securities, referred to as the "Bid Price." The equilibrium price at which a transaction occurs is determined by matching the highest bid with the lowest ask.

Once someone buys securities, they become immediate sellers and can subsequently seek buyers for those securities. This continuous process of buyers and sellers interacting, trying to find agreeable prices for their trades, forms the Bid & Ask process in the stock exchange.

Traditionally, stock trading took place on a physical trading floor, commonly referred to as **"floor trading"** or **"open outcry method."** Traders would gather in a designated area known as the pit and conduct transactions by shouting verbal offers for bid and ask prices while using hand signals to communicate their intentions. This method often led to a chaotic and volatile trading environment, especially during the release of significant market-moving information. Traders taking bullish positions would drive prices higher, while those taking bearish positions would push prices lower.

The floor trading system fostered an informal atmosphere among traders, where trust played a crucial role in ensuring the fulfillment of trades. The exchange displayed information about closed deals, aiding traders in making further decisions. However, this system had limitations, and retail investors were not allowed direct access to the trading floor. They had to conduct their trades through brokers, relying heavily on the broker's advice and expertise.

With the advent of technological advancements in the 1980s, stock trading underwent a significant transformation. Many stock exchanges gradually transitioned from **"floor trading"** to **"screen trading,"** also known as electronic trading. This shift allowed for greater accessibility, transparency, and efficiency in the trading process. The Amsterdam Stock Exchange, one of the oldest stock exchanges in the world, closed its floor trading in December 2002, marking the end of a 400-year-old tradition.

Screen trading enabled global scalability and resulted in the consolidation of stock exchanges, such as the merger of the Brussels and Paris stock exchanges to form Euronext. While most exchanges embraced the benefits of technology, some, like the New York Stock Exchange, still maintained floor trading for specific purposes, such as options trading.

The advent of screen trading democratized stock trading, making it more accessible to retail investors. Prior to this shift, retail investors had to rely on brokers for their trades, often lacking real-time information and decision-making capabilities. With the introduction of trading platforms, commonly web portals, retail investors gained direct access to the stock market and relevant information, allowing them to make informed decisions on their own.

The evolution of stock exchanges from traditional floor trading to modern screen trading has revolutionized the financial landscape. Technology has brought about increased accessibility, transparency, and efficiency, empowering retail investors to participate more actively in the stock market and make informed decisions based on real-time information.

The Indian Stock Market:

The Indian stock market is one of the major financial markets in the world. It comprises two primary exchanges: the Bombay Stock Exchange (BSE) and the National Stock Exchange (NSE). These exchanges facilitate the trading of various financial instruments, including stocks, bonds, derivatives, and other securities. The stock market plays a crucial role in channeling funds from investors to companies, thereby supporting economic growth.

Key Players in the Indian Stock Market:

Stock Exchanges: The BSE and NSE are the two main stock exchanges in India. The BSE, established in 1875, is one of the oldest stock exchanges globally, while the NSE was founded in 1992. Both exchanges operate electronically, offering screen-based trading platforms.

Regulators: The Securities and Exchange Board of India (SEBI) is the regulatory authority governing the Indian securities market. SEBI is responsible for regulating and overseeing all market participants, protecting the interests of investors, and maintaining market integrity.

Brokers: Stockbrokers act as intermediaries between investors and the stock exchange. They facilitate the buying and selling of securities on behalf of their clients and charge a brokerage fee for their services.

Depositories: In India, two depositories, the National Securities Depository Limited (NSDL) and the Central Depository Services Limited (CDSL), provide electronic book-entry depository services. They hold investors' securities in electronic form, making trading and settlement more efficient.

Market Segments:

- **Equity Market:** The equity market is where shares of publicly listed companies are bought and sold. Investors can purchase shares of companies, becoming partial owners and participating in their growth and profit-sharing.

- **Debt Market:** The debt market deals with fixed-income securities, such as government bonds, corporate bonds, and debentures. Investors lend money to issuers in exchange for regular interest payments.
- **Derivatives Market:** The derivatives market comprises futures and options contracts based on underlying securities. These instruments allow investors to speculate on price movements without owning the underlying asset.

Trading Mechanism:

- **Trading Hours:** The regular trading hours for the Indian stock market are from 9:15 am to 3:30 pm Indian Standard Time (IST) on weekdays (Monday to Friday), except on market holidays.
- **Order Types:** Investors can place various types of orders, such as market orders (executed at the prevailing market price), limit orders (executed at a specific price or better), stop-loss orders (triggered when the stock reaches a specified price), etc.
- **Circuit Breakers:** To prevent extreme market volatility, Indian stock exchanges have circuit breakers in place. If the stock price moves beyond a certain percentage in either direction, trading in that particular stock is halted for a specified duration.

Risk and Reward:

- **Volatility:** The stock market can be volatile, and prices of securities may fluctuate significantly over short periods. New traders should be prepared for market fluctuations and understand the risk involved in trading.
- **Potential for Returns:** While the stock market carries risks, it also offers the potential for attractive returns over the long term. Historical data show that, on average, equity investments tend to outperform other asset classes over extended periods.
- **Diversification:** Experienced investors often emphasize the importance of diversification, which involves spreading investments across different assets and industries. Diversification can help reduce risk by minimizing the impact of individual stock price movements on the overall portfolio.

Types of Trading:

- **Intraday Trading:** Intraday trading, also known as day trading, involves buying and selling financial instruments within the same trading day. Intraday traders aim to capitalize on short-term price movements, taking advantage of price fluctuations that occur throughout the day. All positions are typically squared off before the market closes, which means intraday traders do not hold any positions overnight. The trading is on cash basis.

Key Characteristics:

- **Quick buying and selling:** Intraday traders execute multiple trades within a single trading session.
- **Minimal overnight risk:** Since all positions are closed by the end of the day, intraday traders avoid exposure to overnight market events.

- **Focus on Technical analysis:** Day traders often rely on technical indicators and chart patterns to make trading decisions.
- **No Delivery of Stocks:** There is no delivery of stocks transacted in the process. **"Take the Profit, and not the Stocks"** is the mantra.

Swing Trading:

Swing trading involves holding positions for several days to a few weeks, aiming to profit from short-to-medium-term price swings. Swing traders analyze both technical and fundamental factors to identify potential entry and exit points. Unlike intraday traders, swing traders do not need to monitor the markets continuously throughout the day.

Key Characteristics:

- **Short-to-medium-term holding period:** Swing traders hold positions for more extended periods compared to day traders.
- **Risk management:** Swing traders typically use stop-loss orders to limit potential losses on trades.
- **Potential for higher returns:** Since swing traders aim to capture larger price moves, there is potential for higher returns compared to day trading.

Positional Trading:

Positional trading is a longer-term trading approach where traders hold positions for several weeks to months. Positional traders aim to capitalize on significant price trends and tend to focus on macroeconomic factors and fundamental analysis.

Key Characteristics:

- **Longer holding period:** Positional traders hold positions for an extended period, often waiting for a substantial price move to materialize.
- **Less frequent trading:** Unlike day traders or swing traders, positional traders execute fewer trades over time.
- **Patience and conviction:** Positional traders need to be patient and have confidence in their analysis, as they may experience periods of short-term volatility before the expected trend unfolds.

Long-term Investing:

Long-term investing, also known as "buy and hold" investing, involves purchasing assets with the intention of holding them for an extended period, typically years or even decades. Long-term investors focus on the underlying fundamentals of a company, sector, or asset class and expect their investments to grow steadily over time.

Key Characteristics:

- **Low turnover:** Long-term investors have a buy-and-hold approach, so they do not frequently trade or churn their portfolios.

- **Emphasis on fundamental analysis:** Investors focus on the financial health and performance of the companies or assets they invest in.
- **Potential for compounding:** Long-term investors benefit from the power of compounding, as their investments grow over time and generate returns on reinvested gains.

Other Types:

Apart from the primary types mentioned above, there are several other specialized trading strategies:

Scalping: Scalpers aim to make small profits from frequent, rapid trades. They hold positions for a very short time, often just seconds or minutes, and focus on high-volume, liquid assets. These trades are part of the Intraday.

Algorithmic Trading: Also known as algo trading or black-box trading, algorithmic trading involves using computer algorithms to execute trades based on predefined rules and criteria. It is prevalent among institutional investors and hedge funds.

High-Frequency Trading (HFT): HFT is a subset of algorithmic trading that involves executing a large number of orders at incredibly high speeds. HFT firms seek to profit from small price discrepancies in fractions of a second.

Contrarian Trading: Contrarian traders take positions against prevailing market trends, believing that crowd sentiment often leads to overreactions and mispricing.

Event-Driven Trading: Event-driven traders focus on specific events, such as earnings announcements, mergers, or economic releases, aiming to profit from price movements resulting from these events.

Each type of trading has its advantages and challenges, and traders should select a strategy that aligns with their risk tolerance, time commitment, and trading goals. Successful trading requires discipline, risk management, and a deep understanding of market dynamics. Additionally, traders should continuously educate themselves and adapt to changing market conditions to improve their chances of success.

In this book, we are focusing only on Intraday trading - **"Take the Profit, and not the Stocks".**

Types of Orders:

- **Market Order:** A market order is an order to buy or sell a stock at the best available market price at the time the order is placed. The execution of the order is immediate.
- **Limit Order:** A limit order is an order to buy or sell a stock at a specific price or better. It allows you to set a maximum price for a buy order or a minimum price for a sell order.
- **Stop Loss Order:** A stop-loss order is designed to limit your losses on a particular stock position. It becomes a market order to buy or sell a stock when the stock reaches a specified stop price.
- **Stop-Loss Limit Order:** This order combines the features of a stop-loss order and a limit order. It triggers a limit order to buy or sell a stock once the stock price reaches the specified stop price.
- **Bracket Order:** A bracket order is a type of order that allows you to place a target price and a stop-loss order along with the main order in one go. It helps you to set a profit target and limit potential losses simultaneously.

- **Cover Order:** A cover order is a type of order where you place a market or limit order along with a compulsory stop-loss order. It is mainly used for intraday trading.
- **After Market Order (AMO):** An AMO allows you to place order after the regular market hours. These orders get queued for execution when the market opens the next trading day.
- **Good Till Cancelled (GTC) Order:** A GTC order remains valid until it gets executed or canceled explicitly by the trader.
- **Immediate or Cancel (IOC) Order:** An IOC order requires that all or part of the order must be executed immediately. Any portion of the order that remains unfulfilled is canceled.
- **Regular Order:** A regular order is an order placed during the normal trading hours.

The different trading platforms may have variations in the available order types and their functionalities. Always ensure you understand the terms and conditions of each order type before placing any trades.

Brokers:

The Indian stock market has numerous brokerage firms that offer trading services to investors. Some of the popular brokers available for trading in India are as follows.

1. **Zerodha:** India's largest discount broker, offers a top-rated trading platform with low fees and advanced tools. Their proprietary platform, Kite, provides real-time data, advanced charts, one-click orders, and custom price alerts. They offer stocks, derivatives, mutual funds, bonds, and unique zero-commission direct mutual fund investment through Zerodha Coin. Excellent customer support and a flat fee of ₹20 per trade or 0.03% transaction value make it highly affordable. They also provide educational resources and webinars.
2. **Upstox:** Upstox is a popular discount broker, gaining popularity for its low fees and user-friendly platform. The platform offers real-time data, advanced charts, one-click orders, and price alerts. Upstox MF enables commission-free direct mutual fund investment. It provides stocks, derivatives, mutual funds, and bonds. Their mobile app is highly rated and offers all desktop features. Educational resources, including webinars, tutorials, and a dedicated trading academy, are also available.
3. **Angel Broking:** Angel Broking, a full-service broker since 1987, offers stocks, derivatives, mutual funds, and bonds. Known for advanced charting tools, research reports, and user-friendly interface. Angel Broking's ARQ, an AI-based investment engine, provides personalized investment recommendations. Pricing is a percentage of the transaction value (0.04% to 0.50%), with value-added services like research reports and investment advisory. They also provide educational resources and webinars.
4. **5Paisa:** 5Paisa is a popular discount broker with low fees and user-friendly platform. Offering stocks, derivatives, mutual funds, and bonds. The platform provides real-time data, advanced charts, one-click orders, and price alerts. They also offer TradeStation for real-time market updates and analysis. The flat fee is ₹20 per trade or 0.05% transaction value. They provide educational resources and webinars.
5. **Sharekhan:** Sharekhan, a full-service broker since 2000, offers stocks, derivatives, mutual funds, and bonds. Known for advanced charting tools, research reports, and a user-friendly interface. The platform provides real-time data and a variety of order types. Pricing ranges from 0.10% to

0.50% of the transaction value, with value-added services like research reports and investment advisory. They also offer educational resources and webinars.

6. **HDFC Securities:** HDFC Securities, part of HDFC Bank group, offers stocks, derivatives, mutual funds, and bonds. Known for advanced charting tools, research reports, and a user-friendly interface. The platform provides real-time data and various order types. Pricing ranges from 0.05% to 0.50% of the transaction value, with value-added services like research reports and investment advisory. Educational resources and webinars are also available.
7. **ICICI Direct:** ICICI Direct, part of ICICI Bank group, offers stocks, derivatives, mutual funds, and bonds. Known for advanced charting tools, research reports, and a user-friendly interface. The platform provides real-time data and various order types. Pricing ranges from 0.25% to 0.75% of the transaction value, with value-added services like research reports and investment advisory. Educational resources and webinars are also available.
8. **Fyers:** Fyers is a comprehensive desktop-based trading platform by Fyers Securities, offering advanced charting, real-time data, and integrated TradingView tools. Flat fee of Rs. 20 per trade across all segments.
9. **Motilal Oswal Trader:** Motilal Oswal Trader is a web-based platform by Motilal Oswal Financial Services, offering advanced charting, third-party tool integration, and a user-friendly interface. Flat fee of Rs. 20 per trade across all segments.
10. **NSE NOW:** NSE NOW, developed by NSE, is a web-based platform offering advanced charting, direct exchange access, and real-time data. Available through NSE-associated brokerage firms, charges may vary.

I recommend checking with the respective brokerage firms for the most up-to-date information, including brokerage rates, account opening requirements, and available investment products. Additionally, it is essential to consider factors such as brokerage fees, trading platforms, customer support, and research offerings before choosing a brokerage firm that best suits your trading and investment needs.

Charting softwares:

Charting software enables traders to generate charts and conduct technical analysis on stock charts, crypto charts, and forex charts. Charting software platforms provide an important trading tool for asset traders to test and execute trading strategies. Here are some of the most popular charting softwares.

11. **TradingView:** TradingView stands out as the premier choice among traders, investors, and market analysts for its unparalleled technical analysis capabilities and a thriving social community. The platform's advanced charting features enable users to create unique chart layouts, integrate numerous indicators and overlays, and utilize a diverse array of drawing tools. Whether you're interested in analyzing stocks, forex, cryptocurrencies, or other asset classes, TradingView offers an exceptional level of customization and flexibility.
12. **ChartIQ:** ChartIQ serves as a versatile financial charting and data visualization platform for technical analysis, catering to users across desktops, web browsers, tablets, and smartphones. The platform's visualizations are aesthetically appealing and facilitate a seamless engagement

with financial data. Through customized charts and innovative data visualization tools, ChartIQ simplifies and enhances the effectiveness of technical analysis for users at all levels.

13. **Investar:** Geared towards window-based systems, Investar is a comprehensive technical analysis software that caters specifically to intraday traders. While it offers a range of free tools, users can also opt for paid versions that provide an extensive array of in-depth analysis features. For beginners, Investar may initially appear overwhelming due to the abundance of tools and options available, but with time and practice, users can fully harness its potential.
14. **NinjaTrader:** Tailored for experienced traders active in stocks, futures, and forex markets, NinjaTrader boasts outstanding charting tools and supports the utilization of 125 technical indicators for precise market trend analysis. Offering an array of features like advanced charting, backtesting, and automation capabilities, NinjaTrader's true strength lies in its flexibility, allowing traders to customize the platform to suit their individual needs and preferences.
15. **Investing.com:** Investing.com's real-time charting tool stands as a robust and technically advanced resource, striking a perfect balance between user-friendliness and powerful functionality. This platform caters to both beginners and advanced users, offering an intuitive interface for ease of use while providing a wide range of sophisticated tools and resources for comprehensive market analysis.

CHAPTER – 03

Understanding the Market

1. Market:

The National Stock Exchange of India (NSE) is one of the largest stock exchanges in Asia, located in Mumbai, India. Established in 1994, it is the first electronic exchange in India. NSE offers trading in a range of financial instruments including equities, derivatives, currency derivatives, debt instruments, and exchange-traded funds (ETFs). The exchange uses cutting-edge technology to provide a transparent, fair, and efficient marketplace for securities trading. NSE has a broad shareholder base and is widely recognized as one of the leading stock exchanges in the world, offering a range of services to stakeholders, including corporations, financial institutions, and individual investors.

The Bombay Stock Exchange (BSE) is one of the oldest and largest stock exchanges in Asia. Established in 1875, the BSE has a rich history and has played a crucial role in the growth and development of the Indian capital market. The BSE operates on a fully automated trading system, known as BSE On-Line Trading (BOLT), which provides a transparent, fast, and efficient platform for trading. The BSE offers a wide range of investment products, including equities, derivatives, and debt securities, and has a well-diversified shareholder base that includes both domestic and foreign investors. The BSE also provides a range of value-added services, including market data, research and analytics, and investment education, to help investors make informed investment decisions. With a strong focus on technology and innovation, the BSE is well positioned to meet the evolving needs of the Indian capital market and provide a world-class platform for trading and investing.

Understand that you can't directly trade at NSE /BSE, but you have to trade through a broker. The broker provides all the stocks and other financial products for trading which are available on NSE/ BSE. The broker has all the access of data at NSE/BSE being a member of the exchange. You are considered as a Retail Trader in the market.

2. Market Timing:

Market opens at 9.00 AM, but, from 9:00 AM to 9:15 AM (IST), the National Stock Exchange of India (NSE) is in the pre-open session. During this time, the exchange's systems are open and market participants can place orders, but trading does not officially commence. The pre-open session is a crucial period during which market participants can review their orders, assess market conditions, and make any necessary adjustments before the start of the trading session. The pre-open session allows traders to prepare for the day's market activity, and to make informed decisions about their trades before the official start of trading. Pre-open session decide the Opening Price of the stocks. More precisely, the period between 9:00 AM to 9:07 AM is called the pre-open session in the Indian stock market. During this period, traders can place orders, modify or cancel them. However, no trades are executed. This is a time for traders to assess the market conditions and place their orders before the market opens. You can't place or modify your orders after 9.07 AM. Then, 9.07 am to 9.08 am is the time for order matching (there could be difference of 1 minute). At 9.08 AM, the opening price is declared. For Intraday traders, this is the most important phase of 7 minutes to identify few stocks. You can gauge where your "fish" lie. At 9.08 AM, when pre-open session is over, the opening price is declared to the public. NSE also declares Top Gainers and Top losers. This is the time where you can select such stocks which are expected to have volume, volatility and momentum. However, this is not all that the intraday trader should stop at. But, this is one area where you can "**find your fish**".

Here are some of the things that happen during the pre-open session:

1. **Order collection:** During the pre-open session, traders can place orders for buying or selling stocks. These orders can be limit orders or market orders. Limit orders specify the maximum price that the trader is willing to pay for a stock, while market orders buy or sell the stock at the best available price.
2. **Order matching:** During the call auction session, the exchange matches all the buy and sell orders that have been placed during the pre-open session. The opening price is the price at which the stock will start trading once the market opens at 9:15 AM.
3. **Trade confirmation:** Once the opening price has been determined, all the trades that were executed during the call auction session are confirmed. Traders can then start trading the stock at the opening price.
4. The pre-open session is an important part of the stock market trading process. It helps to ensure that the market opens at a fair price and that all trades are executed in a transparent manner.

3. Index:

The SENSEX (short for Sensitive Index) is the stock market index of the Bombay Stock Exchange (BSE) in India. The SENSEX is considered to be one of the leading indicators of the Indian stock market and is widely followed by investors, analysts, and the media. The SENSEX is a market capitalization weighted index, which means that the companies with the largest market capitalization (i.e. the total value of all their outstanding shares) have the largest weight in the index. The SENSEX comprises 30 of the largest and most actively traded stocks listed on the BSE, and is designed to reflect the performance of the Indian stock market as a whole. The SENSEX is often used as a benchmark for the Indian stock market and is considered to be one of the most reliable indicators of the Indian economy. The performance of the SENSEX is closely watched by investors, as it provides a useful tool for evaluating the overall performance of the Indian stock market and the health of the Indian economy.

The Nifty 50 is a stock market index in India, maintained by the National Stock Exchange of India (NSE). The index represents the performance of 50 leading stocks from various sectors of the Indian economy. It is a widely recognized and closely watched benchmark for the Indian stock market, and is considered a barometer of the overall health of the Indian economy.

The Nifty 50 is computed using a free float market capitalization weighted methodology, where the level of the index reflects the total market value of all the stocks in the index relative to a particular base period. The stocks included in the index are selected based on their liquidity, depth of market, and representativeness of the broader market.

Investors use the Nifty 50 as a benchmark to track the performance of their portfolios and to make investment decisions. The index is widely followed by both domestic and international investors, and is considered an important indicator of the Indian stock market's overall performance.

The weightage of different companies in the Nifty 50 index is determined by their market capitalization, which is calculated as the number of outstanding shares multiplied by the current market price of each share. The market capitalization of a company represents its total value, and the Nifty 50 is a market capitalization weighted index, meaning that the weightage of each company in the index is proportional to its market capitalization.

The companies with a higher market capitalization will have a higher weightage in the Nifty 50, while those with a lower market capitalization will have a lower weightage. This ensures that the index accurately reflects the performance of the overall market, taking into account the impact of larger and more established companies. The weightage of each company in the Nifty 50 is reviewed and adjusted periodically to ensure that it continues to accurately reflect the market.

It's worth noting that the weightage of each company in the Nifty 50 can fluctuate due to changes in market conditions, company performance, and other factors. Investors who track the Nifty 50 should regularly monitor the weightage of individual companies to gain a better understanding of the index's performance and make informed investment decisions.

The sectors represented in the Nifty 50, the benchmark index of the National Stock Exchange of India (NSE), are considered to be important for a number of reasons.

Firstly, the sectors represented in the Nifty provide a broad representation of the Indian economy. The Nifty includes companies from a variety of sectors, including financials, information technology (IT), consumer goods, energy, and healthcare, among others. This diversity allows investors to gain exposure to a range of industries and sectors, and helps to mitigate sector-specific risk.

Secondly, the performance of the Nifty is seen as a barometer of the overall health of the Indian economy. The Nifty provides a snapshot of the performance of India's top companies, and fluctuations in the index are often seen as an indicator of the economic and business environment in India.

Additionally, the sectors represented in the Nifty provide investors with a range of investment opportunities, from low-risk to high-risk. For example, blue-chip companies in the financial and consumer goods sectors are generally considered to be low-risk investments, while technology and healthcare companies are often seen as higher-risk investments with greater potential for growth.

Thus, the sectors represented in the Nifty are important for providing a broad representation of the Indian economy, for serving as a barometer of the overall health of the Indian economy, and for providing a range of investment opportunities to investors.

NSE acts as a lighthouse where you can see the trend of the stock market as well as get data of each listed company.

4. Knowing the Economy and Trends

There are many components of the economy that can affect stock prices, but some of the most important for intraday traders include following components. Amongst all, Interest Rate is the most important component for Intraday Trader as it shows its reaction instantly from which huge benefit can be derived.

> **Interest Rates** are the cost of borrowing money. When interest rates are low, it is cheaper for businesses to borrow money and invest, which can lead to economic growth and higher stock prices. Conversely, high interest rates can make it more expensive for businesses to borrow money, which can slow down economic growth and lead to lower stock prices.

The stock market reacts when the Reserve Bank of India (RBI) increases interest rates because it makes it more expensive for businesses to borrow money.

Few reasons why stock market reacts when RBI increases interest rates:

1. **Cost of borrowing increases:** When the RBI increases interest rates, it makes it more expensive for businesses to borrow money. This can lead to a slowdown in investment and economic growth, which can hurt corporate profits and stock prices.
2. **Demand for stocks decreases:** When interest rates rise, the opportunity cost of investing in stocks also rises. This is because investors can earn a higher return by investing in other assets, such as bonds, which are considered to be less risky.
3. **Valuation of stocks decreases:** When interest rates rise, the present value of future cash flows decreases. This is because the higher discount rate used to calculate the present value of future cash flows reduces the value of those cash flows.

The Indian stock market reacts **when the US increases the interest rate** because India is a major emerging market and is closely linked to the US economy. When the US interest rate rises, it makes it more expensive for Indian companies to borrow money, which can lead to a slowdown in investment and economic growth. This can hurt corporate profits and stock prices in India.

Few reasons why Indian stock market reacts when US increases interest rate:

1. **Capital outflow:** When the US interest rate rises, it becomes more attractive for foreign investors to invest in US assets, such as bonds and treasury bills. This can lead to capital outflow from India, which can put downward pressure on the Indian stock market.
2. **Currency depreciation:** When the US interest rate rises, the US dollar strengthens, which can lead to currency depreciation in India. This can make Indian exports less competitive and can also hurt corporate profits.
3. **Reduced liquidity:** When the US interest rate rises, it can lead to a reduction in liquidity in the global financial markets. This can make it more difficult for Indian companies to raise capital, which can also hurt stock prices.

There are other components which can affect stock prices, but, relatively, they are long term in nature.

a. **Gross domestic product (GDP)** is the total value of goods and services produced in a country in a given year. A growing GDP is generally seen as positive for stock prices, as it indicates that the economy is expanding and businesses are doing well.
b. **Inflation** is the rate at which prices are rising. Inflation can erode the value of stocks over time, so traders should be aware of it and factor it into their investment decisions.
c. **Unemployment** is the percentage of the labor force that is unemployed. Low unemployment is generally seen as positive for stock prices, as it means that there are more people with jobs and spending money, which can boost economic growth.
d. **Consumer confidence** is a measure of how confident consumers are about the economy. When consumer confidence is high, people are more likely to spend money, which can lead to economic growth and higher stock prices.
e. **Corporate earnings** are the profits that companies make. Strong corporate earnings can lead to higher stock prices, as investors are more likely to buy stocks of companies that are doing well.
f. **Political news** can also have a significant impact on stock prices. For example, if there is a change in government or a major policy announcement, it can cause investors to reassess their positions and make changes to their portfolios.

It is important to keep an eye on all of these factors when trading intraday, as they can all have a significant impact on stock prices. By understanding the economic landscape, intraday traders can make more informed decisions and increase their chances of success. Over the experience, it is observed, Interest rate plays a very significant role in Intraday price movement, If you have information on this before the commencement of the market, you can predict the trend of the market reasonably, and decide whether you would like to go for buying or selling. Other components do not have much influence on Intraday price movement, but, they have long-term effect.

5. India VIX:

India VIX, (India Volatility Index), is a measure that reflects the market's expectation of volatility over the near term. Specifically, it focuses on the NIFTY 50 index and is calculated by the National Stock Exchange (NSE) using the order book of NIFTY options.

The index provides insights into the market's sentiment and the anticipated level of volatility in the Indian stock market. A higher India VIX value indicates higher expected volatility, suggesting that investors foresee significant fluctuations in the market. Conversely, a lower value indicates lower expected volatility, implying more stable market conditions.

India VIX is an important tool for traders and investors as it helps in gauging market risk. It is often referred to as the "fear gauge" because it tends to rise during periods of market uncertainty and decline during more stable periods.

India VIX and Nifty have a generally inverse relationship.

Negative Correlation: When the India VIX rises, it indicates an increase in expected market volatility, which often corresponds to a decline in the Nifty index. Conversely, when India VIX falls, it suggests reduced market volatility, often leading to a rise in the Nifty index. This negative correlation is due to the heightened uncertainty and risk aversion during times of higher volatility, prompting investors to sell off stocks, thereby pushing the Nifty down.

Market Sentiment Indicator: India VIX is also referred to as a "fear gauge." A spike in India VIX typically reflects market anxiety or fear, which can lead to bearish sentiment in the stock market, affecting the Nifty negatively. Conversely, a lower India VIX reflects investor confidence, which usually supports a rising Nifty.

Understanding this relationship helps Intraday traders to anticipate market movements and manage risks more effectively. The general practice is to google "India VIX" when market opens. When India VIX is in the range of 10 – 16 (It's a bullish stable market. No big movement is expected. You can follow the strategy of "Buy on Dip". The preferable timeframe is 15 or 30 minutes). When India VIX is in the range of 16 – 22 (It's a volatile market. It's good for momentum scalping. Market will go up and down. The preferable timeframe is 1 or 3 or 5 minutes). When India VIX is in the range of 22 – 30 (It's a panic market. Market is falling. The only strategy is to "Sell on Rise". The preferable timeframe is 5 or 15 minutes).

However, India VIX helps to build a view on the market movement. It does not indicate the direction of the market. It only indicates stability or volatility. Therefore, you have to follow your Trade set-up strictly. The view helps you to go for buy or sell in your chosen Trade Set-up.

6. GiftNifty Index:

GiftNifty (formerly SGX Nifty) is a derivative product based on the Nifty 50 Index traded on the GIFT City International Financial Services Centre (IFSC) in Gujarat, India. This product can be beneficial for intraday traders in India in several ways.

Intraday traders of the NSE market can use GiftNifty's pre-market and early trading data to inform their trading decisions when the NSE market opens at 9:00 AM. Since GiftNifty trades nearly 21 hours a day and covers global market movements during the overnight period, its performance can act as an early indicator of market sentiment. Here's how intraday traders can utilize GiftNifty's data to make informed decisions.

1. Market Sentiment Analysis:

By observing how GiftNifty futures have performed in the hours leading up to the NSE market opening, traders can gauge the overall sentiment toward Indian equities. If GiftNifty is trading significantly higher or lower, it could suggest a positive or negative market sentiment based on global developments, such as U.S. market movements, economic data releases, or geopolitical events. Traders can adjust their strategies based on GiftNifty's movement. For example, if GiftNifty has shown a strong upward trend, NSE traders may anticipate a bullish start and plan long positions. Conversely, if GiftNifty has fallen, traders may expect a bearish opening and prepare for shorting opportunities.

2. Anticipating Gaps:

GiftNifty's performance can indicate whether the NSE market will open with a gap up (higher than the previous day's close) or gap down (lower than the previous day's close). Traders can use this information to set up their trades in advance. If GiftNifty has been steadily rising, it suggests a possible gap-up opening for the NSE market. Intraday traders might then focus on buying opportunities in sectors that are expected to benefit from the market's momentum. Similarly, a declining GiftNifty could indicate a gap down, and traders may focus on short-selling opportunities.

3. Pre-Opening Strategy:

GiftNifty is influenced by global events occurring overnight, such as U.S. market performance, Asian markets, or global economic data releases. Analyzing GiftNifty's reaction to these events can give intraday traders a head start before the Indian market opens. By tracking global market events through GiftNifty, traders can prepare strategies for sector-specific stocks that might be impacted. For instance, if U.S. tech stocks surged overnight and GiftNifty reacted positively, traders might anticipate gains in Indian IT stocks and plan their trades accordingly.

4. Volatility & Risk Management:

GiftNifty can provide early signs of volatility or stability in the market. If GiftNifty is fluctuating widely in the pre-market, it might suggest higher volatility when NSE opens. Traders can plan for risk management strategies like tightening stop losses or adjusting position sizes based on the expected volatility indicated by GiftNifty. High volatility can offer more opportunities for intraday trades but also requires cautious risk management.

5. Tracking Global Correlations:

GiftNifty reflects the performance of the Nifty 50 index based on global markets' sentiment. If U.S. or European markets had significant movements overnight, GiftNifty will factor this in, allowing intraday traders to better understand potential NSE market reactions. Traders can monitor the correlation between GiftNifty and key global indices, such as the S&P 500 or FTSE 100, to predict the potential impact on Indian markets. If U.S. indices are down and GiftNifty has dropped in response, it may indicate weaker market conditions at the NSE open.

6. Sectoral Insights:

While GiftNifty provides an index-level view, its performance can be an indicator of sectoral trends influenced by global events. If GiftNifty is up or down significantly, traders may look at which sectors are driving the movement, such as banking, IT, or energy. This allows intraday traders to focus on specific sectors for buying or selling opportunities when the NSE opens.

7. Tracking Foreign Institutional Investors (FII) Activity:

GiftNifty's movement often mirrors the activities of FIIs who may be adjusting their positions based on global trends. This is particularly useful for intraday traders since FIIs have a significant influence on Indian markets. If GiftNifty is moving strongly in a certain direction due to FII buying or selling, it could suggest similar movements in the NSE market. Traders can adjust their strategies based on anticipated FII flows at market open.

8. Using GiftNifty for Stop-Loss Adjustments:

By monitoring GiftNifty's price action before NSE opens, intraday traders can fine-tune their stop-loss levels and exit strategies for the Indian market. If GiftNifty indicates a sudden shift in sentiment, traders can adjust their stop-loss orders accordingly to protect against sudden adverse movements at the NSE open.

GiftNifty offers critical early indicators that intraday traders on NSE can use to predict market behavior, spot opportunities, and manage risks before the Indian market opens. By monitoring GiftNifty's overnight performance, traders can prepare strategies for anticipated gaps, volatility, and sector-specific movements, enabling them to make more informed decisions when the NSE market starts trading at 9:00 AM.

7. Selecting an On-line Broker:

When it comes to selection of a broker, it is recommended only an on-line broker as it is expected you to do "fishing", i.e., trade yourself.

There are many factors to consider when choosing an online broker for trading in the Indian stock market. Some of the most important factors include:

1. **Brokerage charges:** The brokerage charges are the fees that you pay to the broker for each trade that you make. These charges can vary significantly from broker to broker, so it is important to compare them before you choose one.
2. **Account opening fees:** Some brokers charge an account opening fee, while others do not. This is another fee that you need to factor into your decision.
3. **Account Types and Investment Options:** Verify the types of accounts available (e.g., individual, joint, retirement) and the range of investment products offered, such as stocks, bonds, mutual funds, ETFs, and options. This ensures the broker can accommodate your investment needs and goals.
4. **Minimum balance requirements:** Some brokers have minimum balance requirements, which means that you need to maintain a certain amount of money in your account in order to trade. This is another important factor to consider, especially if you are a small investor.
5. **Trading platforms:** The trading platform is the software that you use to place trades. Different brokers offer different trading platforms, so it is important to choose one that is user-friendly and meets your needs.
6. **Account Protection:** Ensure the broker provides robust security measures to protect your investments and personal information. Look for features such as two-factor authentication and encryption. Additionally, verify that the broker is a member of a regulatory body that offers investor protection schemes.
7. **Research and educational resources:** Some brokers offer research and educational resources to help you make informed trading decisions. This is a valuable feature, especially if you are a beginner.

8. **Customer support:** It is important to choose a broker that offers good customer support. This is especially important if you have any questions or problems with your account.
9. **The broker's reputation:** Do some research to find out what other investors have to say about the broker.
10. **The broker's track record:** Look at the broker's track record of execution and customer service.
11. **The broker's trading hours:** Make sure that the broker's trading hours are convenient for you.
12. **The broker's compliance with regulations:** Make sure that the broker is registered with the Securities and Exchange Board of India (SEBI) and is in compliance with all applicable regulations.

By considering these factors, you can choose an online stock broker that best fits your needs, enhancing your trading experience and helping you achieve your financial goals.

There are some of the popular online brokers in India, like Zerodha, Upstox, 5Paisa, Angel Broking, ICICI Securities, Kotak Securities, Fyers, etc.

8. Technical Charts

Technical charts are graphical representations of market data that traders and investors use to analyze trends and make informed investment decisions. They are an essential tool for technical analysis, which is a method of evaluating securities by analyzing statistics generated by market activity, such as past prices and volume. Technical charts are used by traders and investors to identify patterns, trends, and opportunities in the market.

There are several types of technical charts, including line charts, bar charts, candlestick charts, and point and figure charts, among others. Each type of chart provides a unique representation of market data and has its own strengths and weaknesses. For example, line charts are simple and easy to read, but they provide limited information, while candlestick charts provide a wealth of information, but they can be more difficult to interpret.

Technical charts are often used in combination with other technical indicators, such as moving averages, momentum indicators, and oscillators, to help traders and investors make more informed investment decisions. These indicators provide additional information about market trends and can help traders and investors identify entry and exit points, set stop-loss orders, and determine their overall market outlook.

7. Candlestick Charts

Candlestick charts were invented in Japan in the late 1700s by a legendary rice trader named Homma Munehisa. Homma was one of the most successful traders of his time, and he is credited with developing the first candlestick charts to help him make informed trading decisions.

Homma's candlestick charts used the same basic format that is used today, with each candlestick representing a single day's worth of price data. The body of the candlestick showed the difference between the opening and closing prices, while the wick, shadow, and tail represented the high and low prices for the day.

Over time, Homma's candlestick charts spread to other parts of the world, and they have become a popular tool for traders and investors. Today, candlestick charts are used by traders and investors to gain valuable insights into market trends and sentiment, and they are considered an essential tool in many technical analysis systems.

Candlestick charts are a type of technical chart that is used to represent the price movement of securities over a given period of time. They originated in Japan in the 17th century and have since become a popular tool for traders and investors around the world. Candlestick charts provide a wealth of information about market trends and sentiment and are often used in conjunction with other technical indicators to make informed investment decisions.

Each candlestick on a chart represents a single period of time, such as a day, week, or month. The body of the candlestick shows the difference between the opening and closing prices for that period, while the "wick" or "shadow" shows the high and low prices. If the closing price is higher than the opening price, the body of the candlestick is typically white or hollow or green or blue and is referred to as a "bullish" candlestick. If the closing price is lower than the opening price, the body is typically black or filled with red colour, and is referred to as a "bearish" candlestick. This is just an introduction. Nore we will see in the coming chapter.

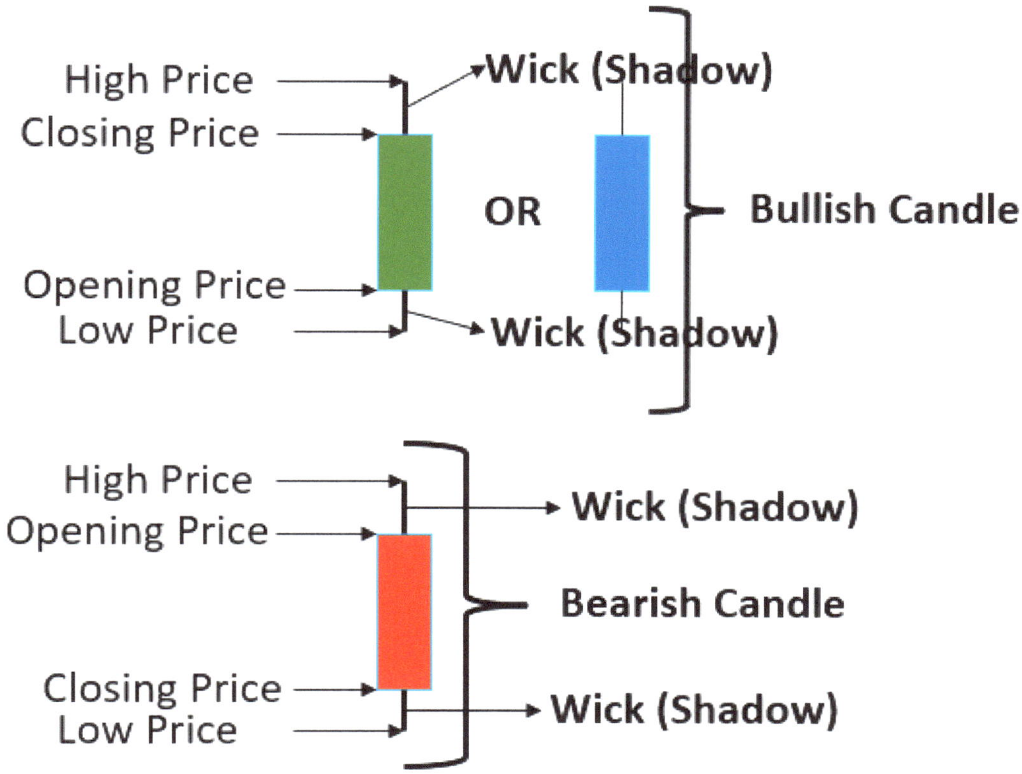

Candlestick charts provide valuable information about market sentiment and trends. For example, a series of bullish candlesticks may indicate that a security is in an uptrend, while a series of bearish candlesticks may indicate that a security is in a downtrend. The length of the body and the shadow of a candlestick can also provide important information about market volatility and momentum.

Candlestick charts are an important tool for traders and investors who want to gain a deeper understanding of market trends and sentiment. They provide a visual representation of market data and can be used in combination with other technical indicators to make informed investment decisions.

By looking at the formation of multiple candlesticks, traders and investors can gain valuable insights into market trends and sentiment. For example, a series of bullish candlesticks may indicate that a security is in an uptrend, while a series of bearish candlesticks may indicate that a security is in a downtrend. Additionally, the length of the body, the shadow, and the tail can provide information about market volatility and momentum.

Candlesticks are a visual representation of daily price data and provide valuable insights into market trends and sentiment.

There are other chart patterns also like Heikin Ashi, Renko, etc. But, I intend to use only one chart pattern, i.e., Candlestick in order to avoid complexity in reading the various types of charts.

CHAPTER – 04

Understanding Price and its Action

Let me tell you a story. In the enchanted kingdom of *Financia*, two legendary creatures, the Bulls and the Bears, often met in the grand arena to test their strength. The kingdom's people would gather around the arena, watching with bated breath, placing bets on the outcome. The arena's ground was painted with magical candlesticks that shifted and changed based on the ongoing tussle.

One sunny day, the Bulls, full of optimism, charged fiercely, pushing the Bears back. As they surged forward, the candlesticks on the arena turned bright blue, growing taller, showing the Bulls' might. The citizens cheered as their predictions of a Bull win seemed accurate.

But just as the day turned to night, the Bears, symbolizing pessimism, roared back with vengeance. They clawed and pushed the Bulls, turning the arena's candlesticks to a deep red. These red candlesticks grew long shadows, signaling the Bears' rising strength. Amidst the fight, there were moments of pause, where neither the Bulls nor the Bears had the upper hand. During these moments, the candlesticks became smaller, their colors uncertain, depicting the indecision in the game.

The spectators were often confused. Some had bet their gold coins on the Bulls, while others had staked their fortunes on the Bears. As the battle raged on, many regretted their choices, while a few celebrated their foresight.

In the end, the duels served as a reminder that in the unpredictable world of *Financia*, predictions and emotions always go hand in hand. And, while the candlesticks in the arena might offer clues, no one truly knows which creature – the Bull or the Bear – would dominate the day.

In light of the story, let us try to understand the market.

Price:

Trading in the stock market is a process wherein the trader is in exploring the "right" price of the stock to buy or sell. The "right" price is a very subjective element because it depends on individual's choice influenced by personal goals, financial and non-financial. Price is the outcome of demand and supply of the stock. When demand is more than the supply, price increases, and when supply is more than demand, price decreases. So, price is always determined by those who control demand and supply, and they are major financial institutions – foreign institutional investors (FIIs), and domestic institutional investors (DIIs). In emerging economies, Foreign Portfolio Investment (FPI) and Foreign Institutional Investment (FII) are two terms used frequently. These terms are used in the context of international investments in the financial markets of a country. Traders and investors often track the

FII and FPI inflows to tap the opportunities and predict stock price movements. Though both are foreign investments, they differ in their structure, scope, and regulatory aspects. However, we will use FIIs as a term in the book which will include FPI.

DIIs are a particular class of investors that undertake to invest in financial assets and securities/stocks of the country they are currently residing in. These investment decisions of DIIs are impacted by both political and economic trends. Similar to foreign institutional investors (FIIs), domestic institutional investors (DIIs) can also impact the economy's net investment flows.

In India, domestic institutional investors have quite a decisive role when it comes to the performance of the Indian stock market, especially when foreign institutional investors are the county's net sellers. DIIs include Indian Mutual Funds, Indian Insurance Companies, Local Pension Funds, Banking and Financial Institutions.

The share of retail investors in the total turnover of the NSE as on June 30, 2023 was 7.49%. This is according to data from the National Stock Exchange (NSE). The share of retail investors has been declining in recent years, from a high of 40.7% in FY22. This is due to a number of factors, including the rising cost of investing, the volatility of the stock market, and the increasing popularity of other investment options, such as mutual funds and exchange-traded funds (ETFs).

Despite the decline in their share, retail investors still play an important role in the Indian stock market. They account for a large number of trading volumes and contribute to the liquidity of the market. Retail investors are also becoming more sophisticated in their investment strategies, and they are increasingly investing in long-term growth stocks.

It is important to note that the share of retail investors in the total turnover of the NSE is just one measure of their participation in the market. Other measures, such as the number of retail investors and the amount of money they invest, are also important. Overall, retail investors are a significant force in the Indian stock market, and their participation is likely to continue to grow in the years to come.

Individual Investors as on June 2023

Sr. No.	Name of the Country	Adult Population (in Millions)	Population invested in Stock Market (in Millions)	% of Adult Population, invested in the Stock Market
1	India	923	8.4	0.91
2	USA	254	50	19.68
3	UK	57	6.3	11.05
4	Canada	44	3.2	0.73
5	Australia	25	2.1	8.4
6	China	1004	78	7.77
7	Europe	548	75	13.69
8	Japan	107	40	37.38

(Note: 1. As per NSE's monthly 'Market Pulse' report, the number of retail investors rose sharply from three million in January 2020 to nearly 12 million in January 2022. Thereafter, it fell to 6.7 million in April 2023, before rising to 8.4 million in May 2023 in India. 2. The figures represent investment in Stocks only. In case of USA, individual investors in the stocks, mutual funds, retirement funds, etc, stand at 158 millions. 3. The percentage may vary with changes in parameters, like for India, individual investors stand at 3% of population as per one report. However, the purpose of the data is to reflect the scale of individual investment in the stocks in different countries.)

The purpose of the discussion is to show you that individual investors don't have influential role to drive the stock market as they trade in low volumes individually. FIIs/DIIs have the power to move the market as they trade in huge volumes. Price moves with volume, and the volume is driven by FIIs/DIIs. Our approach is to observe the market where it is going with momentum and volatility, and take the trade to make profit, exactly like we drive the car looking at the traffic.

One important fact that is to be noted by the readers is that any prediction to the price movement is probabilistic. We take the trade when there is high probability. Hence, we need to learn to find out the high probabilistic trades.

Capturing the Movement of Price

In order to understand the price movement, it must be captured in a form which gives a scope for understanding and analysis. Hence, the price movement is captured in the form of a chart/graph. Traditionally, there have been Line charts or Bar charts which were used by the Western investors. But, they never knew that other form of chart was being used by the Far Eastern investors, particularly from Japan.

Japanese candlestick charts were introduced to the United States in 1991 by Steve Nison, a technical analyst and author. His book, *Japanese Candlestick Charting Techniques*, was a bestseller and helped to popularize the use of candlestick charts in the West. Candle charts display accurate map of the market than the bar charts.

1. Candle charts pictorially display the supply-demand situation by showing who is winning the battle between the bulls and the bears.
2. Candle charts show the trend of the market, and add another dimension of analysis by revealing the force behind the move.
3. Candle charts often send out signals of imminent reversals.

It is a very revealing history of Candlestick charts. As narrated by Steve Nison in his book, there is a Japanese saying, "A clever hawk hides its claws." For over a century, the claws of Japanese technical analysis, that is candlestick charts, were a secret hidden from the western world.

The Japanese pioneered the use of technical analysis in one of the world's inaugural futures markets: rice futures. Initiated in the 1600s, the development of the Japanese rice futures market can be attributed to the nation's military past. This market fostered considerable speculation, leading to the emergence of Japanese technical analysis. Homma, a renowned trader from the 1700s, made a profound observation.

He noted that beyond the basic supply-demand dynamics, market emotions significantly influenced rice prices. Occasionally, market sentiment diverged from actual harvest results. Homma deduced that understanding these market sentiments could offer predictive insights into price movements. He recognized a distinction between rice's inherent value and its market price — a concept that remains relevant in today's financial markets encompassing stocks, bonds, etc.

Over time, Homma's candlestick charts spread to other parts of the world, and they have become a popular tool for traders and investors. Today, candlestick charts are used by traders and investors to gain valuable insights into market trends and sentiment, and they are considered an essential tool in many technical analysis systems.

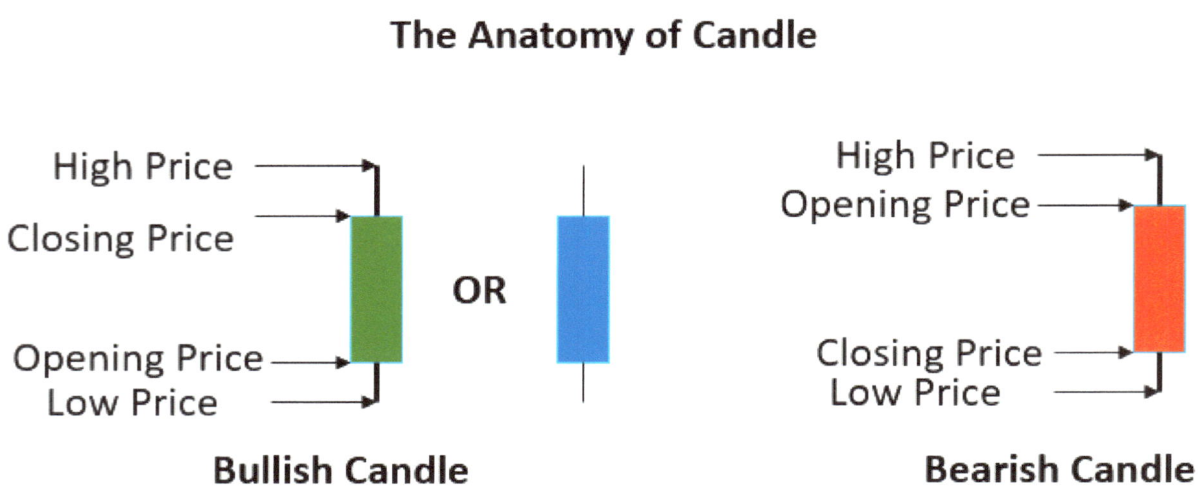

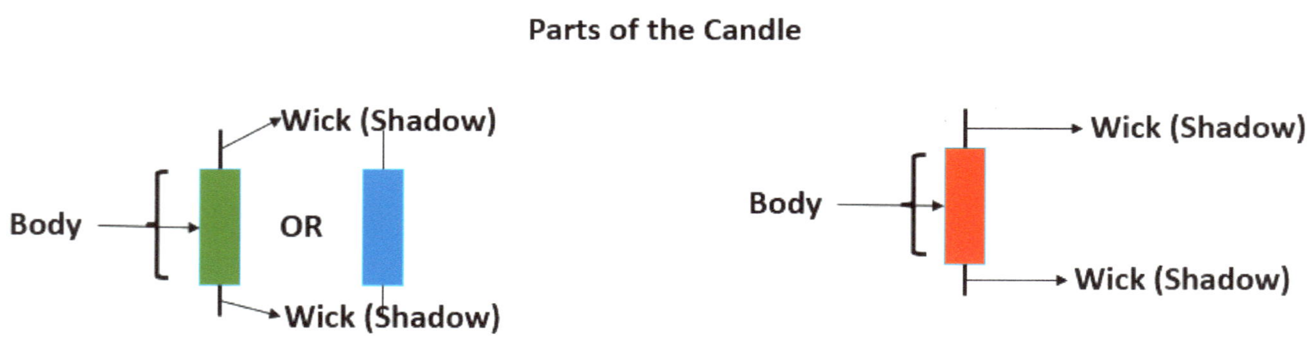

Candlestick charts are the improvisation over Line chart, Pole chart, Bar chart, Anchor chart. Each candlestick on a chart represents a single period of time, such as a day, week, or month. The body of the candlestick shows the difference between the opening and closing prices for that period, while the "wick" or "shadow" shows the high and low prices. If the closing price is higher than the opening price, the body of the candlestick is typically white or hollow or green or blue and is referred to as a "bullish" candlestick. If the closing price is lower than the opening price, the body is typically black or red and is referred to as a "bearish" candlestick.

However, in the fight between Bulls and Bears, different patterns of the candlesticks emerge which represent the power of the bulls and bears which help the investor to predict the future price movement. At this juncture, readers must know that price does not move in a straight line, i.e., price never goes up or goes down like a straight-line. Following picture will make it clear. Price always oscillates. After some rise, there is a fall, and after some fall, there is a rise.

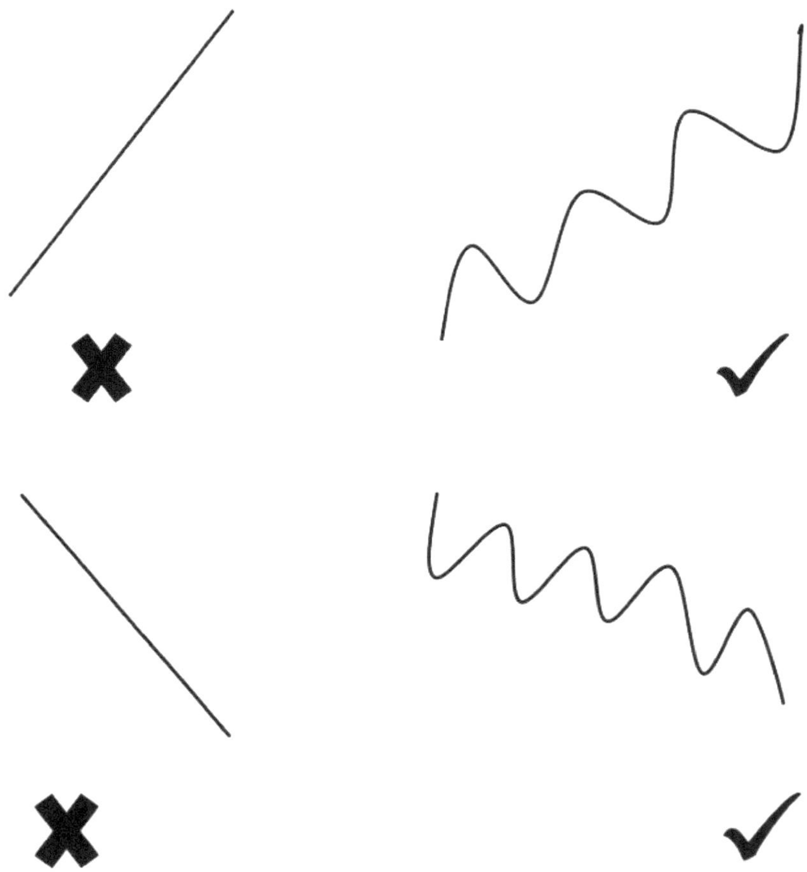

This is the most fascinating aspect of stock trading, as this nature of price movement gives several opportunities to trade. The price movement is captured on various time frames. As a trader or investor, you can follow any time frame which you are comfortable with. Here, we are talking of Intraday trading, and hence, we will trade on 1 minute, or 3 minutes, or 5 minutes, or 15 minutes, time frame. However, we may check the trend of the price movement on higher time frame, like, 1 hour or 1 day. Therefore, on a higher time frame, say, 1-day time frame, the trend is up, but on a lower time frame, say, 5-minutes, we may see the price oscillation where we have many trade-opportunities. Let me show you as follows.

Reliance – Day-chart: You can see the price movement. Price is not going in the straight – line, but it oscillates which is the nature of price movement.

Reliance – 15- minutes chart: You can see the price oscillation. It goes up and goes down. So, in any time frame, you will find this movement-pattern. This gives opportunity to the trader to make profit with right decision. This happens because there is always profit booking at certain level. Hence, there is always a rotation of bullishness and bearishness which means that, within each bull market, there is a bear market, and within a bear market, there is a bull market.

Candle-pattern: The power of Bull and Bear creates patterns. Each candle tells the story of that power. Such story gives wealth of information to the trader, and helps in predicting the movement of price. The Japanese have a saying, "With the fall of one leaf, we know that autumn has come to the world." In this sense, a single candle has a significant indication of price movement.

There are around 45 patterns. However, some traders have categorized over 65 patterns. But, there are 16 patterns which a trader should know. We will discuss those patterns with proper understanding. Remember, the pattern itself may not help much to predict the price movement, but when such patterns are analysed with other dimensions, like place where they are occurring, or with signals given by other indicators, they give proper perspective of probability.

BUY Candles:

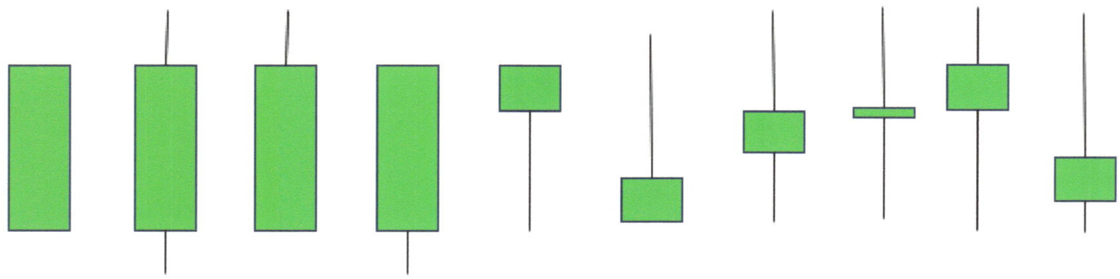

Bullish Candle (as they show upward price movement)

SELL Candles:

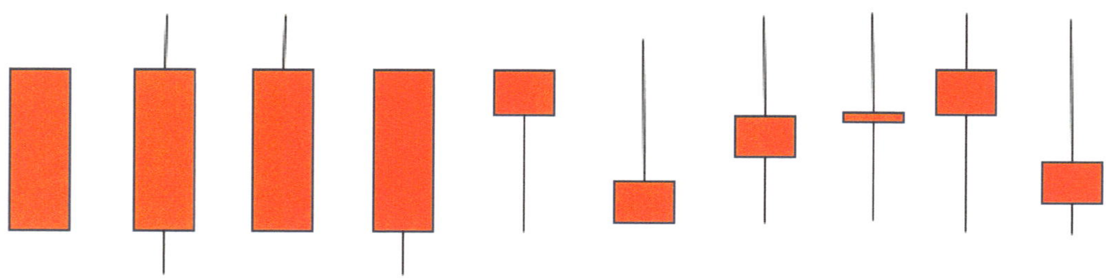

Bearish Candle (as they show downward price movement)

Story of the Candles:

Each candle has its own story to tell about who was powerful – Bull of Bear. Understanding this story, we can predict the future movement of price. Remember, each candle will have one common thing to tell – Opening Price, Closing Price, Highest Price and the Lowest Price. But, more important is to know who is powerful, and hence, where the price is likely to go.

1	Bullish – **Marubozu** (means – “Bald” , “Head-Shaven”)	Bearish – **Marubozu** (means – “Bald” , “Head-Shaven”)
		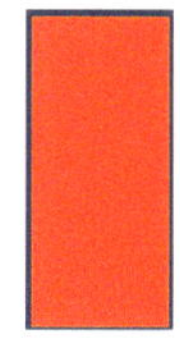
	• A bullish Marubozu candle is a candlestick pattern that indicates strong buying pressure, signaling a potential upward trend or trend reversal. • Long white body represents continuous price growth from opening to closing. • No upper shadow signifies the closing price equaled the highest price of the period. • No lower shadow indicates the opening price was equal to the lowest price of the period. • Such structure indicates strong buying sentiment, i.e., Buyers dominated the trading, pushing prices higher. Buyers are in control. They are ready to pay any higher price for the stock at that time duration. • This suggests a potential upward trend continuation if found within an uptrend, or a possible trend reversal if seen after a downtrend.	• A Bearish Marubozu candle is a candlestick pattern that indicates strong selling pressure, signaling a potential upward trend or trend reversal. • Long black body represents continuous price fall from opening to closing. • No upper shadow signifies the opening price equaled the highest price of the period. • No lower shadow indicates the closing price was equal to the lowest price of the period. • Such structure indicates strong **selling** sentiment, i.e., Sellers dominated the trading, pushing prices lower. Sellers are in control. They are ready to offer any lower price for the stock at that time duration. • This suggests a potential upward trend continuation if found within an uptrend, or a possible trend reversal if seen after a downtrend.
2	Bullish candle with small upper and lower wicks	Bearish candle with small upper and lower wicks

	• A bullish candle with small upper and lower wicks generally signals strong buying pressure and decisive control by buyers.	• A bearish candle with small upper and lower wicks generally signals strong selling pressure and decisive control by sellers.

	• The long white body indicates that the closing price was significantly higher than the opening price, suggesting a sustained buying momentum. • Small Upper Wick means the price briefly tested higher levels but quickly retreated, implying that buyers were eager to buy at any slight dips. • Small Lower Wick signifies that sellers attempted to push the price lower, but buyers quickly stepped in to absorb the selling pressure, demonstrating a strong buying presence. • The market is dominated by buyers, and there's a strong belief that prices will continue to rise. • The lack of significant upper and lower wicks implies that there was little resistance from sellers, further reinforcing the bullish outlook. • This also means Demand is more than the Supply.	• The long black body indicates that the closing price was significantly lower than the opening price, suggesting a sustained selling momentum. • Small Upper Wick means the price briefly tested higher levels but quickly retreated, implying that sellers were ready to sell at any slight dips. • Small Lower Wick signifies that buyers attempted to push the price higher, but sellers quickly stepped in to absorb the buying pressure, demonstrating a strong selling presence. • The market is dominated by sellers, and there's a strong belief that prices will continue to fall.. • The lack of significant upper and lower wicks implies that the support from the buyers was weak, further reinforcing the bearish outlook. • This also means Supply is more than the Demand.
3	Bullish candle with small upper wick	Bearish candle with small upper wick

	• A bullish candle with a small upper wick and no lower wick typically signals strong bullish sentiment and decisive control by buyers. • The long white body indicates that the closing price was significantly higher than the opening price, demonstrating sustained buying pressure. • Small Upper Wick means the price briefly tested higher levels but quickly retreated, suggesting that buyers were eager to buy at any slight dips.	• A bearish candle with a small upper wick and no lower wick typically signals strong bearish sentiment and decisive control by sellers. • The long black body indicates that the closing price was significantly lower than the opening price, demonstrating sustained selling pressure. • Small Upper Wick means the price briefly attempted to move higher but quickly retreated, suggesting that sellers were eager to sell at any slight rallies.

	• No Lower Wick implies that sellers were unable to push the price lower, and buyers absorbed any selling attempts, further solidifying their dominance. • Such structure indicates robust buying pressure signifying buyers are firmly in control, and there's a strong belief that prices will continue to rise. • This also indicates that there is one-sided control. The absence of a lower wick reinforces the lack of resistance from sellers, indicating a potentially powerful uptrend. • If it appears within an existing uptrend, it signals a continuation of the upward momentum. • If it emerges after a downtrend, it could signal a potential reversal to an uptrend.	• No Lower Wick implies that buyers were unable to push the price higher, and sellers absorbed any buying attempts, further solidifying their dominance. • Such structure indicates robust selling pressure and sellers are firmly in control, and there's a strong belief that prices will continue to fall. • This also indicates one-sided control. The absence of a lower wick reinforces the lack of support from buyers, indicating a potentially powerful downtrend. • If it appears within an existing downtrend, it signals a continuation of the downward momentum. • If it emerges after an uptrend, it could signal a potential reversal to a downtrend.
4	Bullish candle with small lower wick	Bearish candle with small lower wick

	• A bullish candle with a small lower wick typically signals strong buying pressure and a potential continuation of an uptrend. • The long white body indicates that the closing price was significantly higher than the opening price, demonstrating sustained buying interest. • Small Lower Wick means that sellers briefly attempted to push the price lower, but buyers quickly stepped in to absorb the selling pressure and drive the price back up. This suggests that buyers are in control and are unwilling to let the price fall.	• A bearish candle with a small lower wick typically signals strong bearish sentiment and a potential continuation of a downtrend or a possible bearish reversal. • The long black body indicates that the closing price was significantly lower than the opening price, demonstrating sustained selling pressure. • Small Lower Wick means that buyers briefly attempted to push the price higher, but sellers quickly regained control and drove the price back down. This suggests that sellers are firmly in control.

	• If it appears within an existing uptrend, it reinforces the bullish momentum and suggests that the uptrend is likely to continue. • If it appears after a period of consolidation or a pullback, it could signal a potential reversal to an uptrend.	• If it appears within an existing downtrend, it reinforces the bearish momentum and suggests that the downtrend is likely to continue. • If it appears after a period of consolidation or a minor uptrend, it could signal a potential reversal to a downtrend.
5	Bullish – (known as Hammer)	Bearish – (known as Hammer)

	• A bullish candle with a long lower wick and no upper wick typically signals strong buying pressure overcoming selling pressure, suggesting a potential bullish reversal or continuation of an uptrend. • The long lower wick indicates that sellers initially pushed the price down, but buyers aggressively stepped in and drove the price back up to close near the high, suggesting a potential shift in momentum towards buyers. • The absence of an upper wick means the price never retreated from its high, reinforcing buyer dominance. • If it appears within an uptrend, it reinforces bullish momentum and suggests the uptrend is likely to continue. • If it appears after a downtrend or consolidation, it could signal a potential reversal to an uptrend.	• A bearish candle with a long lower wick and no upper wick typically signals a potential bearish reversal or continuation of a downtrend, but with some pushback from buyers. • The long lower wick indicates that sellers initially pushed the price down significantly, suggesting strong selling momentum. • However, buyers managed to regain some control and drive the price back up to close near the opening price, forming a bearish candle. • If it appears within a downtrend, it reinforces the downward momentum and suggests the downtrend is likely to continue. • If it appears after a period of consolidation or a minor uptrend, it could signal a potential reversal to a downtrend.

6	Bullish (known as Inverted Hammer)	Bearish (known as Inverted Hammer)
	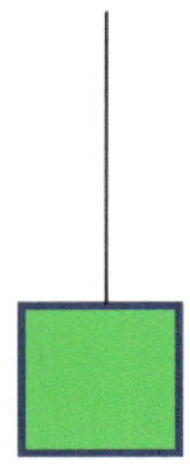	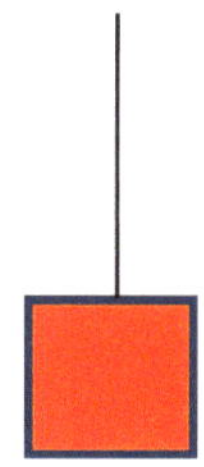
	• A bullish candle with a long upper wick and no lower wick typically signals potential resistance, profit-taking, or a possible reversal, but within a bullish context. • This indicates initial buying pressure. The bullish body indicates buyers initially drove the price up. • The long upper wick suggests that sellers pushed back, capping the price rise and creating resistance. • Some buyers may have exited positions at the high, creating the wick. • The high of the wick could signal a potential resistance level to watch. • If it appears after an uptrend, it could hint at a potential slowdown or reversal. • If it appears within a clear uptrend, it might signal a pause within the trend, not necessarily a reversal.	• A bearish candle with a long upper wick and no lower wick typically signals a potential selling pressure, a possible reversal, or a test of resistance that failed. • The bearish body indicates that sellers initially drove the price down. • The long upper wick suggests that buyers attempted to push the price back up, but sellers ultimately overpowered them, creating resistance. • The high of the wick could mark a resistance level that sellers successfully defended. • If it appears after an uptrend, it could signal a potential slowdown or reversal. • If it appears during the down trend, it could signal a further fall in the price.

7	Bullish (known as Pinbar)	Bearish (known as Pinbar)
	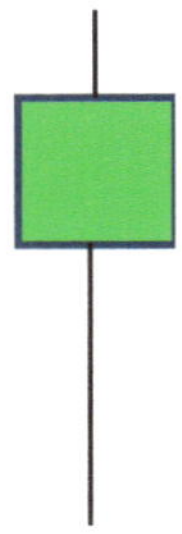	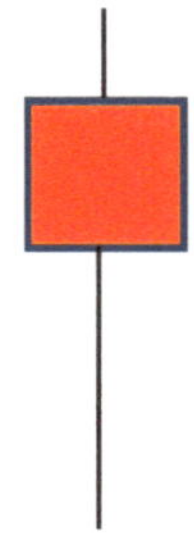
	• Bullish momentum, but not enough to sustain a significant breakout to the upside. • The small upper wick indicates that buyers tried to push the price higher, but sellers resisted, capping the upward movement. • The long lower wick signifies that sellers initially drove the price down, but buyers aggressively stepped in and pushed it back up, closing near the high of the period. This demonstrates strong buying pressure that overpowered the selling pressure. • If this candle pattern appears after a decline, it could signal a potential bullish reversal or at least a pause in the downward trend. • The long lower wick may act as a support level, where buyers are likely to defend against further price drops.	• This suggests potential weakness in the current uptrend and indicates a possible bearish reversal. • The small upper wick signifies that buyers attempted to push the price higher but faced resistance. • The long lower wick suggests that sellers gained control and pushed the price down significantly during the trading period. • This also means a signal to be cautious about the continuation of the upward trend and consider the possibility of a downward move in the market.

8	Bullish (known as Doji)	Bearish (known as Doji)
	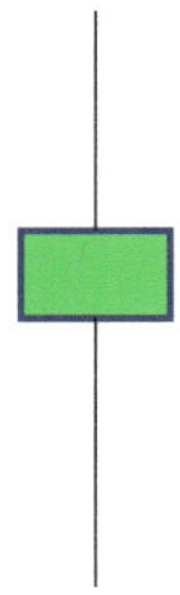	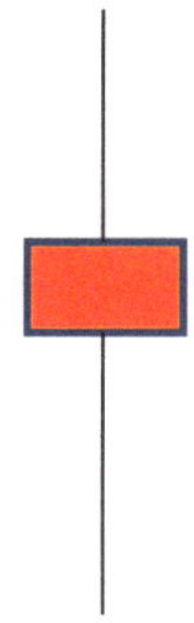
	• This is known as an Indeicision candle. It indicates a change is likely to come in the trend. • The long upper and lower wicks, combined with a small body, indicate a tug-of-war between buyers and sellers, resulting in significant price swings but little net change. • It is a signal either a potential bullish reversal (after a downtrend) or a potential continuation of a bullish trend. The context is crucial for determining the likelihood of either scenario. • The long wicks often highlight important support and resistance levels. The high of the upper wick can act as resistance, while the low of the lower wick can act as support. • Here, colour of the candle is not important as it signifies change.	• This is known as an Indeicision candle. It indicates a change is likely to come in the trend. • The long upper and lower wicks, combined with a small body, indicate a tug-of-war between buyers and sellers, resulting in significant price swings but little net change. • It can signal either a potential bullish reversal (after a downtrend) or a potential continuation of a bearish trend. The context is crucial for determining the likelihood of either scenario. • The long wicks often highlight important support and resistance levels. The high of the upper wick can act as resistance, while the low of the lower wick can act as support. • Here, colour of the candle is not important as it signifies change.

These are the broad formation of candles with price action. The size and shape may differ among these broad formations, but the interpretation largely remains the same. However, there are known important patterns emerge out of the candles during the price action. They are depicted below.

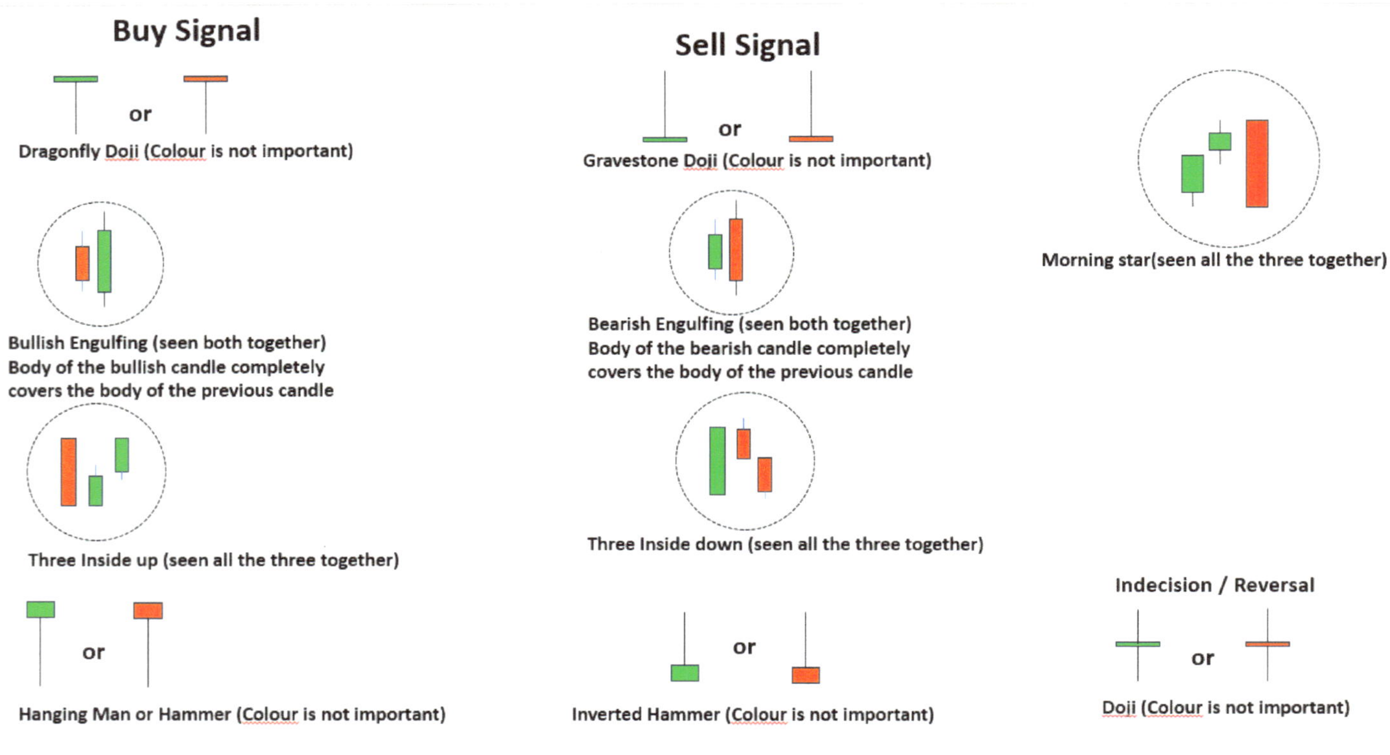

It is very pertinent to note that -

- Analyze these patterns within the broader market context, including recent price action, volume, and other indicators. Its significance and interpretation can vary depending on overall conditions.
- It is advisable to seek additional signals to confirm the potential reversal or support before making trading decisions based solely on this pattern.

Examples:

PVR INOX – Daily Chart
Doji at Resistance level,
and there is Reversal of Trend
Doji at Support level,
and there is Reversal of Trend

PVR INOX – Daily Chart
Bearish Engulfing, happening during the change in trend reversal.
You can see sharp decline thereafter.

Wicks in each candle tell the inside story. Always see from a different perspective, and that is, wicks tell REJECTION. Yes, wicks signify rejection of the price, thus, conveying prominently the Resistance or support. This perspective helps a lot in Intraday trading.

In the book, "The Fountain of Gold-The Three Monkey Record of Money", written by Homma, the author states: "when all are bearish, there is cause for prices to rise. When everyone is bullish, there is cause for the price to fall." This phrase echoes that there is always a rotation of Yang (bullishness) and Yin (bearishness). This means that within each bull market, there is a bear market, and within a bear market, there is a bull market.

Recognizing Chart Patterns:

- Traders identify specific patterns formed by price movements on charts, such as head and shoulders, double tops or bottoms, triangles, and flags. These patterns often indicate potential future price movements, providing traders with opportunities to enter or exit positions. Please understand that these specific patterns in price charts precede certain price movements. For instance, a "head and shoulders" pattern forms when a security's price reaches a peak (the head) with two lower peaks on either side (the shoulders), suggesting a potential trend reversal. Similarly, a "double bottom" pattern occurs when a security's price reaches a low, bounces back, falls again to a similar low, and then rebounds once more, indicating a possible bullish reversal.

    - **Head and Shoulder Pattern**

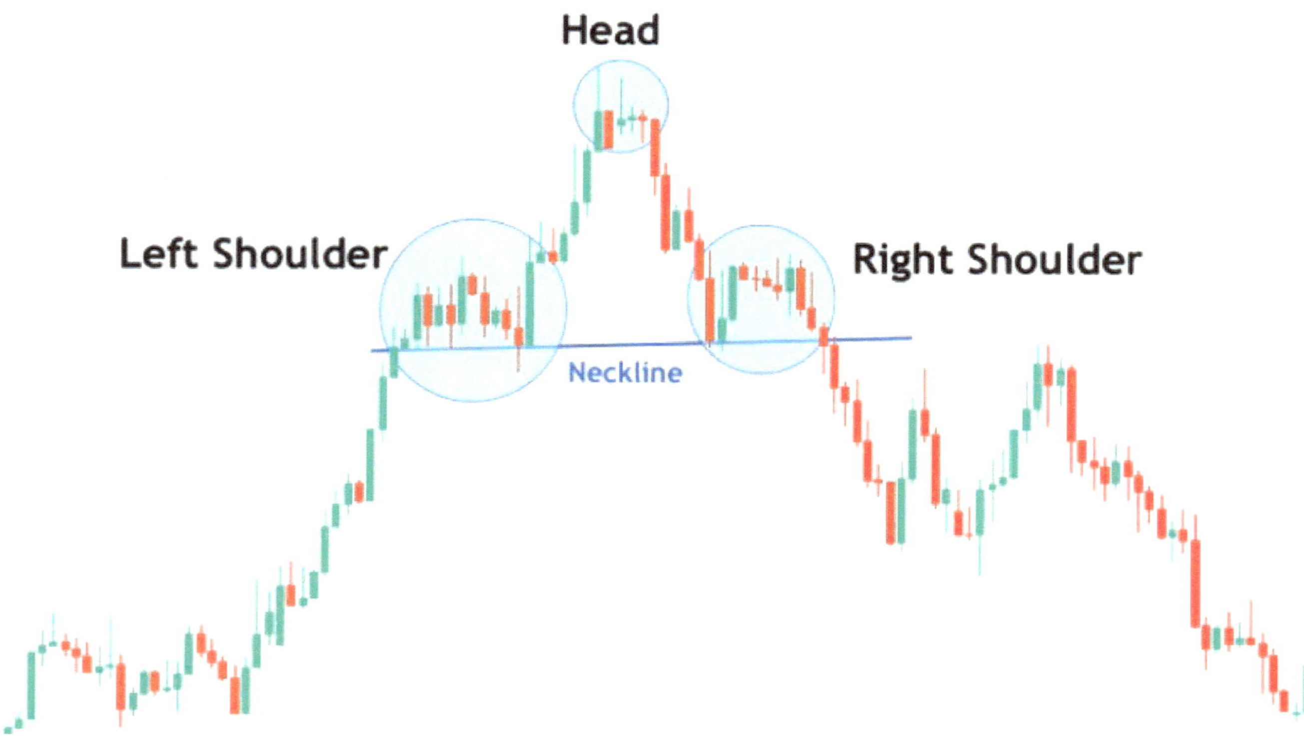

- In the above chart, you can see how price reversal has taken place. One can take the trade during the price reversal from the head, once the neckline is broken.

- **Double Bottom Pattern**

- This is how you take the "BUY" entry.

- **Bullish Flag Pattern**

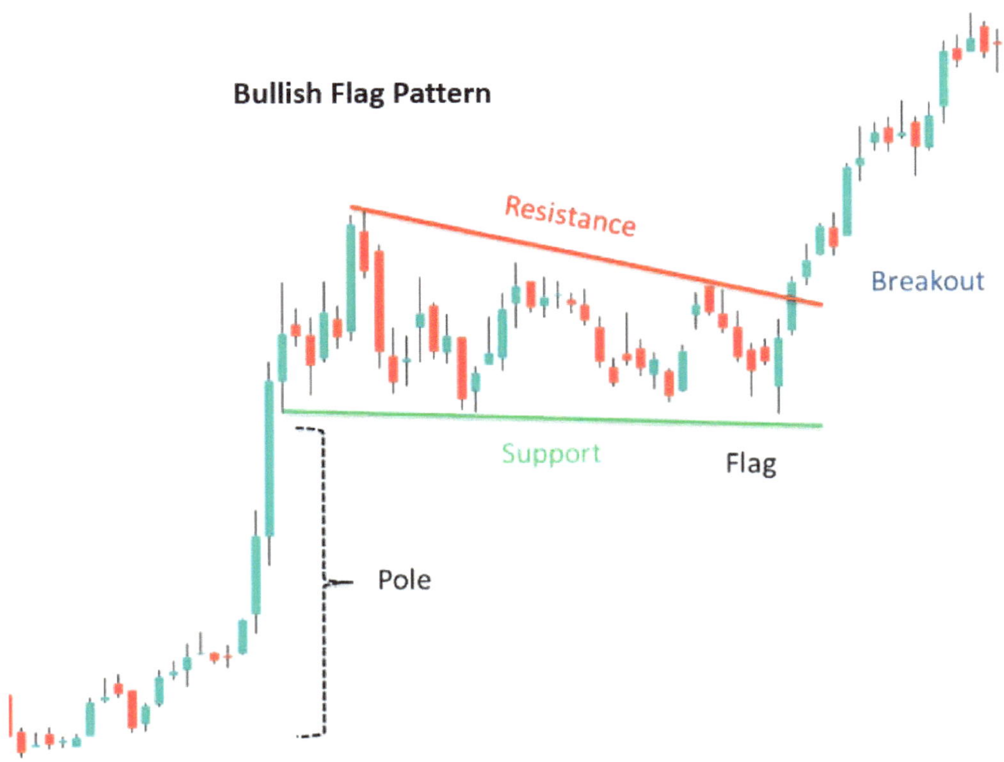

- **Bearish Flag Pattern**

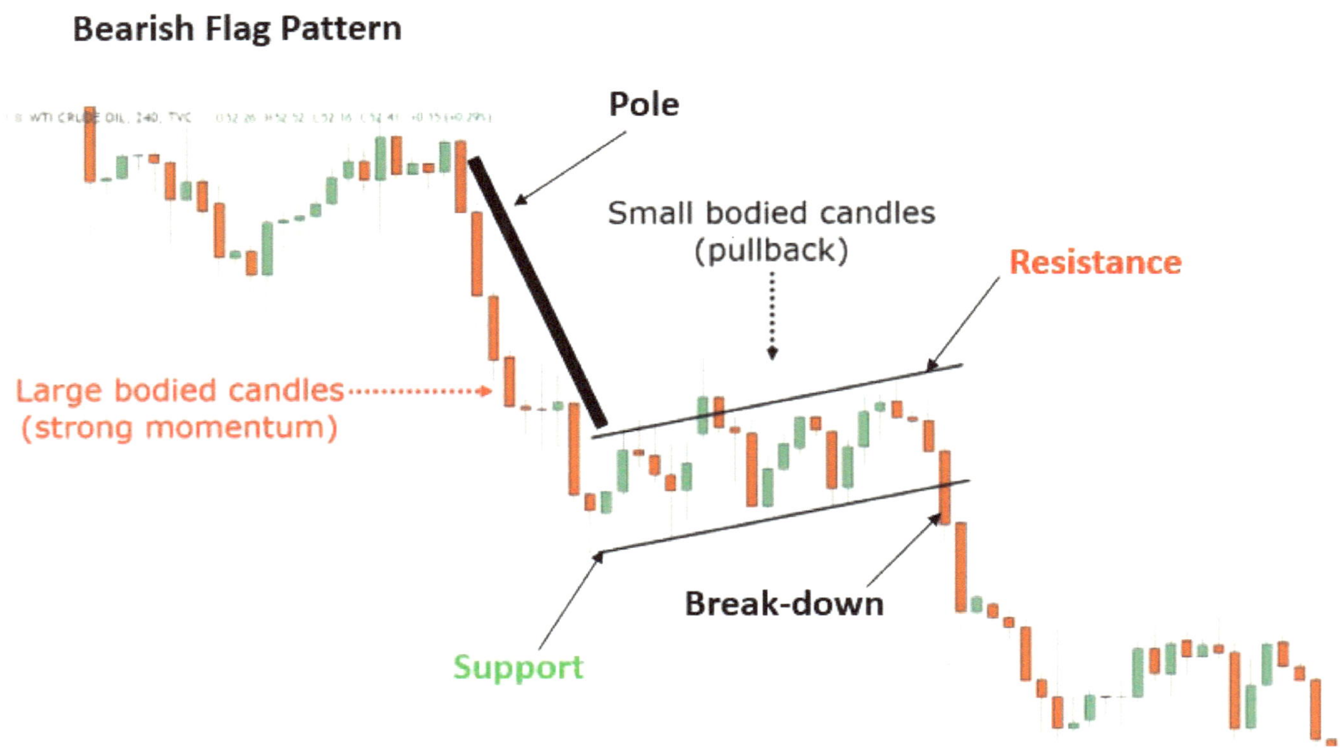

The Core of Price Action:

Traders observe how the price of a stock behaves over different time frames, looking at patterns such as trends, support and resistance levels, and chart formations. Traders study the historical price data of a security, typically represented in candlestick or line charts, to identify trends, support and resistance levels, and chart patterns. By analyzing these movements, they aim to gain insights into the future direction of prices. For example, if a stock's price has been steadily increasing, traders may identify it as an uptrend. Conversely, if the price consistently struggles to rise above a certain level, it could indicate a strong resistance level.

The following aspects of Price action need basic understanding.

- **Demand and Supply:** "Price Action" is dance-play of demand and supply. The stock market, like any other market, lives and breathes on the principles of demand and supply. This fundamental economic force dictates how much investors are willing to pay for a particular stock (**demand**) and how many shares are available for purchase (**supply**). Understanding this interplay is crucial for anyone wanting to understand price action in stock trading.

How it works:

- **Demand:** This reflects the willingness and ability of investors to buy a stock. Factors like positive company news, strong earning reports, industry growth, or economic optimism can **increase**

demand, driving the price **up**. Conversely, negative news, weak financials, industry decline, or wider economic concerns can **decrease demand**, pushing the price **down**.

Supply: This refers to the number of shares available for purchase. Company buybacks, stock splits, can **decrease supply**, making the remaining shares more valuable and pushing the price **up**. In contrast, companies issuing new shares, selling treasury stock, or industry-wide downturns can **increase supply**, making shares more readily available and potentially lowering the price.

Now, let's look at some situations:

- **Situation 1: Positive News Boom:** Imagine Company X announces a groundbreaking product launch. Excitement surges, attracting new investors and increasing demand for the stock. As more buyers chase the limited shares, the price steadily rises, reflecting the strong demand.
- **Situation 2: Earnings Miss:** Company Y reports disappointing earnings, falling short of analyst expectations. Investors lose confidence, leading to selling and decreased demand. With more shares available than buyers, the price dips as supply outweighs demand.
- **Situation 3: Stock Split:** Company Z announces a 2-for-1 stock split. While the total company value remains the same, the individual share price becomes lower. This increased **accessibility** can attract new investors, initially boosting demand and potentially pushing the price slightly higher.
- **Situation 4: New Share Issuance:** Company W needs capital and issues new shares. This directly **increases supply**, diluting the ownership of existing shareholders and potentially lowering the price per share as more shares compete for the same investor pool.
- **Supply and Demand Zones:** Traders often identify areas on charts where buying and selling pressure historically concentrated, called «supply and demand zones.» These zones can provide insights into potential support and resistance levels for future price movements.
- **Technical Indicators:** Tools like Relative Strength Index (RSI) and On-Balance Volume (OBV) can help gauge market sentiment and potential shifts in supply and demand dynamics.

Important to remember:

- While demand and supply are fundamental, the stock market is complex. Other factors like market sentiment, technical analysis, and short-term trading activity can also influence price action.
- Predicting exact price movements based solely on supply and demand is impossible. However, understanding these forces can give you a valuable framework for interpreting price movements and making better investment decisions.
- Demand and supply zones of higher time frames are more reliable for price reversals.

Having understood the demand and supply, let's see on the chart and generate more understanding on buyers' and sellers' behaviour. This will help us to understand why price moves up and moves down.

First of all, understand how we behave as buyers and sellers. We always love to buy at lower price and love to sell always at higher price. Think of, when we go to a vegetable market, we always negotiate to buy at lower price. Think of, when we sell our second-hand car, we always love to sell at higher price. This is the fundamental rule which applies to everything which has demand and supply, means, which has buyers and sellers.

Why Price moves up and moves down ?

You must remember the fact that “Sellers” are most important in the movement of price. They always “offer” their price, and buyers “accept or bid” the price offered by the sellers. However, the buyers’ readiness to pay for the offer decides the sellers’ offer price. For example, the current price of Reliance Industries is Rs. 2800. Sellers will always like to sell at higher price. So, sellers offer at Rs. 2850, and buyers accept the offer, there will be a transaction. Now, sellers will increase their offer price further, say, at Rs. 2900. Here, buyers again accept the offer. Again, sellers will increase the offer price, thinking that buyers are ready to pay higher price. Seller increase the offer price to Rs. 2950, then Rs. 3000. Now, buyers accept the offer at Rs. 2950, but do not accept the offer at Rs. 3000. Therefore, price will not increase further as there are no buyers available at Rs. 3000. So, sellers will decrease the offer price to Rs. 2950. Here, no buyers are interested, so sellers will keep on decreasing their offer price till they get buyers. Hence, no buyers’ price area is an “illiquidity zone”. Therefore, price will always move from “illiquidity zone” to “liquidity zone” where buyers are available. So, when buyers are not interested to sellers’ offer price, sellers will keep on reducing the price. They become active. Sellers are more than buyers. They increase their supply to attract more buyers. This becomes the Supply Zone. This forms a Resistance area, meaning, price is not ready to go up beyond a certain level of price.

Now, the price has reached at Rs. 2500. Here, sellers are not interested to offer lesser than Rs. 2500. Hence, there are no sellers. So, buyers are now ready to pay higher price. Sellers offer Rs. 2550, buyers are ready to pay. Now, sellers, having seen buyers’ interest reviving, they increase their offer price to Rs. 2600. Buyers are accepting the price. Price will go up again. Therefore, at Rs. 2500, sellers are not interested to reduce their offer price further, so buyers will now come into picture as they know stock of Reliance Industries will not be available at Rs. 2500 and less. Hence, they get ready to pay higher price. So, buyers are now becoming more than sellers, which will increase the price further. This becomes a Deman Zone. This forms a Support area.

In the above chart, from point 1 (Rs. 250) , price has moved up to Point 2 (Rs. 300). From Point 2 (Rs. 300) to Point 3 (Rs. 250), the price has moved down – why ?

At Point 1, there are no sellers to sell at below Rs. 250. They decided not to sell below Rs. 250. Now, they are asking for more price. So, buyers are now ready to higher price as they perceive that at this level, the price is cheaper. So, when they are ready to buy at higher price. Now, sellers have understood that buyers are ready to buy at higher price, so, sellers now keep on increasing the price, and buyers are willing to pay higher price. Hence, price is moving up.

Now, their trade reaches at Point 2 – Rs. 300. Now, at this point, buyers are not ready to pay higher price, as they perceive that this stock has become costly. So, there are no buyers at this price of Rs. 300. Sellers have understood that they will not get higher price. So, they are now ready to sell at lower price, and buyers are now ready to buy at less than Rs. 300. Hence, sellers keep on decreasing the price, and buyers keep on buying as they feel that this the cheaper price. Therefore, price is moving down.

Now, their trade reaches at Point 3 – Rs. 250. Sellers are now not ready to sell at less than Rs. 250. Now, buyers are ready to buy at higher price, and the price is moving up once again from Point 3.

A point to understand is – at Point 1, there are no sellers (or lesser sellers than buyers). At point 2, there no buyers (or lesser buyers than sellers). At point 3, there are no sellers (or lesser sellers than buyers). We always interpret this as - at Point 1, there are more buyers, hence, price moves up. At point

2, there more sellers, hence, price moves down. At point 3, there are more buyers, once again, hence, price moves up.

2. Volume Analysis:

Volume analysis involves studying trading volume alongside price action. Changes in trading volume can confirm the strength of a trend or signal potential reversals. High volume during price movements often indicates increased investor interest and conviction, supporting the validity of price action signals. For example, a significant increase in trading volume during an upward price movement suggests strong buying interest, validating the bullish trend. Conversely, a decrease in volume during a price rally may indicate weakening momentum and a potential reversal. Traders use volume analysis to confirm the strength of trends and identify potential trend reversals.

Volumes represent the total number of shares traded within a specified timeframe, reflecting the level of activity in a stock. The higher the volume, the more active the trading. For instance, if you purchase 100 shares of Reliance Industries at Rs. 2700, and another individual sells 100 shares of the same stock at the same price, a trade occurs, contributing 100 shares to the volume. It's essential to note that volume is not doubled by both buying and selling actions; it remains at 100 shares despite the transaction involving two parties. Thus, the correct interpretation of volume focuses on the total number of shares exchanged, rather than summing up buying and selling quantities separately, which can lead to misconceptions about trading activity.

- In the above chart of Gland Pharma (15 minutes time frame), you can see volume candles below and price candles above. Also, there is a blue line on the volume candles which indicate average volume of last 20 candles. Observations:
- The first volume candle and its related price candle, it is a red candle which means there is a fall in the price with more selling volume, but less than average volume. You wait to observe what happens next.
- In the second volume candle, there is selling volume more than average volume causing greater fall in the price which you can see in its related second price candle.
- Third candle is very interesting. The volume is more than the average volume, but less than the previous candle volume, and if you look at the price candle, there is a long lower shadow which means that there is a rejection of the fall in the price. This means that there is a high probability of price reversal. Here you can decide to take the "buy" trade.
- Now, you are in the trade. Look at the 10th candle. Volume is more than the previous candles, and more than the average volume, but the price rise is not adequate as to the increase in the volume. So, some correction is in place. Look at the 11th candle. There is a fall in the volume as to previous candle, and other previous candles, but there is some rise in the price. This means, now, there is a high probability of price reversal. So, you take the exit.
- Please note that trades are not taken by just looking at the volume, but other indicators are also taken into consideration. The point is volume indicates strong signals of trade.

Volume without delivery typically reflects short-term trading activities, such as intraday speculation or arbitrage, which may contribute to short-term price fluctuations due to increased trading activity and liquidity. However, it may not necessarily indicate significant changes in long-term investor sentiment or fundamentals. For example, if investor A buys 500 shares of Company X and sells them later the same day, both transactions contribute to the volume without delivery. For instance, if investor B buys 200 shares of Company Y and holds onto them beyond the trading day, contributing to the delivery volume.

In contrast, volume with delivery reflects genuine investor interest and commitment, as investors hold onto the shares for more extended periods, potentially influencing price action based on fundamental factors, such as earnings reports, industry trends, or macroeconomic conditions.

Understanding the distinction between volume without delivery and volume with delivery can provide insights into the nature of trading activity and its impact on price action, helping investors make better decisions.

As an intraday trader, understanding both volume traded and delivery volume is crucial for assessing demand and supply dynamics in stock markets. Price and volume serve as key indicators for studying stock price movements. Delivery volume, provided by stock exchanges, aids in predicting short-term market trends. Distinguishing between these tools is essential for traders. Not all trades settle, with some being intraday, where positions close within the day. Delivery volume, calculated by deducting intraday volume from total volume, indicates accumulation of shares, signaling investor interest in a stock's prospects. Analyzing delivery volume, particularly during breakouts, helps predict trends. Consider these situations.

Situation 1: Total trading volume: 1000 shares. The price increase is say, 5%. This indicates strong bullish sentiment, yet uncertainty remains about near-term trends.

Situation 2: Total trading volume: 1000 shares. The price increase is say, 10%. 700 shares are with delivery volume. This implies 70% of trades settled, suggesting bullish anticipation for the future.

Situation 3: Total trading volume: 1000 shares. The price increase is say, 12%. The delivery volume is 200 shares. This indicates low delivery volume, signaling mass trader exits, making near-term price uptrend unpredictable.

These scenarios illustrate the significance of delivery volume in understanding market sentiment and predicting price movements.

3. Momentum: Momentum, within the context of price action, refers to the rate at which the price of a share is changing over time. It reflects the strength and velocity of price movements, indicating whether the share is gaining or losing momentum. In price action trading, momentum is crucial for identifying potential trading opportunities and confirming the validity of trends.

Key Aspects of Momentum in Price Action:

- **Rate of Price Change:** Momentum measures the speed of price movements, showing how quickly the price is rising or falling.
- **Strength of Trends:** Strong momentum suggests that a trend is robust and likely to continue, while weakening momentum may signal a potential trend reversal.
- **Confirmation of Patterns:** Momentum can confirm the validity of chart patterns and technical indicators. For example, if a bullish trend is supported by strong upward momentum, it reinforces the bullish bias.
- **Breakouts:** When a stock breaks above a key resistance level with strong momentum, it confirms the breakout and signals a potential uptrend continuation.
- **Divergence:** Divergence between price and the momentum can indicate a weakening trend, suggesting a possible reversal.
- **Trend Strength:** A steadily increasing or decreasing price with consistent momentum indicates a strong trend, providing confidence to traders to enter or hold positions.
- **Volume Confirmation:** High trading volume accompanying price movements reinforces the momentum, validating the strength of the trend.

Momentum trading strategies capitalize on these momentum signals, aiming to buy during upward momentum and sell during downward momentum to profit from price movements. There are indicators like Relative Strength Index (RSI), Moving Average Convergence Divergence (MACD), Average Directional Index (ADX), etc. available reflecting Momentum. These indicators assist traders in analyzing the force behind price movements, identifying potential entry and exit points, and confirming the strength of trends.

You may feel stressed and less confident while studying above price action aspects that how to understand all those points and take the trades. You may feel that such understanding may be acquired after a long time spending in the trading. This feeling is right. So, this is where the technology comes into play for you. You don't require to gain knowledge on these aspects for years, and to wait. But, the technology will help to apply all these with reasonable understanding of price action quickly with sufficient practice in couple of months. You need to understand tools and indicators and application of them. In fact, those tools and indicators possess required knowledge, while you need to understand how to apply. That is why I emphasize that in trading, you require less of knowledge and more of skills. Do you require to understand the mechanism of a car to drive ? No, not at all. Trading View is one of the best platforms which provide that technology which you will understand in the coming chapters.

CHAPTER – 05

The Power of Technology and Tools

Technology has revolutionized the way retail traders participate in the stock market, offering various tools and resources that can significantly impact their trading experience and potential success.

How a Retail Trader is Empowered

1. Information flow for all:

- **Real-time data**: Access to live quotes, news, and market updates empowers informed decision-making, unlike the limited information available in the past. National Stock Exchange website and many other platforms provide real-time data which help in trading.
- **Financial news and analysis**: Online platforms aggregate financial news, analyst reports, and research, providing insights previously reserved for institutional investors. Platforms like Moneycontrol provide valuable reports, and analysis on real-time for better trading decisions.
- **Educational resources**: Online courses, webinars, and educational content allow traders to learn technical analysis, fundamental analysis, and various trading strategies. Hundreds of audio and video material available for continuous learning.

2. Enhanced trading experience:

- **User-friendly charting platforms**: Platforms like Trading View provide excellent charting and analysis tools with real time data for instant trading decisions.
- **User-friendly trading platforms**: Intuitive interfaces and mobile apps enable convenient trading from anywhere, eliminating the need for physical trading floors. You get real-time connected with brokers like Fyers, Zerodha, Motilal Oswal, etc. Now, there is no need to give a call for buy and sell. You yourself can place orders.
- **Fractional shares**: Platforms now allow buying fractions of shares, making expensive stocks more accessible and facilitating portfolio diversification.
- **Order types and automation**: Advanced order types like stop-loss and limit orders help manage risk and automate specific trading strategies.
- **Back-testing and paper trading**: Simulating trades with historical data allows testing strategies without risking real capital.

3. Data analysis and Automation:

- **Algorithmic trading**: Automated trading tools based on technical indicators and quantitative analysis can execute trades based on predefined rules, potentially improving efficiency and removing emotional biases. Platforms like Quantopian and Trade Ideas let you build and automate trading strategies based on technical indicators and quantitative analysis, removing emotions from decision-making.

- **Machine learning**: AI-powered tools can analyze vast amounts of data, identify trading opportunities, and even generate personalized recommendations. Tools like Kensho and Sentifi use AI to analyze vast datasets, identify trading opportunities based on news sentiment, social media buzz, and alternative data sources, providing insights beyond traditional analysis.
- **Chatbots and virtual assistants**: These tools can answer basic trading questions, provide market updates, and even execute simple trades.
- **Writing code for indicators:** AI tools like ChatGPT and Google Jemini can write codes in Pine Script for Trading View platform for your set ups. Now, there is no need to learn coding.

However, it's crucial to remember:

- Technology is a tool, not a guarantee of success. Sound investment principles, risk management, and continuous learning are still essential.
- Over-reliance on technology can lead to impulsive decisions and ignoring fundamental factors.
- Not all tech platforms are created equal. Choose reputable brokers and tools with clear fees and features that align with your trading goals.
- By effectively utilizing technology while maintaining responsible trading practices, retail investors like us can gain a significant edge in the ever-evolving stock market. The technology offers retail traders the means to access information, conduct analysis, automate trading, stay connected to the market, enhance their knowledge, learn from others, and manage their risk exposure more effectively, ultimately helping them to make more informed and strategic trading decisions.

4. Two Platforms:

I am presenting here two platforms which are very popular and used by millions for trading. One is Trading View which is a charting and analysis platform, and other one is FYERS which is a trading platform means it's an online broker. A retail trader has to work on both these platforms for trading activities. On trading View, you analyse and plan, while on FYERS you implement your trade based on the analysis.

1. Trading View (https://in.tradingview.com):

TradingView is a popular online platform that caters to both traders and investors, offering a **combination of charting tools, social networking, and trading capabilities**. There are over 50 million registered users worldwide on the platform. Here's a breakdown of its key features and applications:

a. Charting Tools:

- **Extensive chart types:** Support for line, bar, candlestick, Heikin Ashi, and other chart types.
- **Technical indicators:** Over 400 built-in technical indicators and the ability to create custom ones.

- **Drawing tools:** Over 110 drawing tools for trendlines, Fibonacci retracements, support/resistance levels, and more.
- **Multiple timeframes:** Analyze charts across various timeframes, from seconds to months, for broader context.
- **Alerts and notifications:** Set price alerts, indicator alerts, and custom notifications to stay informed.
- **Paper trading:** Practice trading strategies risk-free with a virtual account and simulated funds.

b. Social Networking:

- **Follow other traders:** Discover and follow successful traders to learn from their strategies.
- **Share ideas and analysis:** Publish your charts, ideas, and analysis with the TradingView community.
- **Discuss markets:** Participate in discussions and forums about specific markets and instruments.
- **Live chat:** Chat with other traders in real-time to exchange ideas and insights.

c. Trading Capabilities:

- **Broker integration:** Trade directly from TradingView charts with integrated brokers (subject to specific broker availability).
- **Paper trading:** As mentioned earlier, practice trading with a virtual account to test strategies before risking real capital.
- **Alerts and notifications:** Utilize these for potential entry and exit points in live trades.

d. Applications:

- **Technical analysis:** Conduct in-depth technical analysis using various indicators, drawing tools, and chart types.
- **Identifying trading opportunities:** Spot potential entries and exits based on technical analysis and chart patterns.
- **Portfolio tracking:** Track the performance of your investments and analyze their behavior.
- **Learning and development:** Explore the platform›s educational resources, community discussions, and expert analysis to enhance your trading knowledge.
- **Staying informed:** Follow relevant markets, news, and economic events to make informed investment decisions.
- **Free and paid plans:** TradingView offers a free basic plan with limited features, and paid plans for more advanced functionalities.
- You can see the following snapshot of the Trading View chart which gives an idea how it works. Different functions are depicted with arrows in the snapshot.

2. FYERS (http://fyers.in)

Among on-line brokers, I have personally found FYERS as one of the most teachnology-savy trading platform which have brilliant features that can be used easily without any complexity and excellent customer support.

FYERS is a trailblazing stockbroking firm founded in 2015, headquartered in Bangalore, India. The company's mission is to simplify trading for retail investors through innovative technology and exceptional customer service. Over the years, FYERS has become one of the fastest-growing, bootstrapped stockbroking firms in India, known for its transparency, low-cost trading, and user-friendly platforms.

3. Technology at FYERS

FYERS harnesses advanced technology to create seamless trading experiences. The key technological aspects and USPs include:

- **First Broker to Provide TradingView:** FYERS was the pioneer in integrating TradingView, offering unparalleled charting and analysis tools.
- **Rapid Account Opening:** FYERS offers an account opening process that takes just 5 minutes, with complete details auto-fetching, making it quick and hassle-free.
- **In-house APIs:** FYERS provides robust in-house APIs for developers and traders, and was the first broker to offer these APIs for free.
- **Disaster Recovery (DR) Servers:** FYERS employs Disaster Recovery servers to mitigate outages and ensure seamless trading experiences.

- **Status Dashboard:** This transparency feature allows users to monitor the status of various services in real-time, enhancing trust and reliability.
- **Colocation Servers:** FYERS provides colocation servers for high-frequency trading, offering traders a significant edge in terms of speed and reliability.
- **Low Latency:** Since most of FYERS' technology is developed in-house, their API latency is the industry's best at 50ms, with plans to optimize it to 20ms.
- **FYERS App:** The mobile application is a one-stop solution for all trading needs, integrating news, fundamental and technical analysis, and trading tools.
- **Traders Journal:** A feature within the app that helps traders track their trades, analyze their performance, and refine their strategies.
- **Industry First Features:** FYERS offers many industry firsts such as trading from charts, verified P&L, FYERS TV, and more.
- **Catering to NRIs:** FYERS offers services tailored for Non-Resident Indians (NRIs).
- **Minor Demat Account:** FYERS supports opening Demat accounts for minors.
- **Multi-lingual Support:** FYERS provides support in up to 8 languages, catering to a diverse client base.

4. Features for Intraday Traders

- FYERS offers several features tailored for intraday traders, particularly those engaged in scalping or day trading:
- **Advanced Charting and Indicators:** Real-time charts with multiple indicators help traders quickly identify trends and make informed decisions.
- **Quick Order Placement:** The platforms support features like one-click order placement and basket orders, which save time during high-volatility trading.
- **High-Speed Execution:** Low latency infrastructure ensures that trades are executed swiftly, minimizing slippage and maximizing profitability.
- **Risk Management Tools:** Features like stop-loss and trailing stop-loss orders help traders manage their risk efficiently.
- **FYERS App:** A one-stop solution for all trading needs, the app integrates news, fundamental and technical analysis, and trading tools, simplifying the trading process for users.
- **Traders Journal:** A feature within the app that helps traders track their trades, analyze their performance, and refine their strategies.

Their founders Tejas Khoday and Yashas Khoday have very impressive entrepreneurial drive in building FYERS as one of the foremost technology on-line broking platforms. At the age of 16, Tejas discovered the dynamic world of stock markets, igniting a passion for trading, investing, and decoding the intricacies of finance. He embarked on a journey of active trading early on, quickly recognizing the limitations of India's conventional brokerage services. Driven by a desire to revolutionize the trading and investing landscape, Tejas set out to create something extraordinary. In 2015, Tejas founded FYERS with his brothers, a technology-driven brokerage firm that has since attracted over 700,000 clients as of October 2023. Drawing from his diverse experiences in both domestic and international firms, Tejas successfully bootstrapped FYERS into a debt-free, profitable company, with a net worth exceeding Rs. 100 crores and a workforce of 300+ adept capital market professionals.Tejas holds Bachelor's and Master's degrees in finance. He has been featured in the "35 under 35" Entrepreneur India Awards. Under his leadership, FYERS has earned numerous accolades, including the title of "Bootstrapped Start-up of the Year" in the 2021 Entrepreneur Awards. His brother, Yashas is an intrepid explorer and astute problem solver, embodying dynamic skill sets that blend technology and financial markets. His adeptness in overcoming technological challenges and constructing scalable, resilient platforms has been a cornerstone in the triumph of FYERS, significantly contributing to its status in the ever-evolving landscape of Indian stock markets. In 2021, Yashas was recognized in Business World Disrupt's esteemed '30 Under 30' list, celebrated as a successful, self-funded entrepreneur and India's youngest stock broker. An accomplished algorithmic trader, Yashas focuses on delivering an unparalleled experience to modern traders and investors, upheld by a formidable team of over 100 dedicated tech professionals. Yashas holds a Bachelor's degree in Economics (Honours), and Portfolio Management from the Indian Institute of Management (IIM), Bangalore.

5. Algorithm-based Trading also known as algo trading or automated trading, is a method of executing orders using pre-programmed trading instructions. Unlike traditional manual trading, algorithmic trading relies on advanced mathematical models and computer algorithms to make trading decisions swiftly and efficiently.

Algorithmic trading leverages technology to automate trading processes, enabling traders to execute large orders at optimal prices with minimal human intervention. This approach enhances speed, accuracy, and efficiency in executing trades, leading to better trade execution and reduced transaction costs.

How Algo Trading is different from Traditional Trading:

Traditional trading relies heavily on human judgment and intuition, whereas algorithmic trading uses predetermined rules and algorithms to execute trades. Algorithmic trading operates at high speeds, enabling timely responses to market changes and exploiting fleeting opportunities that may be missed by human traders. Moreover, algorithmic trading can handle large volumes of data and execute trades across multiple markets simultaneously.

It is a further advancement in technology in which a cloud-based trading platform lets users create, test, and deploy trading strategies without needing to code. Users can easily design their strategies, test them on past data, and launch them in the market. The platform specializes in optimizing and analyzing the performance of strategies. It supports multiple exchanges and offers strong back-testing and live trading features. It includes advanced charting tools, various order types, and a complete environment for algorithmic trading. The platform has many pre-built algorithms and a user-friendly interface for strategy creation and deployment. It also provides advanced tools for order management and execution, suitable for both individual and institutional traders. It focuses on fund management and algorithmic trading with features for strategy development, risk management, and execution. The platform offers a full trading suite with advanced charting, support for multiple strategies, and real-time execution. It supports multiple third-party platforms like TradingView, Amibroker, and Python, and offers free algo trading execution.

Algo Trading Process

1. Market Analysis and Strategy Development:

- Analyze market trends using technical charts and indicators, such as moving averages and volume trends.
- Use your trading set-up which can be easily implemented as an Algo trade.

2. Choosing the Right Stocks:

- Apply any method for selecting the right stocks which is prior to the trading day. This will help to create right alerts which can be implemented as Algos.
- You can refer to the various methods as stated in the forthcoming chapter on Selection of Stocks.

3. Algorithm Creation:

- Create algorithms to execute the strategy. These algorithms include rules for entry and exit points, risk management, and position sizing.
- There are Algo platforms which can easily integrate TradingView or Chartink like Ahmedabad-based Algofox, a leading Algo platform.

4. Backtesting:

- Test the algorithms on historical data to ensure they perform well in different market conditions.
- This helps in refining the strategy and identifying potential issues before real-time trading.

5. Implementation and Execution:

- Use trading software and bots to implement the algorithms.
- These tools automatically execute trades based on the predefined rules without manual intervention.

6. Monitoring and Adjustment:

- Continuously monitor the performance of the algorithms in real-time and make necessary adjustments based on market conditions and performance feedback.

How Algo Trading Resolves Common Intraday Trading Problems

1. Entering Incorrect Types of Orders

- Algorithmic trading automates order placement, ensuring the correct order types (market, limit, etc.) are used based on predefined strategies, reducing human error.

2. Obsolete Online Stock Broker

- Algo trading platforms are typically integrated with technologically advanced on-line brokers, ensuring efficient trade execution, real-time data, and robust infrastructure.

3. Trading with Untested or No Strategy

- Algorithms are back-tested using historical data to validate strategies before live trading, ensuring they are effective and reducing the risk of significant losses from untested methods.

4. Sticking with Traditional (Manual) Trading

- Algorithms can quickly analyze market conditions and execute trades, taking advantage of fleeting opportunities that manual trading might miss due to slower reaction times.

5. Lack of Risk Assessment Knowledge

- Algorithms incorporate risk management rules, such as stop-loss and target-profit levels, to manage risks effectively and protect against significant losses.

6. Inadequate Access to Latest News

4. Some algorithmic trading systems integrate with real-time news feeds and can automatically adjust strategies based on market-moving news, ensuring timely reactions to new information.

7. Trading Against the Trend

- Algorithms can be programmed to follow market trends, adhering to technical indicators and avoiding trades that go against the prevailing market direction.

8. Emotions Overpowering Indicators and Signals

- Algorithms execute trades based on predefined rules and indicators, eliminating emotional biases like fear and greed, and ensuring consistent, rational decision-making.

9. Lack of Trading Discipline

- Automated systems enforce trading discipline by strictly following the programmed strategy without deviations, maintaining consistency and avoiding impulsive trades.

10. Over-trading

- Algorithms can be set to trade only when specific conditions are met, preventing over-trading and reducing unnecessary transaction costs and fatigue.

11. Lack of Patience

- Algorithms wait for optimal trading conditions based on the strategy, ensuring trades are only executed at the right moments, enhancing patience and decision-making accuracy.

12. Lack of Scalability

- Algorithms can handle multiple trades simultaneously across different markets or securities, increasing trading opportunities and potential profits without the limitations of human capacity.

13. Problem of Speed and Slippage while Taking Trades

- Algorithms execute trades at high speeds, reducing the impact of market momentum and slippage. They can place limit orders precisely, ensuring trades occur at desired price levels.

14. More Screen-time

- Algo trading minimizes the need for constant monitoring, as the system operates independently, reducing screen time and associated health issues while providing more personal freedom.

Let me give mention some of the popular platforms which are algo platforms.

1. Tradetron

It is a Cloud-based algo trading platform that allows users to create, back-test, and deploy strategies without coding.

2. Zerodha Streak

It enables users to create trading strategies without coding, back-test them, and deploy them directly to the market.

3. AlgoTest

It focuses on strategy back-testing and optimization, providing a detailed analysis of strategy performance.

4. Algo Bulls

This platform is known for its extensive library of pre-built algorithms and user-friendly interface for strategy creation and deployment.

5. Algofox

This is one of the leading, Ahmedabad-based Algo platform which integrates TradingView and Chartink with its technology. This makes easy for a retail trader to implement pre-defined trading set-ups on a chosen time frame. Algofox is led by Shri Hasmukh Parajapati who plays a very dynamic role in making this more techno-powerful and becomes accessible to small retail traders. This is so much user-friendly that even new comers in the stock trading can easily adopt this platform.

Algorithmic trading has reshaped market dynamics by increasing liquidity, reducing spreads, and improving price discovery. The high-frequency nature of algorithmic trading contributes to market liquidity by facilitating swift order execution and enhancing market depth. However, it also raises concerns about market stability and the potential for flash crashes, highlighting the need for robust risk management measures and regulatory oversight.

Nonetheless, algorithmic trading is a game-changer in modern finance, offering speed, efficiency, and liquidity to financial markets. Such an advanced technology is now accessible to retail traders at low cost which is going to change the way we trade in the coming time. Soon, on-line trading in its present form will become obsolete with more advanced algo platforms.

CHAPTER – 06

Understanding Intraday Trading

Intraday trading represents a distinct approach to stock market trading. Rather than holding onto shares of well-established companies, the goal is to capitalize on price movements within a single trading day. As a result, positions are closed by the end of the day, allowing traders to avoid overnight market risks and uncertainties. This method requires less capital, making it accessible to retail and small traders. Additionally, intraday traders can profit from both rising and falling markets, offering opportunities for gains regardless of market direction.

On average, intraday traders aim for gains of 1% to 2% per trade, depending on market conditions. Due to the high frequency of trades, transaction costs, including brokerage fees, can add up significantly. Additionally, intraday traders must be vigilant about slippage and market volatility, which can impact profitability. Success in intraday trading requires not just a solid understanding of the market but also the discipline to execute trades with precision and the mental fortitude to handle the stress of rapid decision-making.

Below are the fundamental notions, tools and indicators of Intraday Trading that a retail trader must understand.

1. Market Realities: Any retail intraday trader must understand following "Market Realities".

a. **Price is God.** The saying "Price is the God" means that the current stock price reflects all the available information about a company, the market, and the economy. It emphasizes that in the short-term (like intraday trading), trying to predict future prices based on news, analysis, or gut feeling might not be as effective as simply following the price movement itself. In intraday trading, where you buy and sell within the same day, technical analysis based on price charts and trends is often more important than company fundamentals. The highest bidder (buyer) determines the current price. This price reflects all the reasons why someone would be willing to pay that amount.

b. **Retail Gets the News, Whales Make the Moves.** Retail investors often operate at an information disadvantage. Major news or events impacting a stock price might reach professional traders (whales) well before the general public. Hence market discounts all information which is reflected in the current price. The implication is that by the time retail investors hear something through different channels, it's likely already been factored into the stock price by the professionals. Hence, accept that you are not the first to know the news or the event. That's why it is said "Heard it on the Street? It's Probably Old News on Wall Street".

c. **Trend is your Friend.** "Trend is your friend" is a popular saying in the world of trading. This saying emphasizes the importance of trading in the direction of the prevailing trend. As you are the last one to receive the information, or news, the price has already moved, therefore, you should have the ability to make the prevailing trend your friend. Historically, trends once started, tend to extend for some time before reversing. By aligning with the trend, you increase the probability of catching a profitable move. Trending markets often exhibit clear support and resistance levels. These levels can be used to identify potential entry points (buying low in an uptrend or selling high in a downtrend) and exit points (taking profits or minimizing losses when the trend weakens). However, markets don't always trend, and there are periods of consolidation or sideways movement. During these times, you should be cautious. Also, trends can sometimes experience temporary reversals or "false breakouts" before continuing in their original direction. These can lead to losses if you misinterpret the signal. You should remember the fact that all trends eventually end. The key challenge is identifying when a trend is losing momentum and might reverse. Hence, you should know how to use technical analysis tools like moving averages, trendlines, chart patterns, ready-made tools and indicators, etc. to identify the overall direction of the price movement. Don't worry. It's easy to understand and apply with good amount of practice.

d. **Deja Vu on the Charts: Why Prices Like to Rhyme.** Technical analysts believe history whispers on the charts. Price trends tend to repeat themselves, not because of some mystical force, but due to a fascinating dance between human emotions and market psychology. Imagine a stock with a history of surging after positive earnings reports. As the next report approaches, investors get a familiar tingle of optimism. They remember past gains and fear missing out, leading to a buying frenzy that pushes the price up again, mirroring prior trends.

2. Time Frame: The Heartbeat of Intraday Trading

- In the fast-paced world of intraday trading, where positions are opened and closed within the same day, choosing the right time frame is crucial. It acts like a heartbeat, dictating the pace, frequency, and risk profile of your trades. The popular time frames are 1 minute, 3 minutes, 5 minutes, 15 minutes, 30 minutes, 1 hour.

Personality Trait-Time Frame Matrix

Time Frame	Personality Traits	Intraday Trading Style
1 Minute	Intense focus, thrives under pressure, quick decision-making, grasps the situation quickly, fearless, confident	Scalping
3 Minutes	Good focus, Adaptable, reacts well to fast-paced situations, comfortable with short-term risk, fearless, confident	Short-term momentum trading
5 Minutes	Disciplined, good at identifying short-term trends and support/resistance levels, confident	Momentum trading, breakout trading
15 Minutes	Balanced, good at filtering out market noise, comfortable with moderate risk, patience during rice movement, ability to remain seated for a long time.	Swing trading within the day trend
30 Minutes	Good Patience, analyzes broader market context, focuses on larger price movements, no desire for frequent trades	Swing trading with a longer-term view within the day

Shorter time frames, like 1,3,5-minute charts, provides more frequent trading opportunities but requires quicker decisions and potentially more noise from short-term price fluctuations. Conversely, a longer time frames, like 15, 30-Minute charts, offers fewer entries but allows for a more strategic approach based on long-term trends. Highly volatile markets might be better suited for shorter time frames to capture quick movements. Less volatile markets might be better analyzed using longer time frames to identify underlying trends. Your personality and risk tolerance play a role. Do you prefer the fast-paced action of short-term trading or the more cozy approach of long-term swings? The time frame you choose should align with your comfort level and trading style. Smaller time frames give more trading opportunities means more profit and more stop losses which require proper risk management. You can refer to the above table and find out where you fit in. However, to start with, you may choose 5 or 15-minute time frame which will give you more confidence with practice over the time. Practice will make you suited for the time frame you desire.

3. Price and Volume: **Volume Speaks, Price Walks.** This emphasizes the idea that volume confirms the direction of price movement. Understanding the relationship between price and volume is crucial. Price reflects the current value of an asset, while volume indicates the intensity of buying and selling activity at that price. When these two forces interact, they create zones of support and resistance that can guide trading decisions. The volume represents the money entering and leaving the market, influencing price. The price movements can be subtle, but volume provides a stronger confirmation signal.

As such, Price and Volume is a Balancing Act. Imagine a tug-of-war between buyers and sellers.

- **Buyers** are willing to pay a certain price for an asset. The more buyers there are at a specific price level, the higher the **demand**.
- **Sellers** are willing to sell an asset at a certain price. The more sellers there are at a specific price level, the higher the **supply**.

But, the Price movement occurs when one side overpowers the other.

- **Increased buying pressure** (more buyers than sellers) pushes the price **up**.
- **Increased selling pressure** (more sellers than buyers) pushes the price **down**.

Following table gives an idea of price and volume relationship and the probable trend identification.

Price and Volume	**Probable Trend**
Price going UP, Volume going UP	Trend is UP- Bullish
Price going DN, Volume going UP	Trend is DN- Bearish
Price going UP, Volume going DN	Probable Trend reversal
Price going DN, Volume going DN	Probable Trend reversal

- Let us understand why this happens as stated in the above table.

1. Price going UP, Volume going UP – Trend is Bullish

   ○ **Institutional Impact: Volume and Price**

   Unlike retail investors who trade in smaller quantities, institutional giants like FIIs or DIIs move significant blocks of shares. Imagine an FII entering the market to buy stocks of Reliance Industries. Instead of 100 shares, they'd likely acquire 10,00,000 or more. Such sizable purchases can't be discreet – they're reflected in a surge of trading volume.

   Furthermore, these large acquisitions often push the share price upwards. This is why institutional capital is often referred to as "smart money" – the assumption being that these experienced investors make well-informed decisions. So, following the lead of smart money can seem like a sound strategy.

   ○ **Volume and Price Confirmation: A Sign of Bullishness**

   When a stock experiences a simultaneous increase in price and volume, it often indicates significant investor interest. Based on the belief that smart money makes wise choices, this confluence of factors can create a bullish sentiment, suggesting a potential buying opportunity. However, it's important to remember that correlation doesn't equal causation. While substantial volume alongside rising prices can be a positive sign, it shouldn't be the sole factor driving your trading decisions.

2. Price going DN, Volume going UP – Trend is Bearish

   A falling stock price accompanied by a surge in trading volume can be a significant signal in the market. A drop in price indicates that sellers are outweighing buyers. This could be due to various factors, such as negative news about the company or a shift in investor sentiment towards a particular sector. High volume during a price decline suggests a strong conviction from sellers. This increased activity could be driven by institutional investors (often referred to as "smart money") exiting their positions.

   Imagine a company called "Gland Pharma" announces a disappointing clinical trial result. The stock price plummets, and trading volume explodes. This scenario suggests that investors, including potentially some institutional investors, are actively selling their holdings. This heavy selling pressure, alongside the negative news, creates a bearish outlook for the stock.

3. Price going UP, Volume going DN – Probable Trend Reversal

   The scenario, where the price of a stock increases while trading volume shrinks, warrants a cautious approach. This divergence can indicate a potential **bull trap**. On the surface, a rising price might seem positive. However, in the absence of significant buying pressure (represented by volume), the increase could be temporary and misleading. Low volume suggests a lack of conviction from investors. It might be retail investors with limited capital pushing the price up in a short-lived buying spree, rather than larger institutional players making strategic investments.

   Imagine a stock called "IRCTC" experiences a sudden price surge. Excited by the potential, you consider buying in. But upon closer inspection, you notice the trading volume for IRCTC is low. This lack of volume alongside the price increase suggests the rally might be fuelled by speculative retail buying rather than substantial institutional interest. In such a scenario, the price increase could be a bull trap, luring investors in before a potential price decline. Hence, while a rising price can be enticing, don't get caught up in the hype. When price increase is accompanied by low volume, it's a sign to be extra cautious. Look for confirmation from other technical indicators before making any trading decisions.

4. Price going DN, Volume going DN - Probable Trend Reversal

   A decline in price accompanied by decreasing trading volume can be a puzzling situation for investors. A drop in price indicates that sellers are overpowering buyers. However, the lack of significant selling activity (reflected by low volume) can make the situation less clear-cut. Low volume during a price decline suggests a lack of strong conviction from sellers. Nervous retail investors might be exiting their positions, leading to a small price decline without significant institutional involvement. The price dip could be a temporary correction within a larger uptrend.

   Imagine "EaseMyTrip," a company in the travel industry, experiences a small price decline. However, the trading volume for the company also dips. This scenario suggests a few possibilities:

- **Profit-Taking by Retail Investors:** Some retail investors who bought EaseMyTrip earlier might be taking profits on a small price increase, leading to the slight price decline and low volume.

- **Wait-and-See Approach by Institutions:** Institutional investors might be on the sidelines, waiting for a clearer picture before entering or exiting their positions.
- A price decline with low volume doesn't necessarily translate to a bearish outlook. It could be a sign of a temporary pullback or a lack of conviction from sellers, particularly retail investors.

4. The Daily Grind: Using Daily Charts for Intraday Decisions

Le me emphasize the relevance of price and volume relationships on daily charts for intraday traders.

As a fast-paced intraday trader, your focus is on capitalizing on price movements within a single trading day. While real-time charts are crucial for executing trades, don't underestimate the power of daily charts in identifying potential intraday opportunities.

Why Daily Charts Matter for Intraday Trading

Daily charts offer a valuable perspective on a stock's price and volume relationship over a longer timeframe. By analyzing this bigger picture, you can:

- **Identify Trends:** Daily charts can reveal established uptrends or downtrends. These trends can act as a roadmap for potential intraday movements. If a stock is in a strong uptrend on the daily chart, you might look for intraday buying opportunities during pullbacks within that trend.
- **Gauge Support and Resistance:** Daily charts often highlight key support and resistance levels where the price has bounced back in the past. These levels can be significant for intraday trading, as they might act as temporary roadblocks or price targets during the day.

Imagine you're an intraday trader interested in "Tech Mahindra," a company in the technology sector. Looking at the daily chart, you notice Tech Mahindra has been in a steady uptrend for the past few weeks. Additionally, there's a well-defined support level around Rs. 1250 per share that has held multiple times in the past.

Intraday Trading Strategy:

Based on this daily chart analysis, you might consider an intraday long trade (buying) on Tech Mahindra if the price pulls back towards the Rs. 1250 support level during the day. The established uptrend on the daily chart suggests a potential continuation of the upward movement, while the support level might offer a buying opportunity within the intraday timeframe.

Remember, Daily charts provide context, not guarantees. Always use them in conjunction with real-time analysis and other technical indicators to make informed intraday trading decisions.

5. Moving Averages: A moving average (MA) on a chart shows a smoothed-out version of the price movement over a specific period of time. A "smoothed-out version" refers to data that has been processed to remove some of the short-term fluctuations (noise). For example, a stock price chart that looks like a jagged mountain range, with many sharp peaks and valleys. This represents the day-to-day price movements. A "smoothed-out version" of this chart would be like taking a rolling average of the price points. Think of it like smoothing out the mountain range with a giant rolling pin. The overall trend (upward, downward, or sideways) would still be visible, but the sharp peaks and valleys would be less pronounced. The benefit of using a smoothed-out version is that it helps to identify the underlying trend of the price movement more easily. This can be crucial for making informed trading decisions, as short-term fluctuations can be misleading. However, it's important to remember that smoothed-out data can also lag behind the actual price movements, so it's always a good idea to combine it with other technical indicators and analysis for a more complete picture.

The popular moving averages are 9/20/50/100/200 periods. The period depends upon the time frame of the chart. If the time frame is Day-chart, then the period is in days. For example, on a Day-chart, 50 period moving average means the average price of last 50 days, i.e., last 50-cande sticks or on a 15-minutes chart, the 20 period moving average means the average price of last 20 candle sticks of 15 minutes.

By averaging past prices, the moving average creates a line that reflects the overall direction – up, down, or sideways. This can be particularly useful in eliminating short-term price fluctuations and highlighting the underlying trend. Moving averages can act as dynamic zones of support and resistance. In an uptrend, the moving average line often acts as support, with the price bouncing off it after pullbacks. Conversely, in a downtrend, the moving average can act as resistance, with the price struggling to break above it.

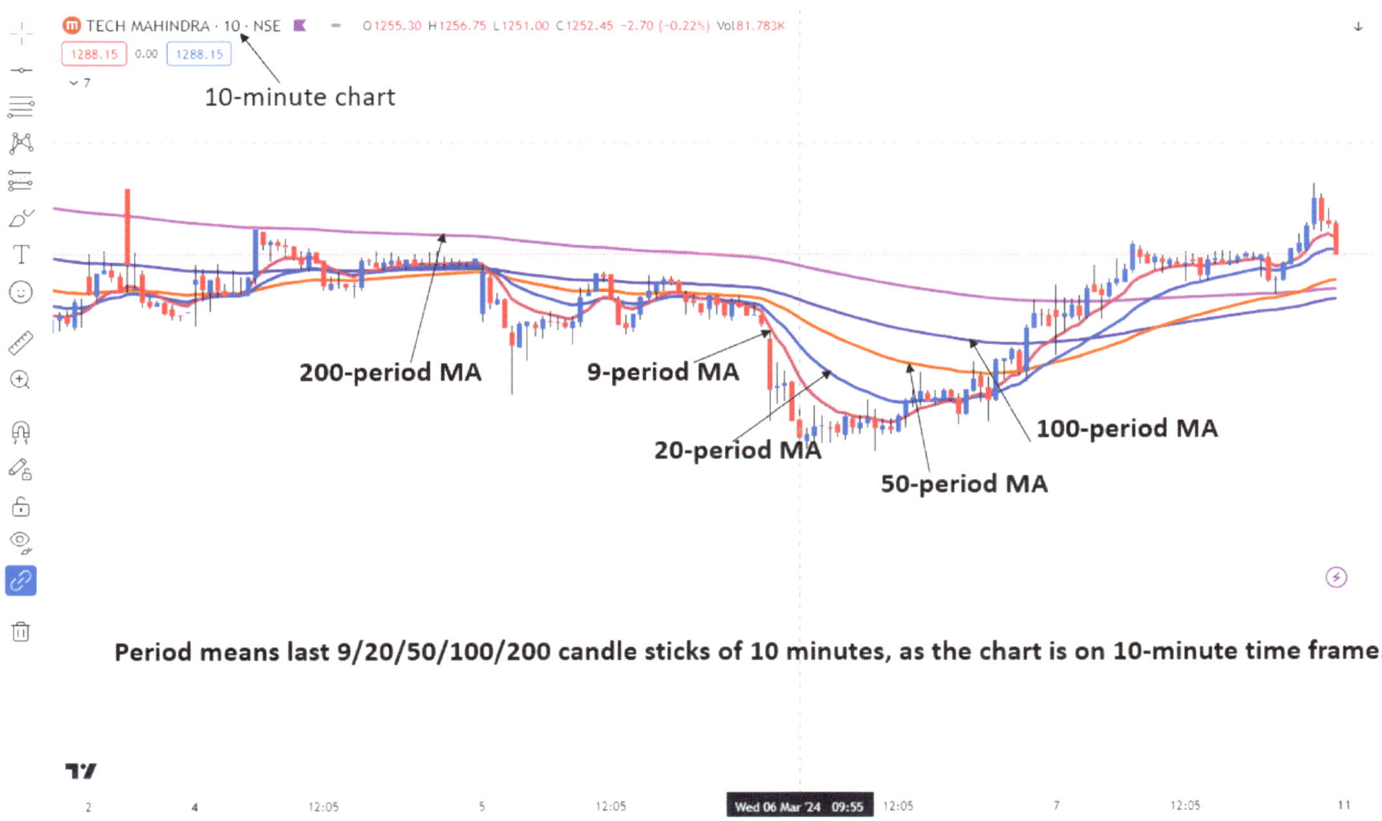

Time Frame	Most Useful Moving Averages	Reasons
1 Minute	9 Period EMA	* Captures very recent price movements. * Suitable for scalping strategies where quick reactions are needed. * Can be quite sensitive to noise, generating more false signals.
3 Minute	9 or 20 Period EMA	* Offers a balance between responsiveness and noise reduction compared to 1-minute charts. * Still suitable for short-term momentum trading strategies.
5 Minute	9 or 20 or Period EMA	* Provides a clearer view of the short-term trend while reducing noise. * Useful for identifying short-term support and resistance levels. * 20 EMA can be used for quicker reactions.
15 Minute	20, 50, or 100 Period EMA	* Offers a good balance between responsiveness and trend identification. * 20 EMA for faster reactions and identifying short-term entries/exits. * 50 EMA for a more established trend confirmation. * 100 EMA can be used as a broader trend filter, especially for swing trading within the day.
30 Minute	50, 100, or 200 Period EMA	* Focuses on identifying the broader trend within the intraday timeframe. * 50 EMA and 100 EMA for trend confirmation and potential swing trading opportunities. * 200 EMA can be used as a strong support/resistance zone for the intraday timeframe.

Different moving averages have different value proposition on different period charts. Shorter time frames like 1/3/5 minute charts have more relevance from 9/20 period moving averages, while longer time frames like 15/30 minute charts have more relevance from 20/50/100/200 period moving averages.

Simple Moving Average(SMA) vs. Exponential Moving Average(EMA)

Both simple moving averages (SMAs) and exponential moving averages (EMAs) are technical analysis tools used to smooth out price fluctuations and identify trends in the market. However, they differ in how they weight past closing prices, leading to slightly different interpretations.

Simple Moving Average (SMA):

- **Calculation:** An SMA is calculated by adding the closing prices of a security for a defined period (e.g., 20 days, 50 days) and then dividing that sum by the number of periods.
- **Example:** Let's say you want to calculate a 10-day SMA for a stock. You would add the closing prices for the last 10 days and then divide that sum by 10.

- **Interpretation:** An SMA reflects the average price over a specific period. It helps visualize the overall trend direction (up, down, or sideways) by filtering out some short-term price movements.

Exponential Moving Average (EMA):

- **Calculation:** An EMA assigns a greater weight to more recent closing prices, giving them a stronger influence on the average. This is achieved through a mathematical formula that considers all past closing prices but assigns a declining weight the further back you go. Newer prices have a more significant impact on the current EMA value.
- **Example:** For example, you assign a weight of 2 to the most recent closing price and then halve that weight for each day prior. You would continue adding these weighted prices for the chosen period (e.g., 20 days) and normalize the sum for a smoother average.
- **Interpretation:** An EMA reacts faster to recent price changes compared to an SMA. It's more sensitive to the latest trends and can provide earlier signals for trend changes.

The analogy for better understanding

- Imagine an moving(automated) walkway at the airport. An SMA is like standing on the moving walkway which is taking you at a constant speed. You'll eventually reach your destination at the speed of the walkway (the average price). An EMA is like walking on the moving walkway with the speed of the walkway itself, constantly adapting to its changes. You'll reach your destination faster, but you might feel the bumps (short-term fluctuations) more intensely.

Which One is Better?

There's no single "better" option. The choice depends on your trading style and the timeframe you're analyzing:

For short-term trading and identifying recent trends: An EMA is generally preferred due to its higher weight on recent prices. It reacts quicker to market movements and can be helpful for capturing short-term opportunities.

- **For longer-term trend analysis:** An SMA can still be a valuable tool. It provides a smoother average and can be helpful for confirming established trends or identifying support and resistance levels.
- **The Recent Perspective:** In the past, any information or news flow was slower and hence, it used take some time to influence the price of the stock. Therefore, simple moving average was a better tool. In today's times, due to media efficiency, information or news flow is rapid fast, hence, it instantly influences the price. The time lag has almost ceased. So, the recent prices carry higher weightage which influence the future price faster. Therefore, traders are using EMA for trading decisions.

6. Trend and Trendlines

- The concept of a trend lies at the heart of technical analysis in the stock market. Trends are formed by a series of consecutive price movements in a particular direction. Imagine a path on a hike – an upward slope signifies an uptrend, a downward slope indicates a downtrend, and a relatively flat path suggests a sideways trend. Trendlines are one of the basic tools used in technical analysis to identify trends in the price of a financial instrument. A trendline is a straight line that connects two or more price points and is used to identify the overall direction of a trend.

- It's important to note that trendlines are not always perfectly straight and may need to be adjusted as new price data becomes available. The slope of the trendline can also provide information about the strength of the trend. A steep trendline indicates a strong trend, while a shallow trendline indicates a weaker trend.

There are **three main types of trends** in the financial markets:

1. **Uptrend:** An uptrend is a situation in which the price of a security, stock, or index is steadily increasing over a period of time. It is identified by a series of higher lows and higher highs.
2. **Downtrend:** A downtrend is a situation in which the price of a security, stock, or index is steadily decreasing over a period of time. It is identified by a series of lower highs and lower lows.
3. **Sideways trend or range-bound:** A sideways trend or range-bound market is a situation in which the price of a security, stock, or index is moving within a defined range and is not showing a clear direction. In this type of market, the price moves up and down but stays within a defined range, without making clear highs or lows.

To determine the prevailing trend, traders pay close attention to the movement of price highs and lows.

- **Upward Trend:** If a series of higher highs and higher lows connect with a rising line, it suggests an uptrend. Imagine the price keeps making new highs and lows that are consistently higher than the previous ones.

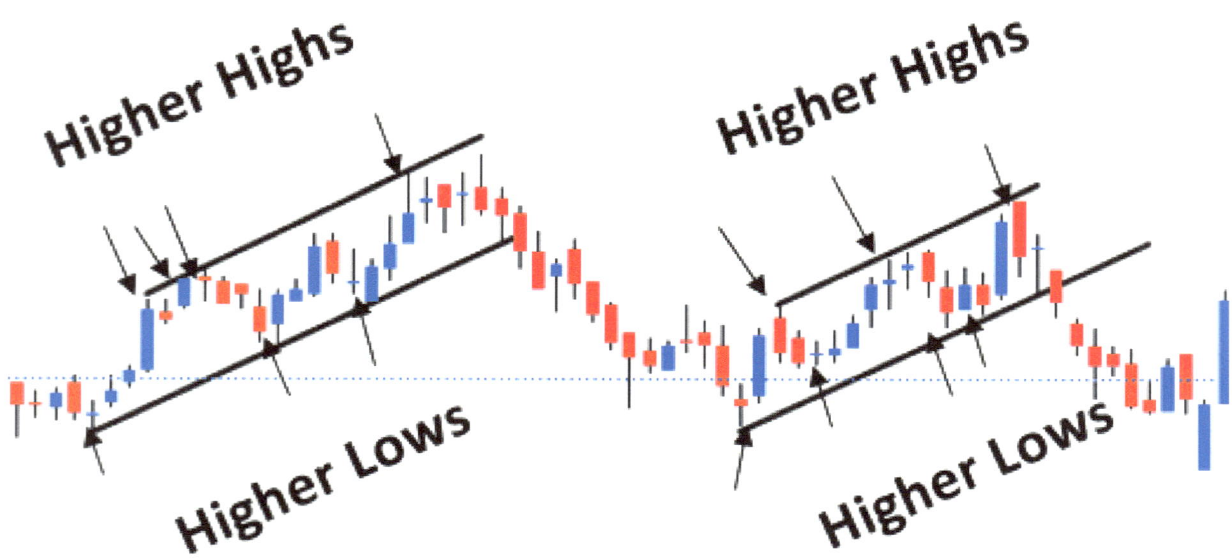

- **Downtrend:** Conversely, a series of lower highs and lower lows connected by a downward line indicates a downtrend. The price keeps making new highs and lows that are consistently lower than the previous ones.

- **Sideways Trend:** When price movements fluctuate within a relatively narrow range, with highs and lows not creating a clear directional bias, it suggests a sideways trend. The price might be choppy but remains within a defined horizontal zone.

- **Drawing of Trendlines**

  To have a valid trendline, minimum three points of higher highs, and higher lows need to be connected for defining up-trend, while minimum three points of higher lows, and lower lows need to be connected for defining down-trend.

By connecting these significant highs and lows with trendlines, you can visually represent the underlying trend direction. Trendlines act as a roadmap, helping you identify potential support and resistance levels during the trend's continuation.

Remember that Trends don't last forever, and prices eventually break out of established trends. However, trendline analysis is a valuable tool for understanding the market's overall direction and making informed trading decisions.

- **Trendlines: Guiding Lights for Intraday Traders**

Trendlines are a fundamental tool in a technical analyst's toolbox, and for intraday traders navigating the fast-paced world of stock prices, they hold particular value. Here's how trendlines can be used effectively in intraday trading:

1. Identifying Trend Direction:

The most basic function of a trendline is to visually represent the prevailing trend – uptrend, downtrend, or sideways. By connecting a series of swing highs (highest points) in an uptrend or swing lows (lowest points) in a downtrend, you can establish a trendline. This helps intraday traders understand the overall market direction and identify potential trading opportunities.

2. Support and Resistance Levels:

Trendlines often act as dynamic support and resistance zones.

- In an **uptrend**, the trendline acts as **support**. If the price dips towards the trendline during the day, it might find buyers and bounce back up, reinforcing the uptrend. This can be a potential buying opportunity for intraday traders anticipating a continuation of the upward movement.
- Conversely, in a **downtrend**, the trendline acts as **resistance**. If the price rallies towards the trendline, it might face selling pressure and struggle to break above it. This can be a potential selling opportunity for short-term traders looking to profit from a potential price decline.
- Support and Resistance levels of higher time frames are more reliable while taking trades. Therefore, when you are trading on a 5-minutes time frame, you must draw supply and resistance zones on higher time frames – weekly, daily, 1-hour time frames.

3. Entry and Exit Points:

Intraday traders can use trendlines to generate potential entry and exit signals for their trades. Here are a few examples:

- **Breakouts:** If the price decisively breaks above a trendline in an uptrend or below a trendline in a downtrend, it might signal a potential acceleration of the trend. This could be an entry point for intraday traders looking to ride the momentum.
- **Retracements and Pullbacks:** During trends, there are often temporary pullbacks (in uptrends) or retracements (in downtrends) where the price moves against the trend. If these retracements

reach the trendline and find support/resistance as expected, it can be a re-entry opportunity for traders who are already positioned in line with the trend.

4. Managing Risk:

Trendlines can also help with risk management. By placing stop-loss orders below the trendline in an uptrend or above the trendline in a downtrend, traders can limit their potential losses if the price movement goes against their expectations.

Important Considerations while using Trendlines

- **Trendline Validity:** Not all trendlines are created equal. The more times the price touches or bounces off the trendline, the stronger its validity. A single touch might be a coincidence, while multiple touches suggest a more reliable support/resistance zone.
- **False Signals:** Trendlines can generate false breakouts or failed support/resistance tests. Always use them in conjunction with other technical indicators and confirmation signals before entering or exiting trades.
- **Trendlines are Not Guarantees:** Trends eventually change, and trendlines can be broken. Use them as a guide, not a foolproof prediction tool.

5. Support and Resistance

Support and resistance are key concepts in technical analysis and are used to identify potential turning points in the price of a financial instrument.

Support refers to a price level at which a security has had difficulty falling below in the past. It acts as a floor for the price and is seen as a level where buyers are likely to enter the market and prevent the price from falling further. If the price does fall below the support level, it is seen as a bearish sign and may indicate that the trend is changing. At this price-level, sellers are not interested to sell the stocks.

On the other hand, resistance refers to a price level at which a security has had difficulty rising above in the past. It acts as a ceiling for the price and is seen as a level where sellers are likely to enter the market and prevent the price from rising further. If the price does rise above the resistance level, it is seen as a bullish sign and may indicate that the trend is changing. At this price-level, buyers are not interested to buy.

In the above chart of ICICIBank on 30-Mimutes chart, you can see how Resistance and Support are formed. At resistance level, the Price often wanted to cross, but it couldn't, because the buyers were not ready to buy at higher price. Hence, sellers reduced the price, became dominant, and the price went down. You can see the five attempts to break the Resistance. Similarly, at the Support level, the price went four times, and bounced back, because, sellers were not ready to sell at lower price than the support price. Hence, buyers were buying at higher price. That fight was going on between buyers and sellers. The fight became intense at the end (see the box). At last, sellers had to reduce the price which led further decline in the price. When Support and Resistance are formed, it gives an indication of price movement and becomes easier to understand the price reversal.

Support and resistance levels can be identified by analyzing historical price data and are used by traders and investors to make informed trading decisions. For example, if a trader believes that a security is likely to find support at a certain price level, they may enter a long position at that level with the expectation that the price will rise.

6. Fibonacci Ratios: Support & Resistance during the Trend

The Fibonacci sequence, a captivating series of numbers, boasts a rich history that stretches back centuries. While some credit its discovery to Leonardo Fibonacci, an Italian mathematician in the 12th century, whispers of its presence can be traced back to even earlier Indian mathematical texts, possibly dating as far back as 200 BC.

The magic of Fibonacci lies in its inherent simplicity: each number is the sum of the two preceding ones, creating a sequence that unfolds like nature itself (0, 1, 1, 2, 3, 5, 8, 13, and so on). But the true wonder unfolds when we delve deeper. Dividing any number in the sequence by the one before it reveals a captivating ratio, approximately equal to 1.618, known as the Golden Ratio. This ratio, often considered nature's divine proportion, appears remarkably consistent throughout the natural world, from the spiral of a seashell to the branching patterns of trees.

Intriguingly, similar consistency emerges within the Fibonacci sequence itself. When a number is divided by its immediate successor, the result is close to 0.618 (or 61.8%). This consistency extends further – dividing a Fibonacci number by the one two places ahead yields a value close to 0.382 (or 38.2%), and dividing by the number three places ahead approaches 0.236 (or 23.6%).

These Fibonacci ratios (61.8%, 38.2%, and 23.6%) have captivated the minds of traders for decades. The theory goes that these ratios can be applied to stock charts, acting as potential support and resistance levels. Imagine a stock price experiencing a sharp rise or fall. Fibonacci analysis suggests that the price might retrace (pull back) to one of these Fibonacci levels before continuing its trend.

This "Pull-back level Prediction" becomes a tool for traders to identify potential entry points. By understanding these Fibonacci ratios, traders can position themselves for trades aligned with the overall trend. While not a crystal ball, the Fibonacci sequence offers a fascinating lens through which to view market behavior, potentially aiding traders in making informed decisions.

Fibonacci retracements are a technical analysis tool derived from the Fibonacci sequence. They are percentages applied to a swing high and low (significant price movements in a specific direction) to identify potential support and resistance levels. The most commonly used Fibonacci retracement levels are:

- **50%**
- **62%**

The theory behind Fibonacci retracements is that, after a strong price move (up or down), the price might retrace (pull back) to one of these Fibonacci levels before continuing the trend.

Why ? We have discussed earlier that price does not move in a straight line, but it moves in a stepped manner as shown below.

1.

3.

2.

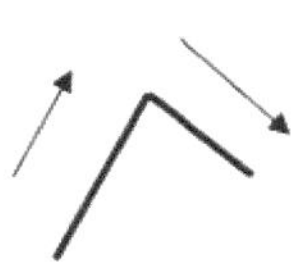

4.

As figure-1 shows, price moves up like this which is called up-trend, and figure-3 shows down-trend. In the up-trend, there is a pull-back, known as correction in the price as shown in figure-2. In the down-trend also, there is a pull-back means after a decline, there is a retracement on the up side. This the price behaviour. However, as a trader, we don't know how much it will retrace or pull- back.

Therefore, in an up-trend and down-trend, we use Fibonacci tool and we look at the numbers – 50% or 62%. Normally, price retraces upto these levels, and using price action, we take a decision of trading. This gives us confidence while trading. These levels act as support and resistance. If price breaks 62% level, it is inferred as change of trend.

7. Volume Weighted Average Price (VWAP) is an excellent tool meant for Intraday trading. It is the average price of a stock, over a given time frame, taking into account both the price and the volume of trades during that time frame. This indicator provides a comprehensive reflection of the market's price action, as it integrates volume data to the price of a given time frame.. By doing so, VWAP offers a more precise measure of a stock's average price compared to moving average price calculations, which do not account for variations in trading volume. It means unlike a simple average that just takes the average of all prices, VWAP gives more weight to prices at which higher volumes were traded.

Three Major Benefits of VWAP

1. **Reflects the Trend**:

   VWAP can be used to identify the underlying trend. If the current market price is consistently above the VWAP, it suggests a bullish trend, while the price below VWAP indicates a bearish trend. So, intraday traders often look for opportunities to go for buying when the price is above VWAP and to go for short selling, when it's below.

2. **Support and Resistance Levels**:

   VWAP act as a dynamic support or resistance levels during the trading day. The Entry/Exit can be easily predicted considering VWAP as support or resistance.

3. **Point of Control:**

   VWAP can be considered a type of POC (Point of Control) because they both reflect areas of price activity with significant trading volume. However, there's a subtle difference:

   - **VWAP:** Represents the average price weighted by volume throughout the trading day.
   - **POC:** Represents the single price level with the highest trading volume during a specific period.

However, both indicate areas of potential price influence. When the current price goes beyond two deviations of VWAP on either side, it indicates potential price reversal.

8. The Relative Strength Index (RSI) is a popular tool used by traders to gauge the momentum of price movement of the stock in the market. It helps to identify **overbought** and **oversold** conditions, which can be valuable for making intraday trading decisions. However, over a period of time, practitioners have found out many other ways of using RSI for trading.

How RSI works:

- It measures the ratio between the average gains and average losses over a chosen period (typically 14 days).
- The RSI is displayed as a value between 0 and 100.
- Generally, an RSI above 70 suggests the stock might be overbought (price has risen quickly).
- Conversely, an RSI below 30 indicates a potentially oversold stock (price has fallen rapidly).

Applying RSI in Intraday Trading:

You can use RSI to identify potential entry and exit points for intraday trades:

- **Buy Signal:** When the RSI dips below 30 (oversold), it might suggest a buying opportunity as the price might be due for a rebound.
- **Sell Signal:** Conversely, an RSI exceeding 70 (overbought) suggests a potential selling opportunity as the price might be ripe for a correction.

Important Considerations:

- **RSI is not a foolproof indicator:** Markets don›t always follow these textbook RSI levels. The RSI can generate false signals, especially in volatile markets.
- **Combine RSI with other indicators:** For a more comprehensive analysis, consider using RSI along with other technical indicators like support and resistance levels, moving averages, or price patterns.

The credit for inventing the Relative Strength Index (RSI) goes to **J. Welles Wilder**. Who introduced it to the world in **1978**. Wilder, a mechanical engineer turned technical analyst, detailed the RSI in his book titled "New Concepts in Technical Trading Systems" published in 1978. The RSI has since become one of the most widely used technical analysis tools for traders.

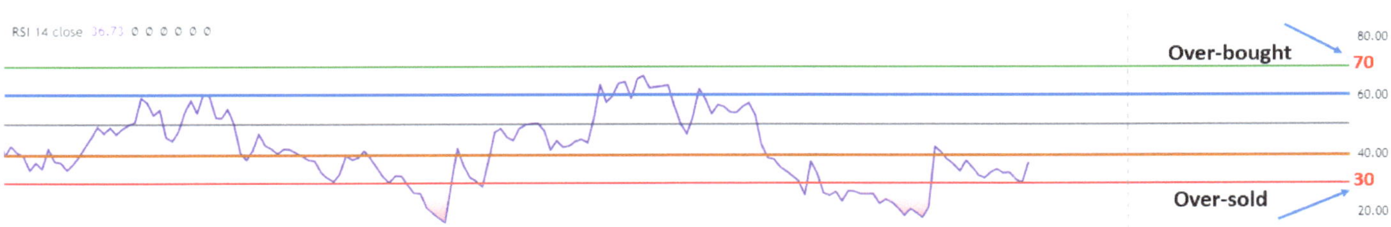

RSI's Versatility

- It is a fundamental indicator available on all charting and trading platforms.
- It is an indicator without which successful trading is not possible.
- It can be used on any time frames.
- Though it is stated that above 70 level, it is over bought, practically, it has been proved that it is not correct. In fact, once RSI reaches at 70, it increases rapidly, and hence, 70 level is considered to be a super-bullish level.

- Similarly, when RSI reaches at 30 level, it is actually not an over sold position, but 30 level is considered to be a super-bearish level.
- The level between 60 and 70 is a Bullish phase, the level between 70 and 80 is a super-bullish phase, the level greater than 80 is actually an over-bought area. You have to observe along with price action, and other indicators, and take the trade for reversal.
- The level between 40 and 30 is a Bearish phase, the level between 30 and 20 is a super-bearish phase, the level lesser than 20 is an over-sold area. You have to observe along with price action, and other indicators, and take the trade for reversal.
- The level between 60 and 40 reflects sideways trend.
- There is also a concept of Divergence associated with RSI which gives high probability signal for Buy and Sell. So, when Price continues to fall below the level of 30, but the RSI continues to rise, it is a bullish divergence which is a signal that strength of momentum is increasing, which is a Buy signal. Conversely, when above the level of 70 when price continues to rise, but RSI continues to fall, there is a bearish divergence.

Example of Bullish Divergence:

You can see in the chart that price is going down, but related RSI (as seen in the indicator below the chart) is going up, which is a bullish signal. You can see what happens thereafter, there is a rise in the Price.

Example of Bearish Divergence:

You can see in the chart that price is going up, but related RSI (as seen in the indicator below the chart) is going down, which is a bearish signal. You can see what happens thereafter, there is a decline in the Price.

11. ADX (Average Directional Index) is a technical analysis indicator used to measure the strength of a trend in the stock market, regardless of its direction. Developed by Welles Wilder, ADX helps traders identify whether a market is trending or ranging, which is crucial for making informed trading decisions.

ADX calculates trend strength based on a moving average of price range expansion over a specified period (usually 14 bars). ADX values range from 0 to 100, with higher values indicating stronger trends. ADX is non-directional, meaning it measures trend strength whether prices are moving up or down. It is usually plotted alongside the two directional movement indicator (DMI) lines, from which ADX is derived.

When +DMI (positive directional movement indicator) is above -DMI (negative directional movement indicator), prices are moving up, and ADX measures the strength of the uptrend. Conversely, when -DMI is above +DMI, prices are moving down, and ADX measures the strength of the downtrend.

ADX readings above 25 suggest a strong trend, making it suitable for trend-trading strategies. Readings below 25 indicate weak or absent trends, and traders may avoid trend-trading strategies.

The following table summarizes ADX value interpretations:

ADX Value	**Trend Strength**
0-25	Absent or Weak Trend
25-50	Strong Trend
50-75	Very Strong Trend
75-100	Extremely Strong Trend

Low ADX values often indicate accumulation or distribution phases.

When ADX remains below 25 for an extended period (more than 30 bars), prices enter range conditions. During low ADX, price patterns are easier to identify as they move between resistance and support levels.

Eventually, price breaks out into a trend when ADX rises above 25. Traders can use ADX to identify strong trends for intraday trading.

When ADX is rising and above 25, consider trend-following strategies.

Conversely, during low ADX, intraday traders may focus on range-bound strategies.

ADX is one such tool without which no one can go for Intraday trading. It is the first tool which conveys whether to enter the trade or not even if other indicators give positive signals. Even, many traders use this as only tool in Intraday trading using +DMI and -DMI.

The above is a 15 – Minute chart of Reliance Industries. You can see in the above picture ADX indicator below the chart. At point no. 1, ADX is rising meaning strength in the trend is increasing, and +DMI (Green line) is crossing above -DMI (Red line) which indicates Buy signal. Price is going up, and you can see in the chart that Price is going up. At point no. 2, ADX is falling meaning strength in the trend is decreasing below value 20. +DMI and -DMI are not opening up and remain close to each other which indicates the trend is sideways which you can see in the chart and Price is range-bound. At point no. 3, ADX value is above 20 means there is strength in the trend. -DMI is crossing +DMI which gives a Sell signal, and the chart indicates Price is declining.

12. Bollinger Bands:

The Empirical Rule, also known as the 68-95-99.7 rule, tells us the probability of finding data within a certain number of standard deviations of the mean in a normal distribution. This means that 68% of data will fall within 1 standard deviation range. Further, 95% of data will fall within 2 standard deviation range, and 99.7% of data will fall within 3 standard deviation range. Bollinger Bands, after a well studied research done by John Bollinger, was brought out as a technical tool in 1980s following the Empirical Rule.

Bollinger Bands are a popular technical analysis tool used by traders to analyze volatility and potential price movements.

Bollinger Bands consist of three lines: a 20-period simple moving average (SMA) in the middle and two outer bands that are standard deviations away from the SMA. Typically, the standard deviation is set to 2, encompassing about 95% of price action within the bands.

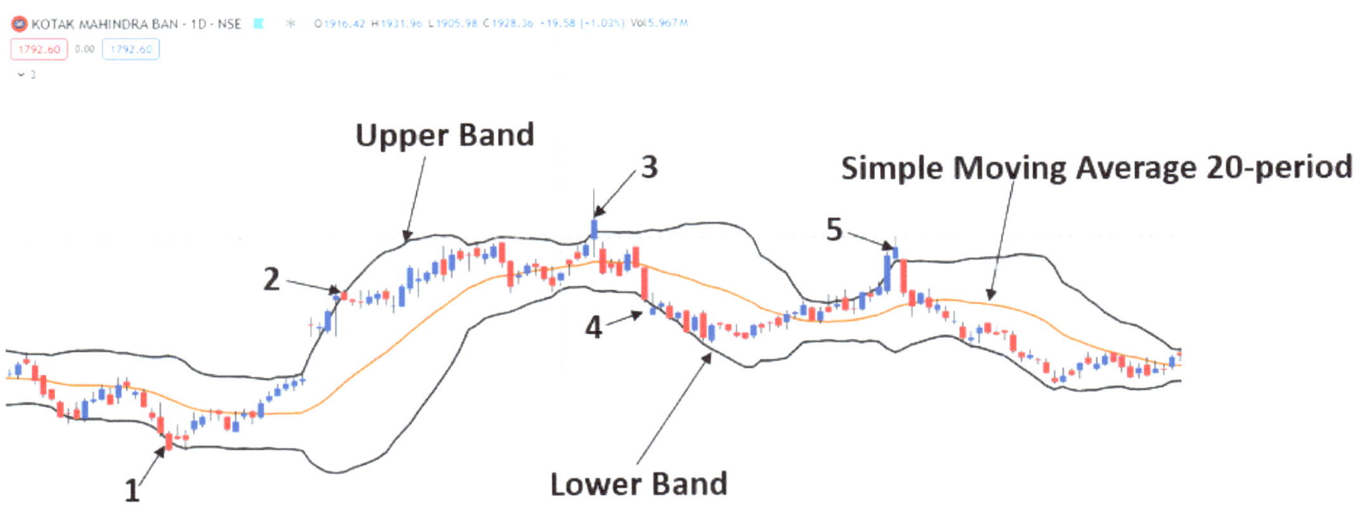

Bollinger Bands with 2 standard deviation. It means that 95% of data will fall in the range. It further means that when price goes beyond the range, there will be price reversal. The Price will go back into the bands. You can see at points 1,2,3,4,5 in the chart.

When the price touches or crosses the upper band, it suggests overbought conditions, indicating a potential sell signal. Conversely, when the price touches or crosses the lower band, it indicates oversold conditions, signalling a potential buy opportunity.

Bollinger Bands expand during periods of high volatility and contract during low volatility. As a Trader, you can use this information to gauge market volatility and anticipate potential breakouts or reversals.

Bollinger Bands can be used in various trading strategies, such as the Bollinger Bands squeeze strategy for trading range-bound markets and the Bollinger Bands bounce strategy for identifying potential reversal points. We will see in the next chapter on Master Setup.

However, it is crucial to combine Bollinger Bands with other technical indicators and risk management principles to make informed trading decisions and manage risk effectively.

CHAPTER – 07

Trading Strategies and Set-Up

Intraday stock trading, also known as day trading, involves buying and selling stocks within the same trading day. The goal is to capitalize on price movements within a day. To succeed in intraday trading, traders need proper resources, solid set-up and effective strategies.

Trading Resources:

1. **Equipment and Software:** A reliable computer and high-speed internet connection are essential. Charting platforms like Tradingview, Trading platfroms like Fyers, Zerodha, Upstox, etc. and Stock Selection platforms like Tradingview and Chartink provide the tools needed for stock selection, charting, analysis and order execution.
2. **Brokerage Account:** Choose a broker that offers low commissions, high-speed trade execution, and access to the markets and stocks you wish to trade.
3. **Trading Plan:** Develop proper trading plan outlining your goals, risk tolerance, and trading strategies. Be consistent with the trading plan. Practice the plan before dealing with large quantities.

Benefits of Intraday Trading:

Intraday trading, or day trading, involves buying and selling stocks within the same trading day. "Take the Profit, and not the Stock" is the basic strategy of Intraday trading. Seven benefits of intraday trading are outlined below.

1. **No Overnight Risk:** Since all positions are closed by the end of the trading day, there is no risk of adverse overnight price movements impacting your stocks. This always saves you from the impact of big market fall next day like we saw on Vote Counting day on 4th June 2024. Since there is no overnight risk involved, you have always peaceful night and joyful morning every day.
2. **Potential for High Returns:** Intraday trading allows traders to capitalize on small price movements throughout the day, offering the potential for significant profits within a short time frame. When you are on a shorter time frame, you always find rewarding Capital Turnover, i.e., with the same capital you can enter into many trades throughout the day.
3. **Good Margin on Capital:** Brokers offer margin facility under the SEBI regulations to Intraday traders. This is also known as Leverage. It means normally you get 5 times of leverage on your capital requirement depending on stocks you trade. For example, Reliance is traded at Rs 3000 per share. If you want to trade with 100 quantity, you require Rs. 3,00,000 in your account with the broker. But, you can trade 100 quantity with just Rs. 60,000 as you get the margin money of

20%. This means you get leverage of 5 times. This facility increases the potential returns. This means you can control a larger position with a relatively small amount of capital. Please note that you don't get margin facility if you take the delivery of stocks, and go for positional or swing or long-term trading. Such trading is called as investing, and not trading.

4. **High Liquidity:** Intraday trading in highly liquid markets ensures that traders can enter and exit positions quickly without significantly affecting the stock's price. Whatever you buy, you can instantly sell off with your desired price, and when you sell, you can instantly buy with desired price. This ensures safety of capital as well as returns.
5. **Short Selling Opportunities:** Intraday traders can profit from declining markets by short selling, which is the practice of selling stocks that the trader does not currently own, anticipating a price drop. This is the greatest advantage of intraday trading. You don't have to worry for market fall. In fact, it's a profit making opportunity for intraday traders. This is actually what happened on 4th June 2024. There was a big fall, but intraday traders made huge profits on that day by short selling.
6. **Flexibility:** Intraday trading can be done from anywhere with an internet connection, allowing traders to work from home or any other location. Once you have a practice, you can trade for intraday for a few hours or when you are on a trip, you can access your online platform from anywhere. Such a flexible trading happens only in the stock market.
7. **Automation:** It is easy to automate your trade for the day with proper algo set-up. This will make your day time free from seating against the computer the whole day. It's like you have a Robot which operates on your behalf under your instructions. If you want, you can monitor your trade and you can discontinue at any time of the day.

However, intraday trading, at the same time, suffers from certain challenges, like -

1. **Stress and Pressure:** The need to monitor the market continuously and make quick decisions can be very stressful and mentally exhausting. However, it depends on the age group also. Youngsters may feel like gaming the trading, and the process becomes joyful. Intraday trading for few hours may be helpful to be away from constant stress and pressure.
2. **Time-Consuming:** Intraday trading requires a significant time commitment to watch the market and execute trades, making it less suitable for those with other commitments. However, adopting this as a profession may not create a feeling like this. But, if undertaken as a side activity may turn out to be time consuming. The Algo trading is a new technology-based trading which saves from time-consumption in trading, and the trader can utilize the same time for another activity.
3. **Emotional Challenges:** The fast-paced nature of intraday trading can lead to emotional trading decisions, which may result in losses. The sudden movement in the price may prompt you to deviate from the rule-based trading which ultimately incur a loss, or the price movement may prompt you to discontinue the trade and you may incur loss in profit.

So, these are few of the challenges. The continuous practice in one set-up will definitely ensure the success in intraday trading and help you to overcome these challenges.

Trading Strategies

The whole day of price movement comprises of momentum, dullness, sudden momentum, or sudden dullness. Therefore, the market can be in uptrend, or down trend or sideways. The various experts on different platforms often say that 70% of the time the market remains sideways, and only 30% of the time it remains in trend. If the market is volatile, then it can show both uptrend and down trend on the same day. Therefore, the intraday traders follow different strategies depending on the market movement conditions. Mainly, there are four strategies which are given below.

1. **Scalping:** Involves making dozens of trades in a day to "scalp" small profits from each trade. Scalpers rely on precise timing and quick execution. The preferred time frame for scalping is 1 minute or 3 minutes or 5 minutes chart. Once it is mastered, then it is the best strategy to make profit in a day. Traders usually go for large quantities and get out of the trade once they reach their profit goal. Since the time frame is shorter, you can trade in one stock or maximum two stocks simultaneously. I call it as "an Adventure Sport of the Financial Markets". Once you get the hold of it, then it becomes fun and entertainment. Once you set-up the right indicators, and understand price action on smaller time frame, then there is no going back from this strategy. You always ensure some profit every day in this strategy.
2. **Momentum Trading:** Momentum in momentum trading refers to the rate of acceleration of a stock's price or volume. It is a key concept that drives the momentum trading strategy, where traders seek to capitalize on the continuation of an existing trend in the market. Traders buy stocks showing upward momentum and sell them when the momentum weakens. The preferred time frame for momentum trading is 15 minutes or 30 minutes or 45 minutes time frame. Even, 1 hour time frame is also preferred in a day trading. However, the best time frame, in my opinion, is 15 minutes time frame. Here, you hold the stock for a longer time till the momentum continues. The advantage over scalping is that you get good time to take a decision, and you can trade simultaneously in more stocks. If you adopt Algo trading, then this becomes the best strategy with proper Risk Management. On this time frame, you get to see proper price action which becomes very useful in trading.
3. **Reversal Trading:** Reversal trading is an intraday strategy that focuses on identifying price points where the price of a stock is likely to change direction. This involves capitalizing on the shifts in market sentiment and trend reversals after a significant price movement. Traders aim to enter at the early stage of the new trend to maximize profit potential. This strategy involves identifying overbought or oversold stocks and betting on a reversal. Identification of reversal patterns such as Head and Shoulders, Double Tops and Bottoms, Doji play a significant role for entering into the trade. A significant increase in volume can indicate the strength of a new trend. Reversal trading when executed properly, it can be a highly profitable intraday strategy. The preferred time frame is 15 minutes or 30 minutes or 1 hour.
4. **Breakout Trading:** Breakout trading is a strategy used in intraday trading where traders look to capitalize on a stock's price moving outside of a defined support or resistance level. When the price "breaks out," it indicates a significant change in market sentiment, often accompanied by increased trading volume. When the price remains in the narrow range for a long time, it indicates a signal of Break-out. Traders find such stocks on different time frames, and execute

the trade on proper Break-out. Increased volume during a breakout is essential for confirming the strength of the breakout. Higher volume indicates greater trader interest and confidence in the new price direction. Not all breakouts lead to sustained price movements. False breakouts occur when the price moves beyond a support or resistance level but then quickly reverses. To avoid false breakouts, traders may wait for a confirmation candle or further validation through volume and other technical indicators. Breakout trading requires careful analysis, patience, and strict adherence to trading rules to be successful. It can be a highly profitable strategy when executed correctly. The time frame you can select is 5 or 15 minutes.

Successful intraday trading requires discipline, quick decision-making, and a deep understanding of market dynamics. Continuously refining your strategies and staying informed are key to navigating the fast-paced world of intraday trading.

Trading Set-up:

The crucial phase in intraday trading is establishing a Set-up that aligns with your chosen strategy. Technical Analysis Tools and Indicators help in creating right set-ups. There can be various permutations and combinations of those technical analysis tools and indicators which can be created for establishing a set-up that suits your requirements and personality. To ensure profitable trading, it's essential to develop your own "Rules of Trading" using those tools and indicators. This practice fosters discipline, maintains profitability, and safeguards against emotional instability during market downturns. It also protects your capital and aligns with your risk tolerance. Therefore, having a well-defined set-up is indispensable for any trader aiming for consistent profits.

There are hundreds of indicators available on Tradingview which help in creating a set up which suits your convenience and emotional personality. The best set-up is the most simple set-up because it is easy to judge and implement trades. Let's see these set-ups.

Before we enter into the world of set-ups, let us make it clear why we need Trading Set-up. The set-up drives us and helps in taking trading decisions of Entry, Exit, Stop Loss, and Target Profit. Trading is not possible with out any set up. All set-ups are good, but they may differ according to the strategy you have selected, your comfort to use the set-up. Choose one, practice for 60 days uninterrupted and you will master the set up. It is just like learning car driving and practicing it for a long time to master.

Another important aspect is that the goal of trading is to make profit using the trading set-up. Our mind is trained to think like that because we always ask to ourself how do we make money, and stock market trading is one area where you can make money with less capital. However, if you want to make profit by trading in the stock market, then you need to change your perspective of making profit completely. You should have a goal - How I protect my capital by using the trading set-up. Once you decide on that, then you make profit without any tension. Remember, you will always make profit in the stock market if your first goal is to protect your capital, and not to make the profit because that will decide your trading plan. For example, you have Rs. 50,000 capital to trade with. Since you are going for Intraday (called as MIS trades). MIS means Margin Intraday Square-off which is an order type designed for intraday traders. In this type, trader can get leverage on capital, i.e., if you have Rs.

50,000 capital, you get leverage normally 5 times depending on the stock as per SEBI Rules. Therefore, with Rs. 50,000 capital, you get Rs. 2,50,000 funds from your broker to trade which means you can trade with more number of shares. Now, you need to decide how much risk you are ready to take on your capital of Rs. 50,000 for the whole day. Normally, it is suggested that you can take 2% risk, i.e., Rs. 1000. That means, you are ready to incur loss of Rs. 1000 for the day on your capital of Rs. 50,000. This is your Risk-appetite or Risk-tolerance. If your risk-appetite is more, you can be ready to incur more loss. Now, the question is, how many trades you can get for the whole day. It depends on the time frame you choose. Lower the time frame, more trading opportunities. Higher the time frame, less number of trading opportunities. Let's say, you want to trade on a time frame of 3 minutes, you may get 4 to 6 trades per day on a particular stock, if there is no movement or trend. But, if there is a good trend, then you may get around 2 trades. Normally, there is always a 50% probability to earn out of the trades. It means that, if you take 4 trades, you will make profit in 2 trades, and you will incur loss in 2 trades. If you take 2 trades, you are likely to make profit in 1 trade. Such a plan makes you clear with what you are going to do. Your loss is certain, and your profit is unlimited.

Let's take an example.

- Stock name: State Bank of India
- You select this stock because you have an understanding that this stock will be in trend tomorrow.
- You select the time frame of 3 minutes.
- You select Supertrend as your indicator.
- You don't know how it will move, so you don't know how many trades will be there.
- But, you have your plan ready. Rs. 50,000 capital, and you get 5 times leverage. So, you have Rs. 2,50,000 funds to trade with.
- The current market price of State Bank of India is Rs. 850.
- The total number of shares you can buy is 294 shares per trade. (Rs. 2,50,000 / Rs. 850).
- Your risk appetite is Rs. 1000 for the whole day.
- It means, if you project 4 trades, then your risk appetite per trade is Rs. 250.
- Normally, you can expect 1% movement in the price on 3-Minute time frame which you can fix it as Stop-loss.(you can use ATR – Average True range for deciding the stop-loss which we will see later.)
- Therefore, your stop-loss can be Rs. 8.50 per share. (Rs. 850 * 1%)
- You can buy 30 shares (Rs. 250 / Rs. 8.50 per share) which will fix your loss for trade at Rs. 250, if your trade goes wrong.
- OR, you consider the first 3-minute candle to assess and take the trade in the second candle.
- You may enter at the high of the first candle, and keep the low as Stop-loss.
- The difference between the High price and the Low price is your stop loss per share.
- Say, the difference is Rs. 5 per share, then 50 shares you can trade with. (Rs. 250 / Rs. 5 per share)
- This type of plan will keep you free from any tension, as you are ready to lose Rs. 250 per trade considering you expect that there will be 4 trades.
- Now, let's see what happens, if you trade in State Bank of India on a particular day when you find there will be a good trend.

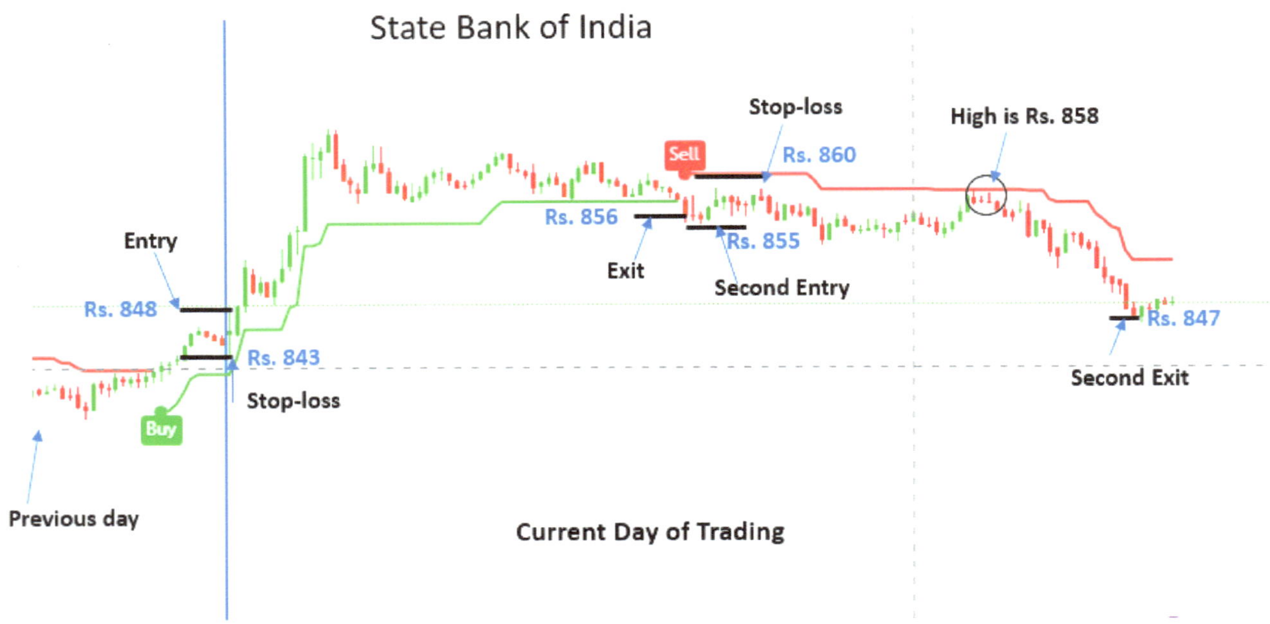

- On a current day, At the second candle, you take the Long (Buy) entry at Rs. 848 (High of the first candle) with a stop-loss of Rs. 843(low of the first candle). This means, the stop-loss is Rs. 5 per share. So, you can buy 50 shares (Rs. 250 / Rs. 5 per share). So, your capital invested will be Rs. 42,500, though you have a fund of Rs. 2,50,000. But, you will not utilize considering your risk-appetite or risk-tolerance.
- You can see a good trend after you enter the trade.
- Now, the trend is changing and going down. So, as per the indicator, you take exit at Rs. 856. You make profit of Rs. 400 (50 shares * Rs. 8 per share).
- Now, you take the Short (Sell) trade (second entry) at Rs. 855, and keep the stop loss at Rs. 860 being the supertrend high. Again, the stop-loss difference is Rs. 5 per share.
- So, you can buy 50 shares (Rs. 250 / Rs. 5 per share).
- The price went up to Rs. 858, and it did not touch the stop-loss, thereafter, you get a good downward trend.
- You take second exit at Rs. 847 as it is reaching end of the day. However, in any case, as an intraday trader you need to take exit before 3.15 pm, otherwise your exit will be made by your broker automatically with a penalty. Hence, it is advisable to take exit by 3.00 pm.
- In the second trade, you make profit of Rs. 400 (50 shares * Rs. 8 per share).
- Hence, there was no stop-loss hit on the day, and you made profit of Rs. 800 on your capital of Rs. 50,000 which is 1.6 % per day.

Now, if you continue your trades like this, and considering 50% of probability of success in the trades in a month of 20 days trading, you are likely to make profit as follows.

• 10 days – profit	Rs. 800 profit per day	Rs. 8000
• 10 days – stop-loss	Rs. 500 stop-loss per day	Rs. 5000

(Assumed 2 trades per day. There can be more trades also.)

You make Profit of Rs. 3000 in a month on your capital of Rs. 50,000 which comes to 6% per month, i.e., 36% for 6 months, whereas interest on Bank FD for this period hovers around 7%.

In reality, with practice, your success rate will increase to 70% to 80%.

This is just a brief scenario given before we dwell into the Trade Set-ups. There numerous Trade Set-ups available by incorporating various indicators. Tradingview is one platform which has unlimited indicators. You can create your own set-up by choosing indicators therefrom. However, a particular set-up will work depending upon whether market is in trend or sideways. It is advisable to use Tradingview for charting and analysis with trade Set-ups.

Few Good Trade Set-ups:

1. Trade Set-up: 1:

a. Time frame: 1 Minute or 3 Minutes. It is not advisable to trade on higher time frame when market is in Trend as you may lose good profit opportunity.
b. Indicators: (1) Supertrend at Tradingview
c. Limitation: It fails to give results when market is sideways. It is not advisable to use this indicator in this situation.

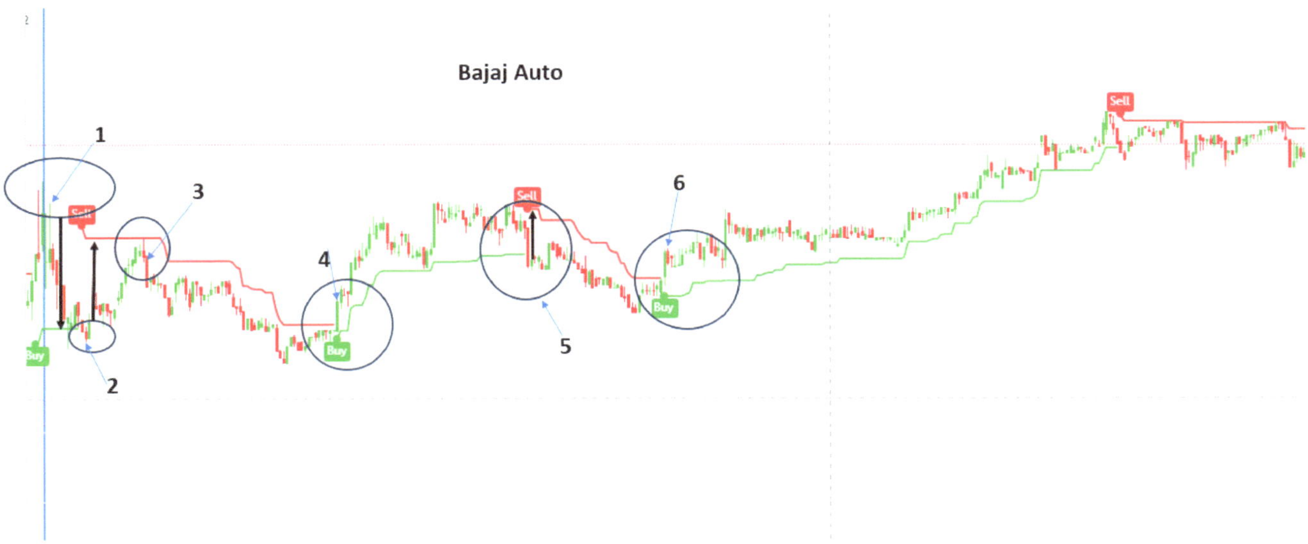

On 1-Minute chart, you have to simply be "mechanical" in buying and selling with the supertrend. This will work the best when there is good trend in the market. Only care to be taken is to ensure that there is no much distance between the breaking candle (the first candle which is becoming bullish or bearish while breaking the supertrend) and the supertrend, otherwise wait for the retracement upto the supertrend. This can be a very good set-up to earn some profit daily without worrying anything about the market. Once you have good practice, it will be much easier for you to trade, and you start understanding the candles more, and your accuracy level increases a lot. It is like, once you learn driving, you start driving comfortably in the traffic with good practice. Those who are like adventure sports can do very well with this set-up.

Above is the 1-Minute chart of Baja Auto. The chart gives you an overview. I have broken the chart on parts for better understanding.

At Point-1, the candle opened up and went high much above the supertrend, but did not become a bullish candle. We always wait for first minute to candle to form, then only we think of taking trade. In case, it became a green candle, then, you can see the down black arrow showing the distance. In such situation, no trade is to be taken at the high of first candle. You have to wait for the retracement at the supertrend level. After touching supertrend, it retraced, and you can enter the trade, but it reversed, and hit the stop-loss. Now, at Point-2, again, the distance between the breaking candle and the bearish supertrend is very high (see the upward arrow), you can not enter the trade, and wait for the retracement. At point no. 3, it again reversed touching the supertrend, and you can enter the trade which has given good fall. At point no. 4, it became a green candle, with no distance with bullish supertrend, hence, you can enter at the high of the first candle.

At point no. 5, much distance is found between bearish supertrend and the breaking candle, so, wait for the retracement. Here, retracement did not happen till the supertrend, but it reversed in-between. You can take the call after waiting for 2 or 3 red candles to happen. At point no. 6, less distance between the green candle and the bullish supertrend, and you can enter the trade at High of the first candle. Thereafter, you can enjoy the ride.

2. Trade Set-up: 2

a. Time frame: 1 Minute or 3-Minutes
b. Indicators: (1) Supertrend
(2) Exponential Moving Average 200 (EMA 200)
c. To be with overall trend as per EMA 200.
d. When EMA 200 shows down trend, then go for SHORT (SELL) trades only, whenever opportunity comes.
e. When EMA 200 shows up trend, then go for LONG (BUY) trades only whenever opportunity comes.

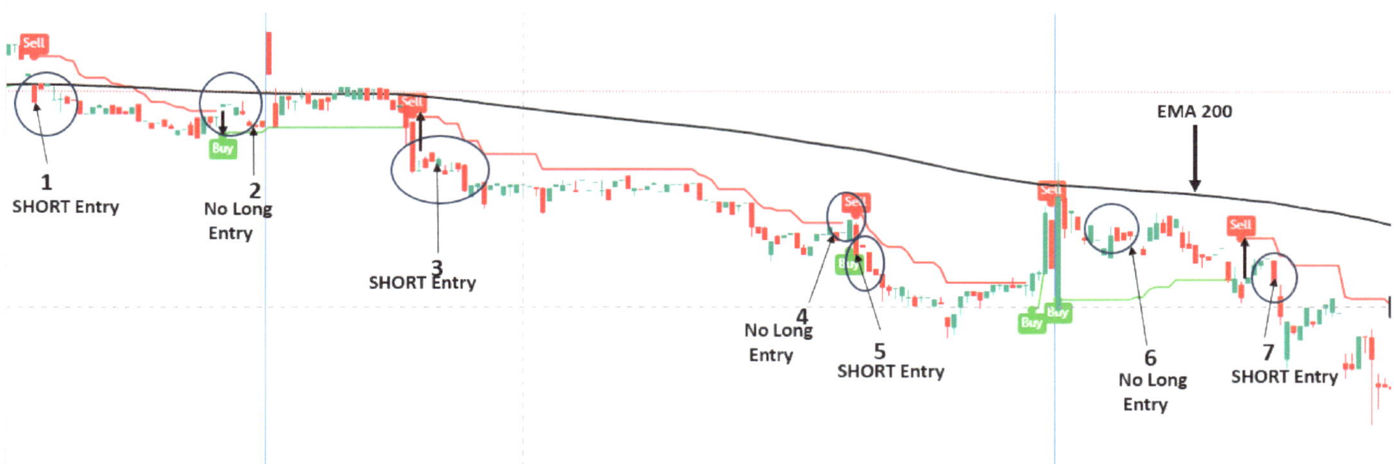

You can see in the above chart that EMA 200 shows down trend, hence, we will plan only SHORT trades, and avoid LONG trades as long as EMA 200 shows down trend. At point no.1, you can take short entry. At point np.2, you avoid the long trade as EMA 200 shows down trend. At point no. 3, again, you can go for short trend. No long entry at point no. 4. You can take short entry at point no. 5. Next day, at point no. 6, there is no long entry as EMA 200 still continues in down trend. At point no. 7, again you can go for short entry. It is advisable to book profits as per your target and situation. Do not wait for the change of trend to book the profits. With practice, you will get an idea when to book the profits.

3. **Trade Set-up – 3**

a. Time frame: 1 or 3-Minutes
b. Indicators: (1) SMA (Simple Moving Average) 9
(2) VWAP (Volume Weighted Average Price) with Upper Band and Lower Band.
(3) MACD (10,50,Close)
c. The cross-over of SMA 9 VWAP alerts the entry.
d. When Price starts moving on the Bands, you go for the entry
e. When SMA9 crosses down VWAP, and Price starts moving below the Lower Band, then go for SHORT (SELL) trades.
f. When SMA9 crosses up VWAP, and Price starts moving above the Upper band, then go for LONG (BUY) trades.
g. Before you enter the trades, get the confirmation from MACD.
h. The width of the upper and lower bands is very important. The broader the width, it shows momentum, while the width is narrow, it shows lack of momentum.

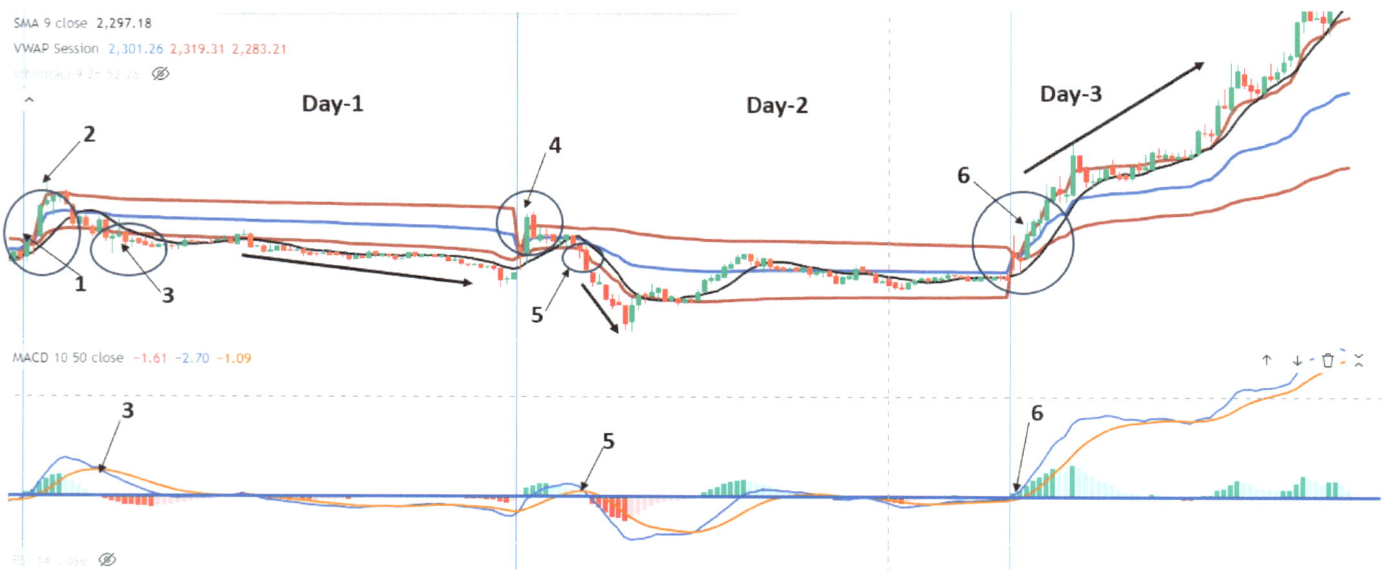

This is the 5-minute chart of CDSL. For better understanding, I have given 3 days' chart. On Day-1, you can see at point no. 1, at beginning of the day, there was already a prior cross-over of SMA9 (black line), and VWAP (blue line) on the previous day, hence, it's a buy opportunity once, the price moves beyond the upper band (brown line). Later, at point no. 2, you can see the momentum rising, but the price is not going above the upper band (brown line). Then, the price retraced, went below the SMA9, and also went below the lower band (brown line). This is an alert for short entry. At point no. 3, below the red candle, there is a short entry. Simultaneously, you get confirmation at MACD, point no. 3. You can see a down trend arrow thereafter. The stop loss will be at above the VWAP. On day-2, the second green candle is a big candle, going above

VWAP, and SMA9. Hence, there is a long alert. But, the next third candle turns red immediately, hence, there is no long trade taking place. At point no. 5, the price goes below SMA9, and VWAP, hence, it's an alert for short entry. Thereafter, it moves beyond lower band (brown line), and there is confirmation from MACD too. Hence, you enter the short trade with a stop loss above VWAP. You can see the down trend thereafter. Later, during the day, there is no trade opportunity as the price remains in the bands. You can book your profit depending upon the target you have fixed. Generally, it is observed that after 4 to 5 green candles or red candles on a time frame of 1 or 3 or 5 minutes, there is a chance of reversal. So, if you are getting a good profit during this ride, it is advisable to book the profit. On Day-3, at point no. 6, you can see the third green candle, going beyond SMA9, and VWAP. So, it is an alert for long trade. You get confirmation from MACD too for a long entry. You can place stop loss at below VWAP. Thereafter, you can see a very good uptrend, and all candles remaining above SMA9. You can also observe the width of the bands. More the width, better is the momentum.

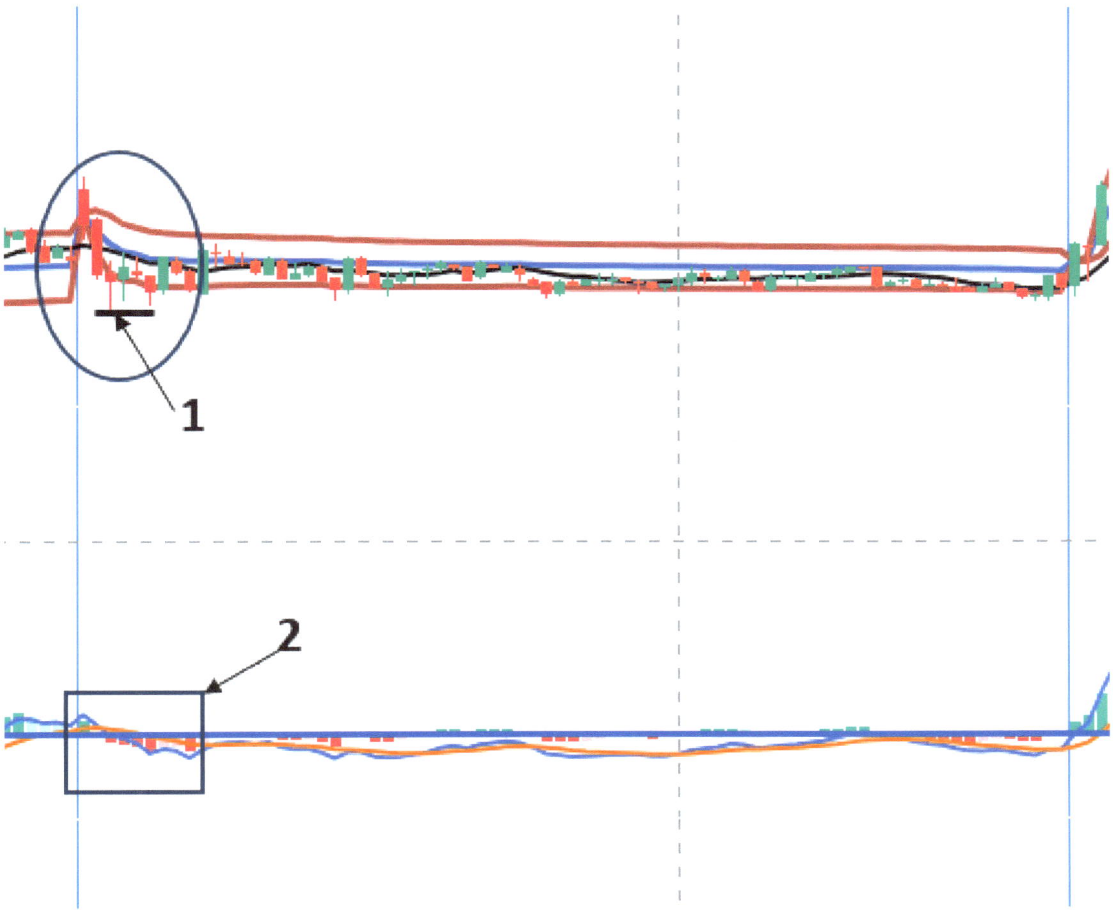

You can see in the above chart. At point no. 1, The second red candle goes below SMA9, and VWAP. Hence, this is an alert for short trade. When the price goes below the lower band (brown line), there is a short entry, and there is confirmation from MACD too at point no. 2. But, the entry does not take place because, the price reversed and formed a green candle, going back to the lower band. Again, the sixth candle becomes red, and goes below the lower band, but the next candle turns green, and goes back to the band. The price remains in the band the whole day, so there is no trade during the day. You can observe that the band remains narrow throughout the day which indicates there is no momentum during the day. Also, MACD remains narrow which also indicates lack of momentum.

5. Trade Set-up – 4

a. Time frame: 3 or 5 – Minutes
b. Indicators: (1) AlphaTrend (1,14) by KivancOzbilgic
(2) ADX (20,20)
c. AlphaTrend works best on lower time frame on 3 or 5 – minutes. Avoid using 15-minutes or higher time frame for intraday.
d. It has very few fake signals on lower time frames. It is a very versatile indicator which incorporates momentum, trend, volatility, and volume.
e. The trader has to follow Buy and Sell signals, and go for the trades.
f. ADX is an excellent confirmatory indicator along with AlphaTrend. But, the setting has to be 20,20 for better accuracy. There is no need to use ADX, but only +DI (Directional Index) and -DI are to be used. The cross-over of +DI and -DI give accurate conformation to take the trades.

The above chart is of Voltas on 3-minutes time frame. You can see AlphaTrend indicator gives Buy and Sell signal. Below the chart is ADX indicator with only +DI and -DI. On Day-1, At point no.1, there is sell signal, and you can enter the short trade at the low of Red candle below sell signal which is conformed by cross-over of +DI and -DI below. The stop loss will be the above red line. You can remain in the trade till the straight red line. At point no. 2, there is buy signal, but no confirmation from ADX, so no trade for us till the confirmation is given. However, after few candles, you can get confirmation from ADX, and you can take the long entry. The stop loss will be the below red line. You can remain in the trade till the straight red line. Again, at point no. 3, there is sell signal. ADX also gives confirmation. You can enter short trade with stop loss above the red line. At point no. 4, you can avoid the trade as it is 2.45 pm. It is advisable not to take any fresh entry after 2.30 pm. In case, you had taken the entry, the stop loss would have ben hit. On Day-2, you can observe that bullish momentum is continuing. You can enter the long trade at point no. 5, as ADX also gives confirmation. You can have stop loss below the red line. You can continue in the trade till straight red line or your target profit. You can see at point no. 6, a long straight red line which shows that there is no momentum, hence, no trade opportunity. You have to wait for the right opportunity. At point no. 7, the momentum has started which is seen in the green filled space. Whenever there is such space filled with green or red colour, it shows momentum, and gives trade opportunities. Here, at point no. 7, you can enter the long trade, and confirmation is also given by ADX.

Let's see one interesting example below.

As seen in the above chart, there is a short trade opportunity at point no. 1 with confirmation by ADX. At point no.2, there is green space which shows that momentum has started, and there is a cross-over of +DI and -DI which gives confirmation of long entry. But, soon, momentum is lost, and the straight red line has started. Below, ADX, there is a cross-over of -DI and +DI which indicates bearish signal. But, you are riding the long trade. This is an interesting situation wherein the trend is bullish, but the ADX shows bearish trend. Here, either you can get out of the trade, or remain in the trade till sell signal comes. If you remained in the long trade, you would have enjoyed good profit.

5. Trade Set-up – 5

a. Time frame: 10 Minutes only
b. Indicators: (1) EMA Crossing (5,55) by Harryla123
(2) Trend Trader Strategy (55,3)
(3) ADX (20,20) with +DI and -DI
c. EMA Crossing works best on 10-minutes time frame. It is a cross-over of Exponential Moving Average 5 and Weighted Moving Average 55 denoted by Red arrow for short and green arrow for long.
d. Trend Trader Strategy indicator shows direction, and works as resistance and support,
e. ADX is an excellent confirmatory indicator. But, the setting has to be 20,20 for better accuracy. There is no need to use ADX, but only +DI (Directional Index) and -DI are to be used. The cross-over of +DI and -DI give accurate confirmation to take the trades.

In the above chart of 10-minutes duration, on Day-1, at point no. 1, you can enter the short trade once the price goes below Trend Trader Strategy Indicator (TTS). You get confirmation from ADX also. On

Day-2, the down trend continues. At point no. 2, you can enter the short trade as the price is below TTS. ADX also confirms the trade. On Day-3 and Day-4, similar trend continues. You can enter the short trade at point no. 3 and point no. 4. ADX also gives confirmation. On all the days, you can place stop loss above TTS. On Day-5, there is a change in trend. EMA Crossing indicator gives buy signal. At point no. 5, you can enter long trade with a stop loss below TTS.

6. Trade Set-up – 6

a. Time frame: 3 or 5 – Minutes
b. Indicators: (1) UT Bot Alerts (3,1) by QuantNomad
(2) NSDT HAMA Candles by NorthStarDayTrading
(3) ADX (20,20) with +DI and -DI
c. UT Bot Alerts indicator gives Buy and Sell signals depending upon Bullish or Bearish trend. You have to change the setting for better accuracy and to avoid many signals which are often fake. The key value should be 3 instead of 1, and ATR period should be 1 instead of 10.
d. NSDT Heiken-Ashi Moving Average (HAMA) candles gives the bullish and bearish direction. The candle size gives the extent of momentum.
e. ADX is an excellent confirmatory indicator. But, the setting has to be 20,20 for better accuracy. There is no need to use ADX, but only +DI (Directional Index) and -DI are to be used. The cross-over of +DI and -DI give accurate confirmation to take the trades.

In the above 5-minute chart, you can see Buy and Sell buttons which represent UT Bot Alerts indicator. The Green and Red candles with a moving average green and red line is NSDT HAMA candles. On Day-1, in the first 5-minutes only you get Sell signal, and red NSDT HAMA candles. The ADX also gives short trade confirmation. At point no. 1, you can enter short trade at the low of the first candle. At point no. 2, you get Buy signal. But NSDT HAMA candles show down trend, ADX also shows down trend, so, long trade is to be avoided. At point no. 3, you can see yellow line under sell button. This shows neutral trend, hence, the short trade is to be avoided. At point no. 4, there is buy signal with green line and green candles. Hence, long trade is to be initiated at the high of blue candle. At point no. 7, you can see very light HAMA candles which shows lack of strength in momentum. Hence, the trade is to be avoided.

7. Trade Set-up – 7

a. Time frame: 15 – Minutes
b. Indicators: (1) UT Bot Alerts (4,1) by QuantNomad
(2) Linear Regression Candles
(3) SALMA (RedK Slow and Lazy Moving Average) by RedKTrader
c. SALMA indicator is placed on the main chart. UT Bot Alerts and Linear Regression Candles are to be placed on the New Pane in the chart.
d. UT Bot Alerts indicator will work with Linear Regression candles and will give Buy and Sell signals depending upon Bullish or Bearish trend. You have to change the setting for UT Bot Alert indicator with key value 4, and ATR period 1 for better accuracy and to avoid many signals which are often fake. This works best on 15-minute chart.
e. When SALMA and UT Bot Alert synchronize with green or red, i.e., bullish or bearish trend, you need to initiate the trade accordingly.

The above chart is a 15-minute chart of Mphasis Ltd. For a period of 9 days. Since it is on a higher time frame, it gives less signals, but strong signals. When there is buy signal, and SALMA is green, you enter the long trade. When there is sell signal, and SALMA is red, you enter the short trade. Stop loss will be below the low or high of the entry candle for buy or sell signal. You exit the trde when you get the opposite signal, or when you reach your target profit or at 3.00 pm.

8. Trade Set-up – 8

a. Time frame: 1 or 3 – Minutes
b. Indicators: (1) AI trend Indicator
(2) MACD (10,50)
c. When there is cross-over of Price Value Line (PVL) and AI Trend Moving Average, it's a trigger for entry. This is a very simple indicator and wrks very well on lower time frame – 1 or 3 minutes time frame.
d. MACD gives confirmation while trigger is taking place.

This is a 3-minute chart of L & T Technology Services Ltd. At point no. 1, there is a trigger as there is a cross-over. You can take short entry at the low of the swing low of the candles which is confirmed by MACD also for short entry. Next day, at point no. 2, the third candle is a green candle with a strong sell rejection. You can take long entry at the high of the third green candle with a stop loss below blue line. MACD also gives confirmation for the long entry. Blue line which is a PVL acts as a strong support and resistance. It is a magnetic line, as price will come back to it, if it goes far from it.

9. Trade Set-up – 9

a. Time frame: 3 or 5 – Minutes
b. Indicators: (1) Bollinger Band (20,2)
(2) EMA 5 - Low
c. Whenever there is cross-over of EMA5 and SMA20 of Bollinger Band, there is a trade opportunity. When EMA 5 crosses up SMA 20 of Bollinger Band, long trade is initiated. When EMA 5 crosses down SMA 20 of Bollinger Band, short trade is initiated. However, if the cross over does not give adequate space between EMA 5 and SMA 20, then the trade is to be avoided, or wait till the space is created.
d. Bollinger Band shows the boundary of price travel. As the 97% of the time price remains in-between the bands, the moment price goes above the upper band or goes below the lower band, it indicates that the price will come back inside the band. Hence, there is a chance of reversal. So, that is a point of profit booking. However, in case of a super-bullish scenario, price will "walk on the band", which can be traded provided there is a cross-over of EMA 5 and SMA 20 on the up-side.

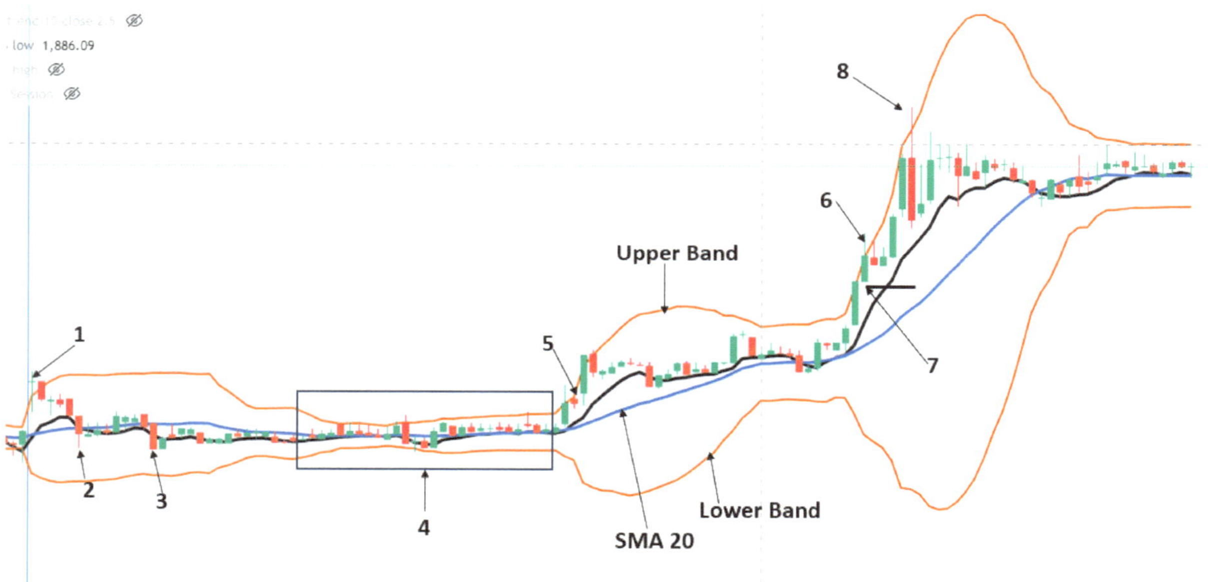

This is a 3-minute chart of DALBHARAT. You can see the first candle at point no. 1. It is going above the upper band, so chances of reversal. Therefore, no long trade opportunity though EMA 5 (black line) is crossing up SMA 20 (blue line). At point no. 2, EMA 5 (black line) is crossing down SMA 20 (blue line), but there is no momentum as it can be seen there is no adequate space between EMA 5 and SMA 20. Hence, you have to wait. At point no. 3, space is created. You can enter the short trade at the low of the red candle, but the price gets reversed, hence, you don't get the short trade. Thereafter, the price remains between EMA 5 and SMA 20 which shows no momentum. Whenever the price remains in between the EMA 5 and SMA 20, no trade is initiated. Then, at point no. 4, you can see there is no momentum, and the bands of Bollinger are squeezed which indicates no momentum. But, at the same time, it also indicates potential break-out. You can see the green candle before the point no. 5 which is giving a break-out, but it is going above the upper band, so, there is a reversal in the next candle at point no. 5. However, the high of the candle, though it is a red candle, can be considered for long trade, as it is above EMA 5 and SMA 20. Secondly, the red candle is a small candle occurring after the green long candle which indicates retracement. The stop loss to be taken below of the SMA 20. You can ride the trend, though it was not a good trend for another 8 to 10 candles, but then, it went up. At point no. 6, there is an opportunity to book the profit as the price is going above the upper band, or you can trail the stop loss below the candle at point no. 7. Thereafter, at point no. 8, the price is going above the upper band, you can book the profit after a good profitable ride without being greedy further.

10. Trade Set-up – 10

a. Time frame: 3 or 5 or 15 – Minutes
b. Indicators: (1) CM SlingShot System by Gibs
(2) Relative Strength Index (RSI 14,21)
c. This is a very interesting set up with high accuracy.
d. In this set up, we are going to use RSI differently. We will take trading confirmation based on the cross-over of RSI and RSI Moving Average (RSI-MA). The RSI-MA will be set up at 21 period. The RSI over bought will be 80 and above, the RSI over sold will be 20 and below. This will help us to predict the price movement, but, no decision will be taken on the basis of over bough or over sold situation. Similarly, we will enable the divergence in the setting of RSI which will again help us to predict the price movement. RSI is one of the best indicator which is very versatile in nature. It helps the traders to monitor the price travel on the chart, and has predictive element in it.
e. The trading decision we will take from CM SlingShot indicator which is also one of the most accurate indicators. If this indicator indicates the trade, we will not enter the trade, if RSI and RSI-MA cross-over does not confirm.

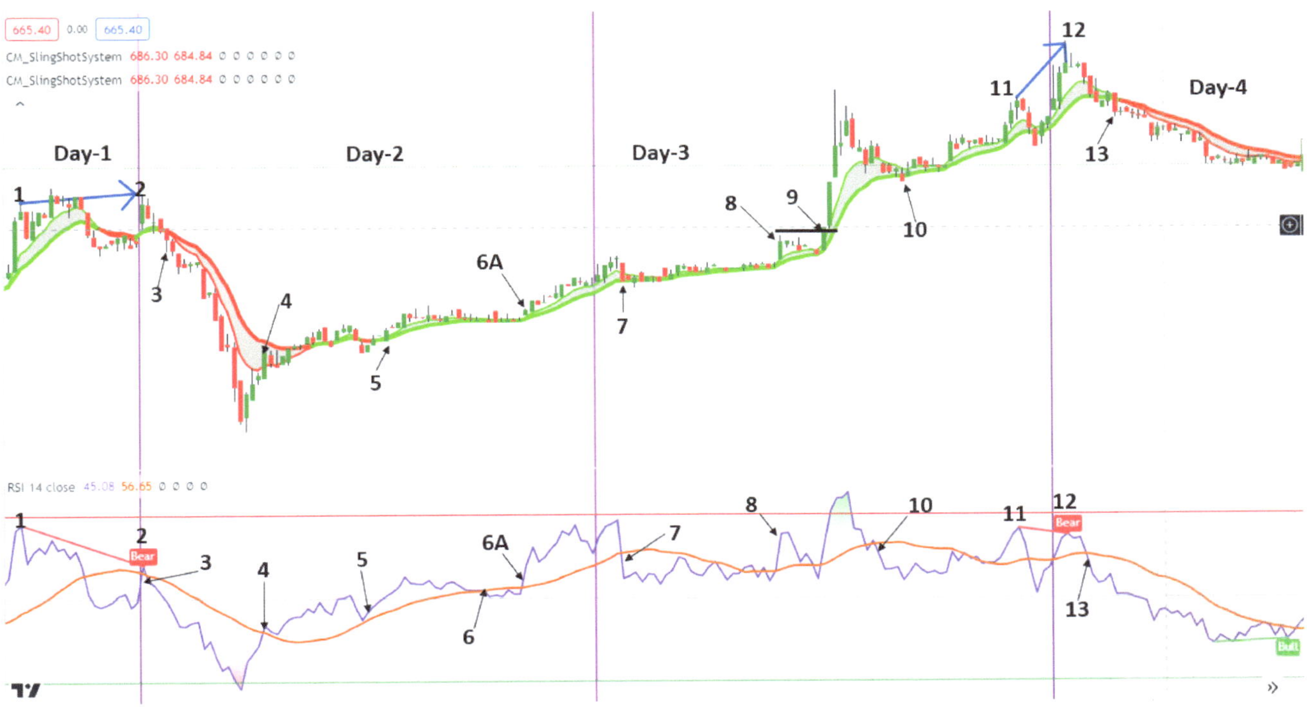

This is a 5-minute chart of Shanti Gears. Day-1 is an example of divergence. Divergence occurs when price rises (from point no. 1 to point no. 2), but RSI declines at the same price level (from point no.1 to point no. 2). This is called Bearish Divergence which predicts that there is a high probability of decline in the price in the coming time. And, next day, Day-2, the price declined. At point no. 3, CM SlingShot indicator, turning red indicates short trade, and RSI is crossing down RSI-MA which confirms the short trade entry. At point no. 4, RSI crosses up RSI-MA which indicates profit booking. At point no. 5, CM SlingShot is green, and RSI is above RSI-MA which confirms the long trade. But, at point no. 6, RSI crosses down RSI-MA which means profit booking, or trail the stop loss. At point no. 6A, you continue with the trade, or you take fresh entry. On Day-3, there is no fresh cross over, so no trade to be initiated. At point no. 7, RSI crosses down RSI-MA, but CM SlingShot is green so, no long trade as RSI cross over does not confirm the long trade. At point no. 8, there is a cross -over which confirms the long trade. So, at point no. 8, the high of the green candle is the entry which you get at point no. 9. At point no. 10, you book the profit or wait and trail the stop loss. You can book the profit at 3.00 pm. Now, price rises from point no. 11 to point no. 12, but corresponding RSI declines which shows Bearish divergence predicting price-fall in the coming time. So, at point no. CM SlingShot turns red which indicates short trade and RSI crosses down RSI-MA which confirms the short trade. The stop loss in each trade will be high or low of the CM SlingShot red or green line.

11. Trade Set-up – 11

a. Time frame: 1 or 3 or 5 Minutes
b. Indicators: (1) EMA 9 (High), and EMA 9 (Low)
   (2) RSI (14,21)
c. On my journey to write this book, I studied and came across various trade set-ups with numerous indicators recommended by many experts and practicing traders. I also carried out experimental research on those set-ups and indicators. What I observed and noticed that cross-over of RSI and RSI Moving Average has not been so emphasized for taking trades. The power of RSI is kept limited to finding reversal through overbought or oversold positions, or locating bullish or bearish phase, or indicating super bullish at 70, or super bearish at 30, or finding bullish or bearish divergence. But, cross-over of RSI and RSI Moving Average gives excellent opportunities for buy and sell at all timeframes which you like. For Intraday trades, I have observed that timeframes 1 or 3 or 5 minutes are giving excellent results. Hence, I have developed a trade set-up using cross-over of RSI and RSI Moving Average and incorporating EMA 9 at High and Low.
d. In this set up, we are going to use RSI differently as used in the set-up 10. We will take trade alert based on the cross-over of RSI and RSI Moving Average (RSI-MA). The RSI-MA will be set up at 21 period. The RSI over bought will be 80 and above, the RSI over sold will be 20 and below. This will help us to predict the price movement, but, no decision will be taken on the basis of over bough or over sold situation. Similarly, we will enable the divergence in the setting of RSI which will again help us to predict the price movement. RSI is one of the best indicator which is very versatile in nature. It helps the traders to monitor the price travel on the chart, and has predictive element in it.

e. The trading decision for buying the stocks will be taken on the basis of RSI is crossing up RSI Moving Average, provided price is closing above EMA 9 (High). Similarly, for shorting the stocks, RSI crossing down RSI Moving Average as an alert, provided price is getting closed below EMA 9 (Low).

Let us look at the chart below.

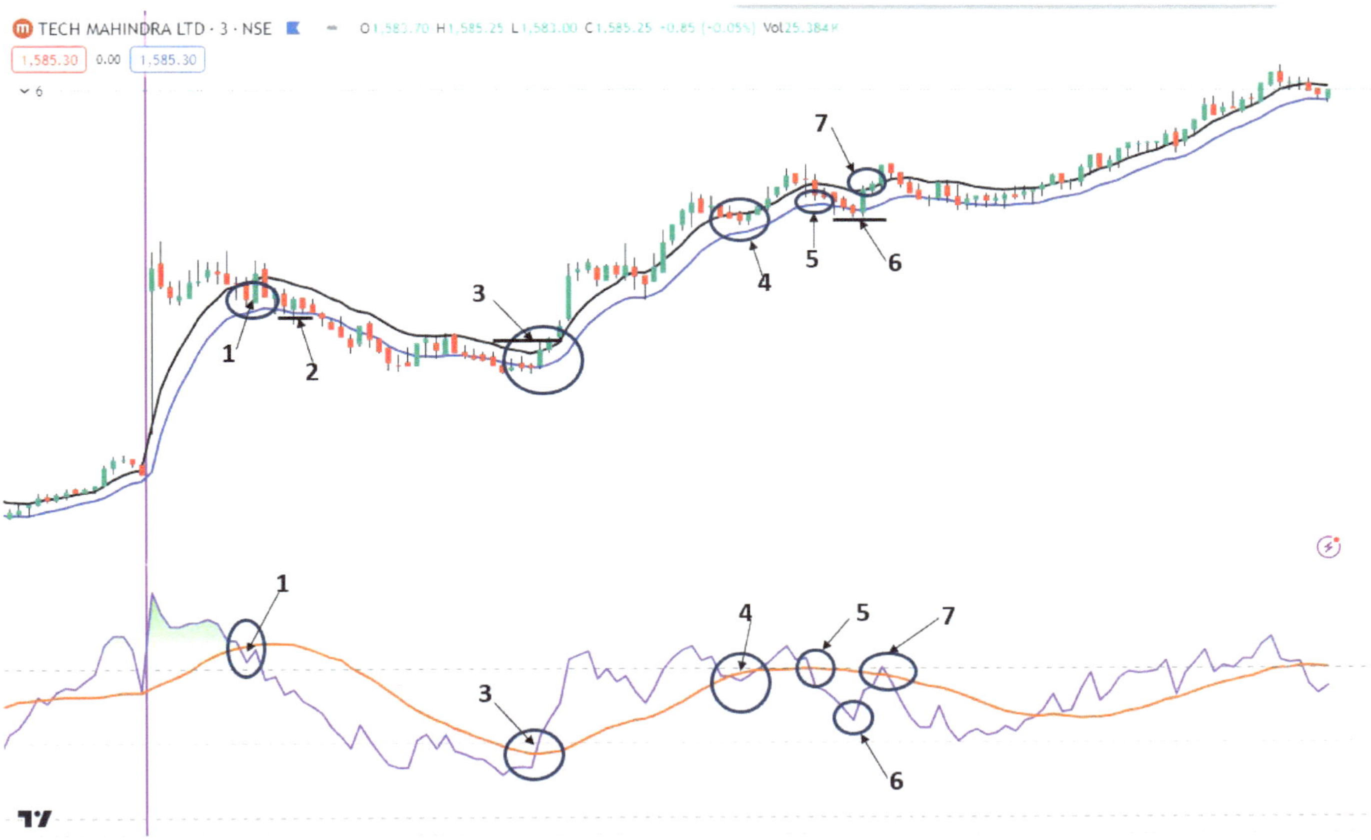

This is a 3-Minute chart of Tech Mahindra. At point 1, there is a cross-over of RSI and RSI MA. But, the price has not gone below EMA 9 (LOW). So, there is no entry for short at point 1. But, at point 2, the price closes below EMA 9 (Low), so, there is an entry with a stop loss above EMA 9 (High). Point 3 is an exit as well as fresh Long entry. You can observe at point 3 and 4. Though there is RSI cross-over with RSI MA. But, the price has not gone below EMA 9 (Low), so, you can remain in the trade. At point 6, you can take exit. But, again at point 7, there is Long trade with a stop loss below EMA 9 (Low). You can take a nice ready though there have been RSI and RSI MA cross-overs, but the price is not visibly below EMA 9 (Low), so you can remain in the trade.

With good practice this set up can become the best set up. It is not necessary that every time you go for the trade. You can take one trade with good quantity and make good profit, provided your risk-reward permits.

12. Trade Set-up – 12

I came across a set-up on a few technical analysis tools developed by a small town boy of Gujarat, Kapadvanj of Kheda District. He is Akar Sharma, Founder, Mindjek Technologies. His set-up is unique in a way that it combines multiple time frame trend, previous day high and low, VWAP, Supertrend, Pivot points, support and resistance levels, RSI with target profit, stop loss, and a dashboard for stock selection. It's a very versatile set-up. Akash is a pine script developer and experimenting with many new technical analysis tools.

a. Time frame: 5 or 10 or 15 Minutes
b. Indicators: RAVAN 2.0, available on TradingView.

In the above of 5 minutes chart of ACC Ltd, you can see how alerts are created for buy and sell, how support and resistance levels are created automatically. I have experimented with this set-up, and the accuracy level is almost 70% to 80%.

13. Trade Set-up – 13

This trade set-up primarily refers to the cross-over of Exponential Moving Averages. They are classic indicators and being followed from ages. Where there are volumes and momentum, they give excellent results.

We will discuss two set-ups here.

Set-up 13A:

a. Timeframe: 1-3-5 Minutes
b. Indicator: EMA 3 with offset +1, and EMA 9 with offset +3

c. Offset is normally zero in every EMA indicator, but small change in offset gives excellent results in terms of better visual interpretation of price movement and signal clarity.
d. Cross-over up and cross-over down will generate alerts for buy and sell respectively.

- In the above 1-minute chart of TCS, there are 7 trade opportunities – 4 are buy opportunities and 3 are sell opportunities on the basis of cross-over of EMA 3 and EMA 9 with some minor changes in offset. You can change the offset by going into the setting of EMA.

Set-up 13B:

a. Timeframe: 5 or 10 or 15 Minutes
b. Indicator: Three Indicators - EMA 8-13-21 with no change in offset.
c. The cross-over of the three indicators gives trade alerts. It also clearly shows the sideway market where you can easily avoid the trade.

In the above 1-minute chart of Mphasis Ltd., you can see how three EMA look like. At point no. 1, all the three EMAs are becoming one, means, the market is sideways. At point no. 2, EMAs are opening and you can see the width which means there is momentum, and you can enter the trade with a Long position. At the point no. 3, you can see the unusual width among EMAs (point no. 4 arrow) which is an indication of reversal, and profit booking at Point no. 4. At point no. 5, there is a cross- over down which means a short trade opportunity till end. These three EMAs give excellent result on lower time frame, especially, when there is trend. But, when there is no trend and sideway market, they save you from stop losses as it is easy to identify the sideway market.

Experts and professional traders often use combinations of EMAs with different periods to gain insights into market trends and improve accuracy. The use of different offsets with EMAs can be applied strategically for better visual interpretation and signal clarity.

You can see below various combinations of EMAs that experts use, along with potential strategies to incorporate offsets for better accuracy:

EMA Combination	Offset Strategy	Application
EMA 9 & EMA 21	Negative offset (-1 or -2) on EMA 9	Short- to mid-term trend signals
EMA 12 & EMA 26	Positive offset (+1 or +2) on EMA 26	MACD and momentum trading
EMA 50 & EMA 200	Negative offset on EMA 50, positive offset on EMA 200	Long-term trend identification
EMA 5, EMA 20, & EMA 50	Negative offset (-1 or -2) on EMA 5, positive on EMA 50	Multi-timeframe trading strategy
EMA 8, EMA 13, & EMA 21	Negative offset on EMA 8, positive on EMA 13 & 21	Scalping or intraday strategies

Important Note:

There are hundreds of indicators available on TradingView platform which traders can use according to comfort and convenience. I have studied many indicators and undergone experimental research as well as back-test studies. Accordingly, I have tried to present best 11 set-ups for trading easily with better accuracy but without much knowledge.

Deliberately, I have not presented other indicators which are reversal based, which are support and resistance based. Too much of knowledge will create confusion, and will make it difficult for you to implement. It is strongly advised to select one or two aet-ups, practice for at least 3 months with 1 quantity of share. The results will create immense confidence in you, thereafter, you can take trade with bigger quantities. I strongly advise not to paper trade. Paper trading will not be able to generate right skills in you. You must lose something in order to gain something. That losing experience is the best teacher in the stock trading.

Another aspect of trading is when there is trend in the market, all indicators will work, but, when trend is missing, it will be difficult to trade with indicators. It's like when there is no traffic, you can drive the car easily and enjoy the ride. But, when there is traffic, it becomes difficult to drive. Hence, practice, practice and practice is the key to master the indicators. Stop loss will help you to protect your capital.

CHAPTER – 08

Data-Driven and Time-Driven Trading – A Different Approach

Data is God: Data-driven Trading – Order flow Analysis

Data-driven intraday trading relies on analyzing various forms of market data to make trading decisions. This includes historical price data, real-time price movements, trading volumes, and other market indicators. Traders often use intraday charts based on different time intervals such as 5-minute, 15-minute, or 60-minute intervals to identify patterns and make timely trades.

Order Flow Trading

Order flow trading is a data-driven strategy that focuses on the recent buy and sell orders in the market to make trading decisions. This method helps traders understand the market's supply and demand dynamics. It offers traders a detailed view of market activity with relevant data, enabling them to make more informed trading decisions. By analyzing the order flow, traders can predict short-term price movements more accurately. This strategy is particularly useful in detecting market imbalances and trading opportunities. Order flow analysis allows traders to detect areas of high liquidity, where large orders are likely to be executed. Trading in these areas can reduce slippage and improve execution efficiency.

In the market Trend is established when the market moves. So, if we get the data of "who moves the market", then we can increase accuracy in the trade. Let us understand who moves the market. Market is made up of two types of orders:

Limit Orders

Market Orders

Limit orders ***make*** the market. The bid and offer orders are limit orders, Market Orders are those orders which are placed at the market price which lift the bid (buy) and ask (sell) orders which are limit orders. Therefore, market orders ***move*** the market because they create imbalance in supply and demand, and price moves up. Buy at market order and sell at market order is also known as aggressive buying and aggressive selling. Therefore, as a trader, if we know only aggressive buy and sell volume, then we the market movement picture becomes clear. An order flow chart will show you exactly how many buy and sell market orders were executed at each price level. Therefore, this is also known as Footprint chart as it detects the footprints of aggressive buyers and aggressive sellers.

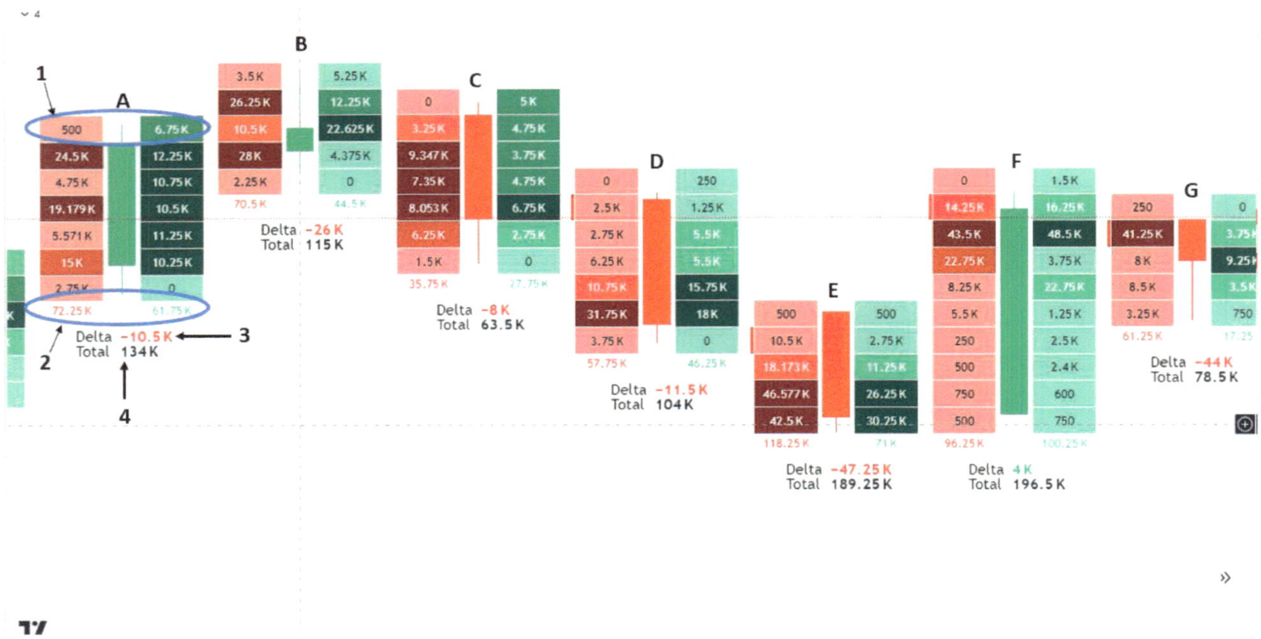

This is a 5-minute chart of Reliance Future (Important note: Those stocks which are in Futures contract can only have Order Flow chart. Therefore, there are around 180 stocks in which we can apply order flow chart. This is a separate chart pattern available on TradingView platform as Volume Footprint chart.)

You can see each candle has data on both the sides. On the right side of the candle, buyers' aggressive volume is seen. On the left side of the candle, sellers' aggressive volume is seen. At each price-level, we get such data. At point no. 1, buyers' volume of 6.75K is seen at a particular price level, while sellers' volume is only 500. This means at this price level, aggressive buyers are more than aggressive sellers. At point no. 2, we can see total volume of aggressive buyers and sellers of that particular candle A. The point no. 3 shows Delta which represents difference between buyers and sellers. This reflects that in a particular candle who is more dominant. Here, sellers are more dominant, so there is negative delta. Similarly, in real-time, you can analyse the candles when they are forming in the live market. At point no. 4, there is total volume of buyers and sellers. This helps to know the trend of volume and market participants.

The interesting part of the data is our prediction becomes more clear and confident. You can see that Candle A has Delta of -10.5K which is negative. But, the candle A is green. This means that though the price has increased, aggressive sellers are more dominant in this candle A. This is called Delta Divergence. This reflects possibility of reversal. You can analyse Candle B. Though the Candle B is green (means price has increased), there is delta Divergence (-26K). This means sellers' are more dominant and their dominance has increased over the previous Candle A. hence, the probability of reversal is more. If we include price action, then we can see that the candle B is a Doji candles which means price reversal as per price action. And, you can see that price has reversed thereafter. So, if price action is combined with data, then the trade becomes more confident.

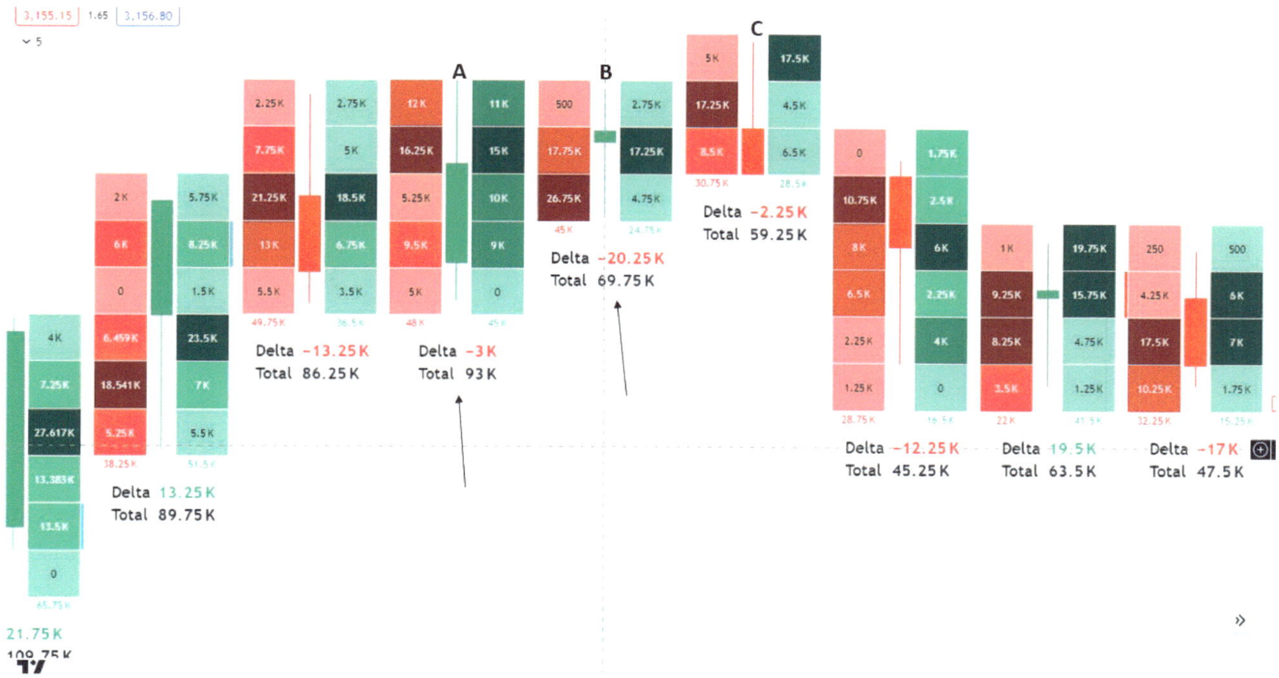

This is also a Reliance Future chart of 5-minutes duration. You can see Delat Divergence in candle A. There is more divergence in candle B, and candle B is becoming a Doji candle which means there is a high probability of reversal. Candle C is becoming like an Inverted Hammer depicting buyers' rejection. You can see data inside the candle C how sellers are becoming more dominant. All these put together, it suggests that there will be price reversal, and you can enter the short trade at the low of candle C.

This is the same chart of Reliance Future given above. You can see how the price has reversed. Thus, data gives you solid information, if combined with price action, then the level of accuracy of the trade is very high.

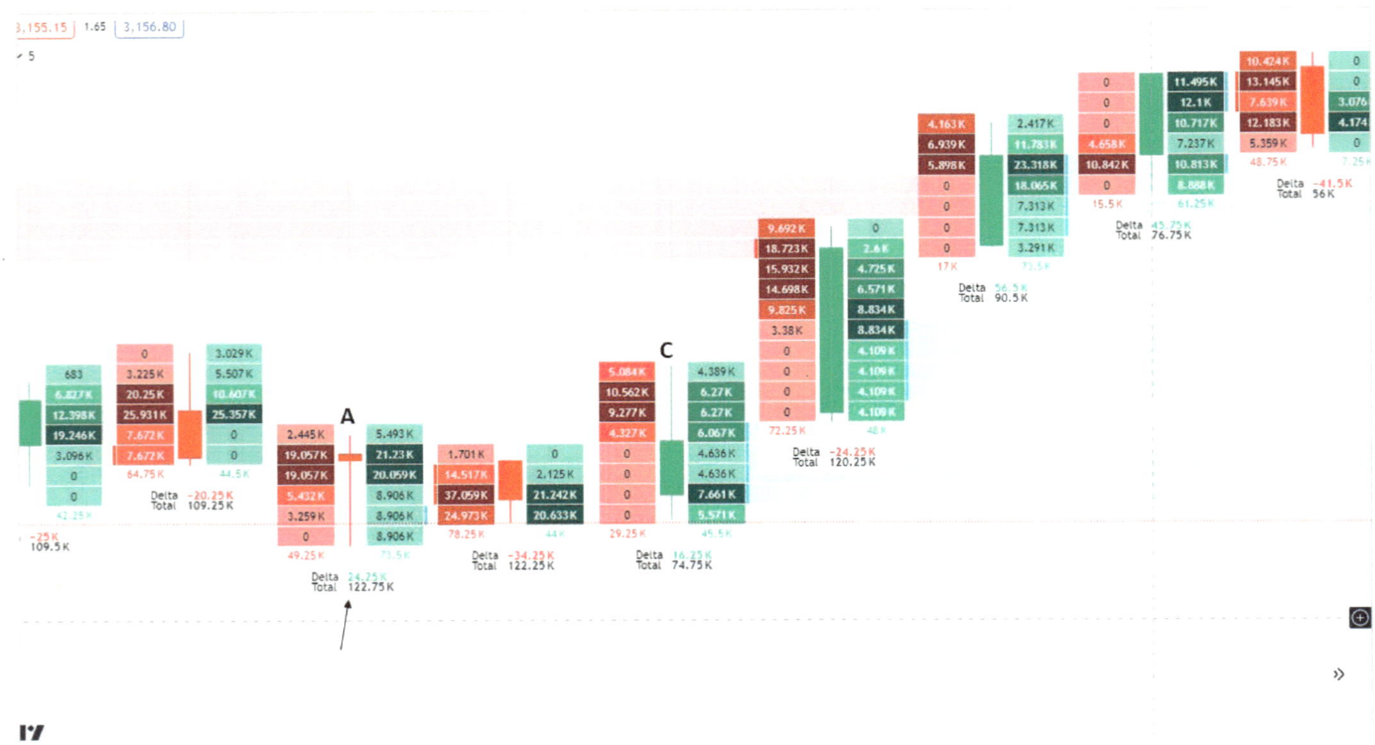

Another example is about upward movement. Candle A has positive Delta Divergence (buyers are more dominant), and the candle A is Red (price has decreased), at the same time, the candle A is becoming a pin bar with a sellers' rejection in a big way. This means there is a probability of price reversal. Now, wait for a green candle. The High of candle C can be an entry. You can see the upward movement thereafter.

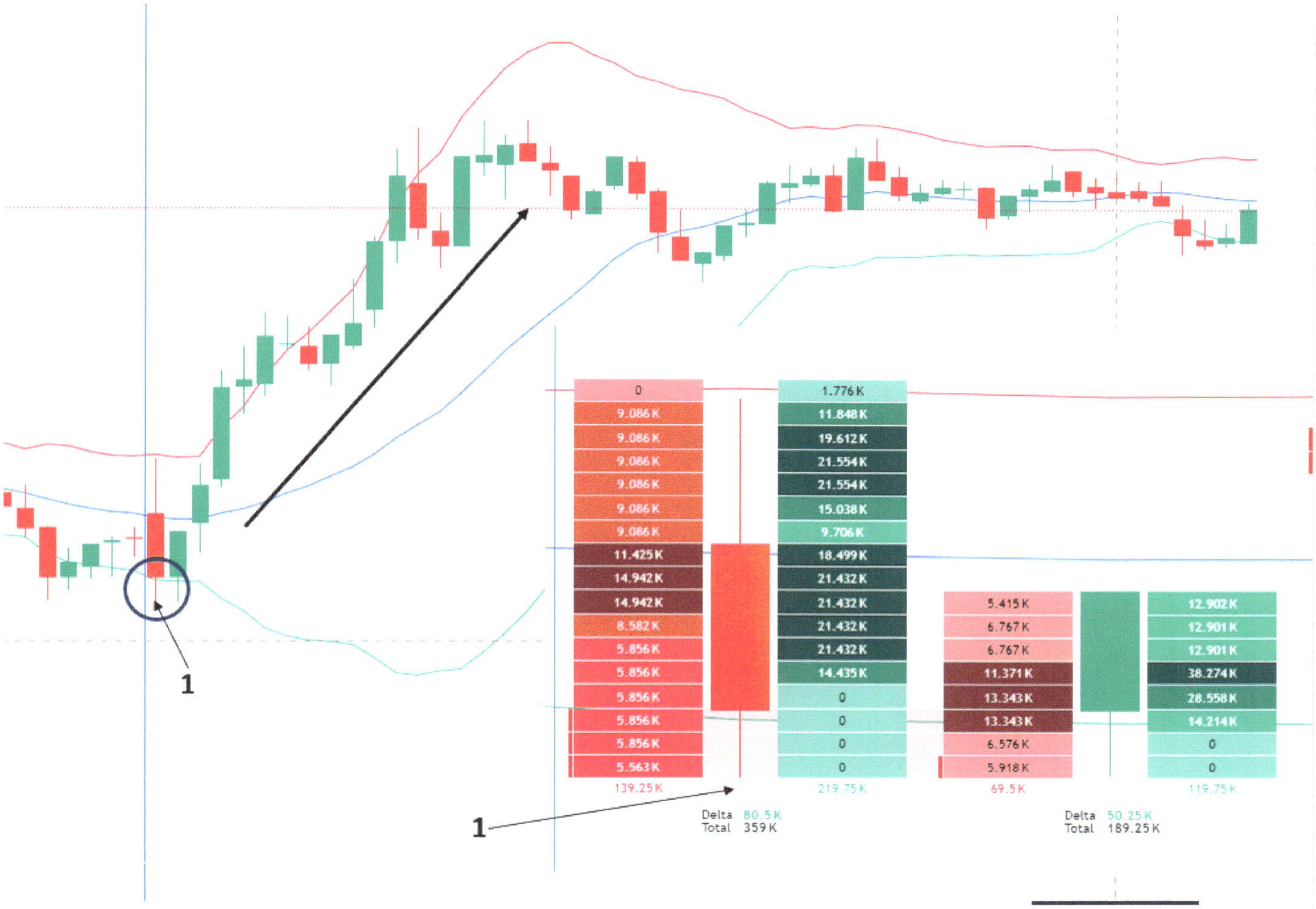

In the chart above, you can see at point no. 1, the price goes out of the lower band, and closes almost on the band. You can also observe the positive Delta Divergence happening in a red candle. So, two things are happening – 1. Candle is on the lower band, and 2. There is positive delta divergence. This is a case of high probability long trade. You can enter the trade in the next candle which is making high and close at the same price level with good positive delta.

Trade Setup – 14

- There is Delta Divergence.
- Positive Delta Divergence at the Support level, or at the lower band of Bollinger band or at the outside of lower band of Bollinger band.
- Candle pattern of Doji, Hammer, Pin Bar, Engulfing

Such a scenario will constitute a high probability trade. However, every Delta Divergence will not create a trade. Therefore, you have to wait for a matured trade set up.

Thus, order flow analysis helps you recognize the final details of the buying and selling volume. It's a microscopic look into candlestick studies. Inside each candlestick, there is a lot of information that can be analyzed through order flow.

There are traders who trade only on the basis of Data. Mr. Lovedeep Garg from Bangalore has created his own set up on the basis of research on data on which he identifies fair price value and break-out candle. Dr Vinay Prakash Tiwari from Varansai has come out with LTP (Last Traded Price) Calculator which is a very popular instrument to identify high probability trade on the basis of Option Chain and Volume data. His extensive research on the same has earned him a Doctorate Degree from a reputed American University. His data identify the support and resistance levels, along with divergence and extension with a high accuracy.

For such traders, Data is God.

B. Time is God: Time-driven Trading (Financial Astrology)

Earlier we saw, **Price is God** where all trading actions centre around Price and we use indicators that are largely price-driven. We also saw the power of data where **Data is God**, how different types of data can be engineered and interpreted for trading decisions which deliver more confidence in trading. Here, we will see **Time is God** which refers to time that drives price and data called Financial Astrology.

Financial astrology, though controversial, has demonstrated notable success in predicting market trends. Historical analyses reveal correlations between planetary movements and major market events, highlighting its unique predictive potential. This has made it an appealing tool for many traders, despite its complexity and the criticism it faces.

Astrologers predicted the 1987 market crash, attributing it to a rare planetary alignment. The crash's timing aligned precisely with the predicted astrological window, showcasing financial astrology's potential accuracy. Similarly, the early 2000s dot-com bubble burst coincided with significant planetary transits, particularly the Saturn-Pluto opposition, which traditionally signals economic downturns and structural changes. These historical correlations suggest that astrological events can often precede major market movements.

Financial astrology's roots trace back to ancient civilizations, where celestial events were linked to agricultural cycles and economic activities. The practice gained prominence in the 20th century through financial astrologers like W.D. Gann, who used astrological cycles to predict market trends. Gann's forecast of the 1929 stock market crash, based on planetary movements, earned him legendary status in financial circles. He developed several astrological indicators still used by traders today, including institutional traders.

Financial astrology connects planetary movements with market volatility, explaining how to interpret planetary and lunar activity for market forecasting. By integrating astrological insights with technical trading patterns, traders can gain a new perspective on market dynamics.

Studies support financial astrology's relevance. The Federal Reserve Bank of Atlanta found that U.S. stock markets tend to be negatively affected by geomagnetic storms, while the Royal Bank of Scotland showed that a trading system based on moon phases would have outperformed the market.

Popular predictive techniques in financial astrology include:

Transits: Tracking planetary movements through the signs to forecast events.

Aspects: Analyzing angles between planets to predict how events will unfold.

Timing: Identifying optimal times for trades by studying natal charts, transits, and aspects.

These techniques enable astrologers to time trades and investments for maximum profit.

I would like to mention the contribution being made by some of the Indian financial astrology experts like Shri Harshubh M Shah. He is making all efforts to popularize this discipline among the traders with his punchline – "Astro is the King". He has done an extensive study in this field and emphatically advocates – "Time is God". He is different from other Astro-experts in a way that he integrates technology with Astro factors. He is practicing using on-line Astrological platforms making the use of financial astrology simpler and understandable. In the one of his approaches to trading decisions, he advocates taking into consideration "Bhadra kaal", i.e., period of change when the market tends to reverse. As a part of my research for this book, I studied "Bhadra kaal" as suggested by him, and I found all those dates falling in, and I could see the reversals in the trend 100% correct on all the dates from the year 2023 to June 2024. Such an information, well-in-advance, prepares you for taking right trading decisions in Intraday stock trading. There are other number of Astro factors that he emphases on for right trading decisions like transit of Moon, Mars, Saturn, Jupiter in Sun.

Financial astrology is a method used by some traders to select stocks for intraday trading based on planetary positions and their influences. The extensive and aggressive research on study of astrological influences on financial markets and stock prices was carried out by Mr. Indrodeep Banerjee, a Trader and Financial Astrologer. He wrote the book "Stock Market Astrology" after 11 years of dedicated aggressive research in application of astrological principles in predicting stock markets.

The data shown in the book are amazing and prove that this can be a very effective tool for selecting the right stocks in advance.

For Intraday, the planet Moon is very important. Studying the Moon's placement in a particular constellation (Nakshatra), in the particular House out of 12 houses, the aspect thrown by other planets on the Moon and the House give valuable information about which sector is going to be Bullish or Bearish. Once the sector is found, you can find a stock of the sector and take the trade accordingly. I am quoting one example from his book for intraday.

"Intraday in Dhanishtha Nakshatra

On 30.09.2009, Wednesday. It was Dhanishtha nakshatra day.

This day Mars was aspected by Saturn. By judging aspect we found that aspect to Mars is unfavorable, so it was decided to trade short in stocks related to infrastructure and cement during this day. Therefore RIIL was short sold at Rs. 1115 per share with opening of market at 09:57, and purchased back near end of day at 15:00, at Rs. 1102, with intraday profit of Rs. 13 per share or 1.20 % profit in intraday trading.(Page no. 102)."

Ther have been many examples in his book that he has experimented.

Similarly, he has also explained about the time of trading during the day on the basis of planetary influence during the time which is called as Hora in Astrology. He has also taken trades successfully on that basis.

Since the science of Astrology is complex to understand, very few are successful in trading on the basis of indications given by Astrological tools. However, these days, this is gaining much attention among the traders. I firmly believe that in the years to come, more and more people will embrace financial astrology in their stock trading.

CHAPTER – 09

Stock Selection

This chapter stands as the cornerstone of this book. Based on insights from various experts and my personal observations over the past three years, stock selection accounts for 80% of trading success, whereas different trading setups contribute the remaining 20%. Even the most optimal trading setup will falter without the correct stock selection, leading traders to inevitable stop-loss hits. Conversely, selecting the right stock allows traders to navigate the market with ease and confidence.

The term "right stock" refers to stocks exhibiting significant momentum and volatility on a given trading day. Thus, identifying such stocks with these characteristics is crucial for traders to maximize their success. According to the Pareto Principle, a small proportion of stocks typically account for the majority of profitable trades, highlighting the importance of careful stock selection. When you catch the fish, fishing spot is very important where fish are flowing. Similarly, you need to find those stocks which are likely to give a big move.

There are two approaches to stock selection.

A. Day prior to the trading day.
B. During the day of trading.

First of all, it is important to understand that this is an Intraday trading.

Now, let us understand how stock selection happens under these two approaches. In both the approaches, those stocks to be selected which are within a price range of Rs 750 to Rs. 4000 only. Any stock which is below Rs. 750 is to be avoided as a rule, because stocks with movement of 2% and above can only be profitable for an Intraday trader. So, stocks with below the price of Rs. 750 can give less than Rs. 15 rise which may be profitable. Similarly, stocks above the price of Rs. 4000 are to be avoided because this will require more funds. If we consider the movement of 2% and above, then it will give the rise from Rs. 15 to Rs. 80 which has a great profit potential for an Intraday trader. Moreover, any stock between this price range with a volume of less than 50,000 is to be avoided because, it will fail to give momentum due to lesser volume to a greater extent. However, with experience, you can change these parameters.

A. Day Prior to the Trading Day.

This approach requires prior preparations for the next day intraday trading. This can be one day before as well as one hour before the commencement of the trading day. It is important to understand that stock selection will take place on Day-timeframe, and trade will take place on lower timeframe (1 or 3 or 5 or 15 minutes depending upon Trading Set-up).

1.Stocks closed on and above EMA 9

Any stock closing above exponential moving average of 9 period is most likely to give momentum. Hence, such stocks need to be identified in advance on a Daily timeframe. You can do this exercise on a previous day evening. It will take maximum one hour initially to do this exercise. Remember, the identified stocks will have a greater probability of giving momentum, it is not 100% that it will move. You can keep these stocks in your watchlist for 3 to 4 days for taking Intraday trades. Such stocks remain in momentum for 3 to 4 days. You can take entry once the high of the previous day is broken. But, you have to follow your trading set up. Break-out of the previous day high is a trigger which will give you an alert to initiate the trade, provided your set-up gives green signal.

There is always a challenge to find such stocks from amongst 6000 stocks. But, the technology has done wonders in the field of stock trading. You can use screeners using different platforms. TradingView is one such powerful platform which helps to identify such stocks easily, and transfer such stocks to your watchlist. Analyze those stocks both for long and short trades on TradingView, and select stocks with highest probability of giving movement. When there is big green and red candle crossing the EMA 9, then it may not give good momentum. So, such stocks are to be avoided. Stocks closing above EMA 9 are for Long trades, while stocks closing below EMA 9 are for short trades. Let me give you one example.

This is the Daily chart of Hindustan Aeronautics Ltd. (HAL). You will find Stock Screener on the left bottom corner as depicted at point no.1 in the above chart. TradingView does not give EMA 9, so, you may select EMA 10 which will not give any much difference. There are other parameters also need to be fixed in the stock screener, such as, selection of Exchange, Price range, Volume, etc. Blue line is the EMA 9 as depicted in the point no. 3. You can see at point no. 2, the price is closing above EMA 9. We can take entry at the high of the *doji*-type candle. You can see the momentum. The trade was available on both the sides (long & short) during the day, if your set-up is of 3 or 5 minutes duration. Similarly, at point no. 4, you can enter the trade at the high of the candle. The care is to be taken that if the green candle is very big, then you should avoid the trade next day as it may not give needed momentum. At point no. 5, you can get a short trade at the low of the previous day Red candle as it has closed below the EMA 9. The best part of Intraday is that we can have trades on both sides – up side and down side, and have opportunity of making profit even in a falling market.

Another way of selection of stock is to use Chartink scanner (chartink.com). You can write your requirements in their specified format, and you get the stocks. Let me give you example.

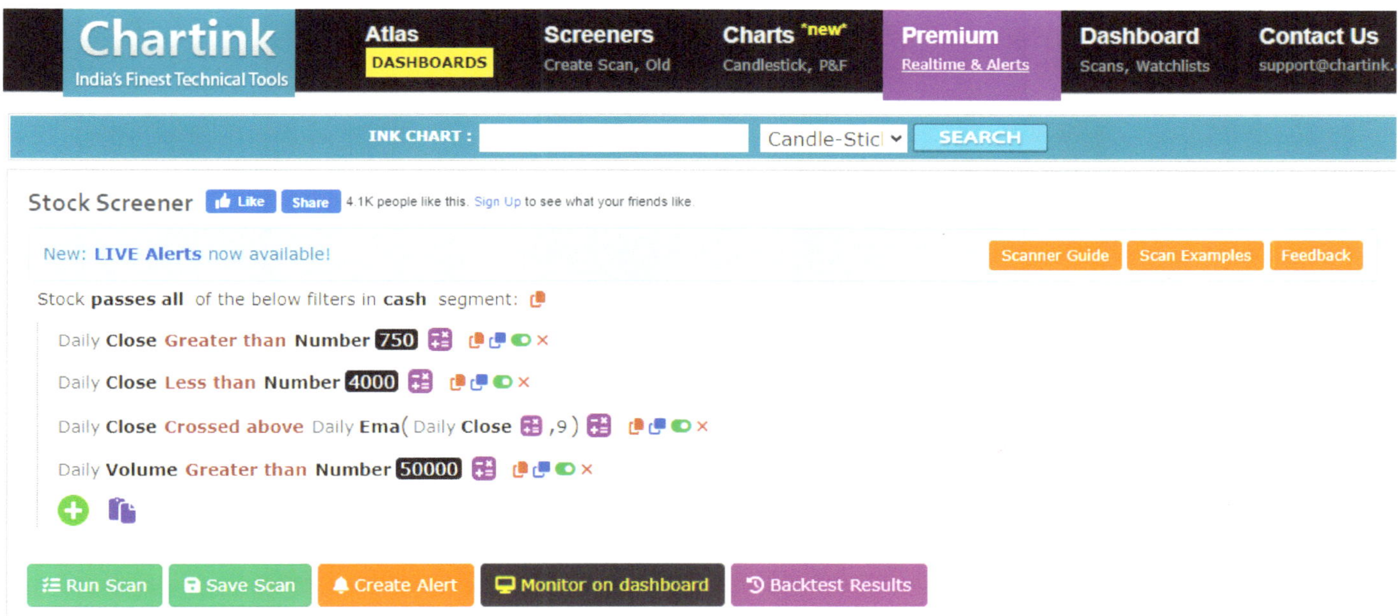

As seen in the stock screener, you can write your requirements in the specified format. When you click on "Run Scan" tab below in the chart, you will get the list of such stocks (may be, 50 stocks out of 6000 stocks). The list you can download and put in the watchlist of TradingView for further analysis and screening for next day trade. For finding stocks for short trade, we have to change only one condition in the screener, i.e., third condition (**Daily Close Crossed below Daily Ema (Daily Close, 9)**

2. Stocks in Trend for last 2 to 3 days

Those stocks which are in up price trend with up volume trend are likely to be in the trend next day. Their probability of being in up trend will increase when overall market is in up trend which you can verify on Nifty chart at 9.21 am after 5 minutes, and you can decide to go for the Long trade in the next candle in the screened stocks. You can get data one day in advance, and create a watchlist, analyze and find out which are the most likely stocks. Next day, when Previous Day High (PDH) is broken, you have alert for a long trade. But, you follow your set up. PDH break-out is just an alert for the trade, but your set up will decide whether you should go for it or not.

Steps to find out such stocks –

a. Google "fatafat screener".
b. Click on it.
c. You will go to the home page of fatafat screener.
d. Click on the button "open free fatafat screener"
e. You will get a large excel sheet.
f. Click on "Daily candle scan" on the bottom of the excel sheet.
g. Go to the column P - "Volume"
h. Sort column with criteria – "2 days up", and "3 days up".
i. Go to the column O – "Closing".
j. Sort column with criteria – "2 days up", and "3 days up".
k. Select those stocks which have common criteria in both the columns.

3. Stocks having pattern of Inside Bar, and NR7 on Daily timeframe.

Inside Bar is a pattern which depicts consolidation with price not going above the high and below the low of the previous day candle.

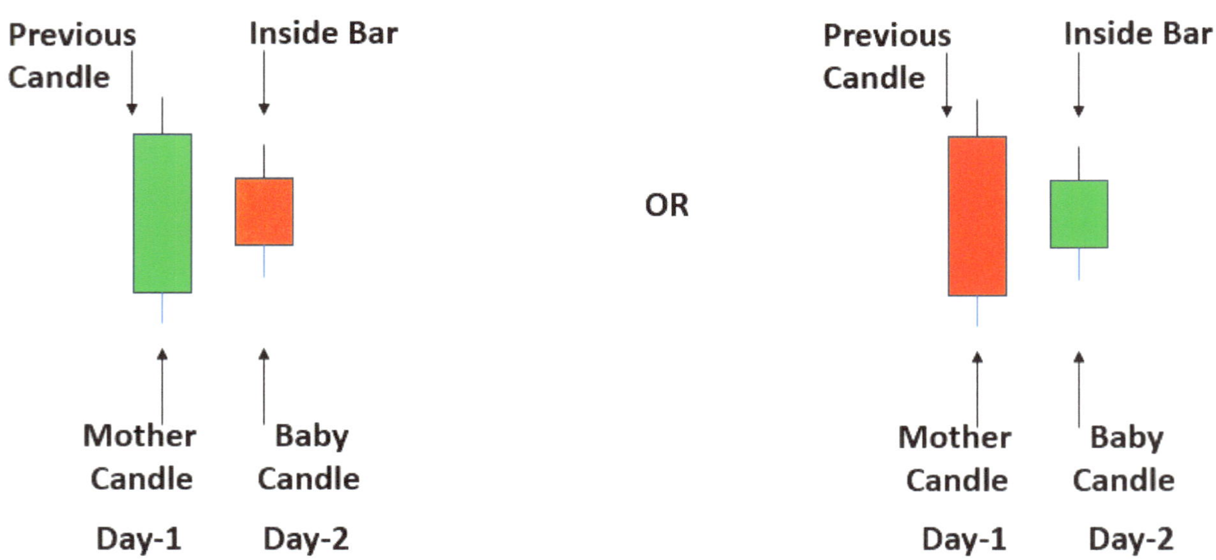

This is a two-candle pattern which is very powerful in terms of high probability of break-out next day, i.e., 3rd day. The break-out can be either on up-side or down-side. Such stocks can be in the watchlist. When on the third day, they give break-out when high or low of the 1st day candle is broken, it is an alert for the trade on the 4th day. Then, on the 4th day, you can go for long or short, when the high or low of the 4th day candle is broken. However, you have to follow your chosen set-up which is on the lower timeframe. You have to keep such stocks in your watchlist for 2 to 3 days, because such stocks have higher probability of giving break-out next 2 to 3 days.

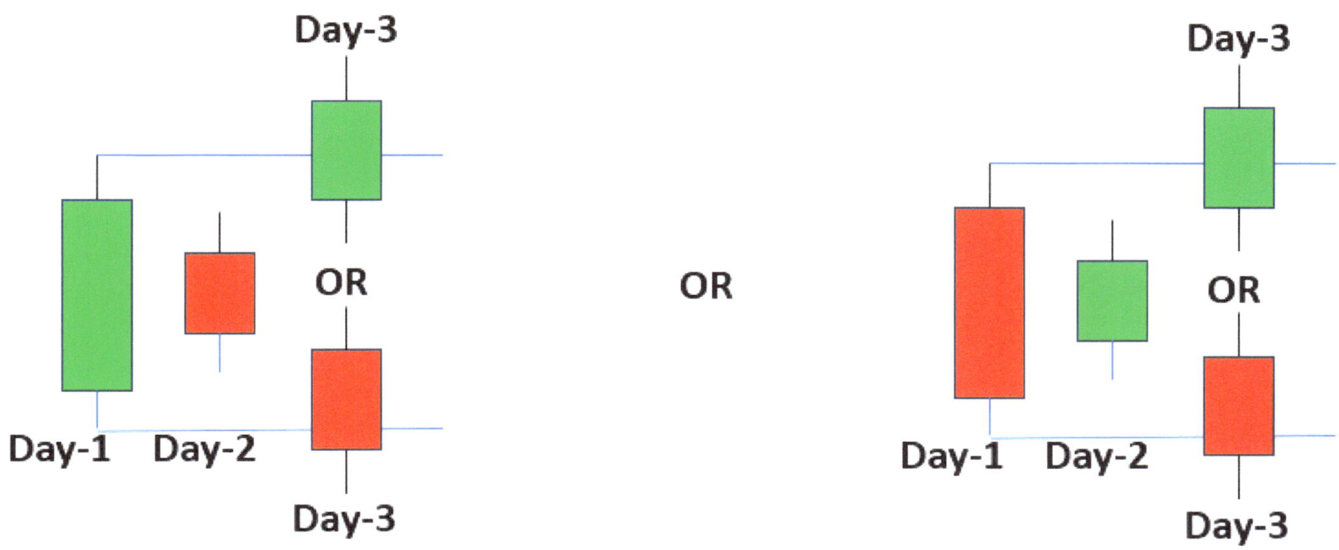

NR7 candle pattern means Narrow Range 7th candle. Range means high minus low. Such stocks with narrow range in the 7th candle compared with previous 6 candles are called NR7. Thus, the 7th candle is narrow in range (High – Low) when compared with previous 6 candles. This means the stock has consolidated much when compared with previous 6 days' period. This increases the probability of a break-out. Now, when Inside bar has also a high probability of giving break-out. But, when Inside Bar becomes NR7 candle, then the probability of a break-out becomes very high. Therefore, such stocks need to be found out and kept in the watchlist.

When such pattern develops at the support or resistance level, then there is a very high probability of break-out. So, you can mark those levels after identifying such stocks, and decide which are those five to six stocks which can have high probability of break-out. Or, you can apply EMA 9 on the chart to find out the trend, whether up trend or down trend is going on. If the pattern is found on the above of EMA 9, then it can give break-out on the buy side. If the pattern is below EMA 9, then it can give break-down below EMA 9. However, there is no rule that it will happen like that. But, such analysis can help you to build a view on the future price movement.

Below is the Chartink screener which can be run at the end of the day to find out such Inside Bar with NR7 candle patterns. When you click on "Run Scan" button, you will get list of stocks which are from Nifty 500 stocks. You may get 15-20 stocks. Keep them in a separate watchlist with a name "InsideBar and NR7-Date:__________". Date of the stocks when you found out will be very important for further analysis.

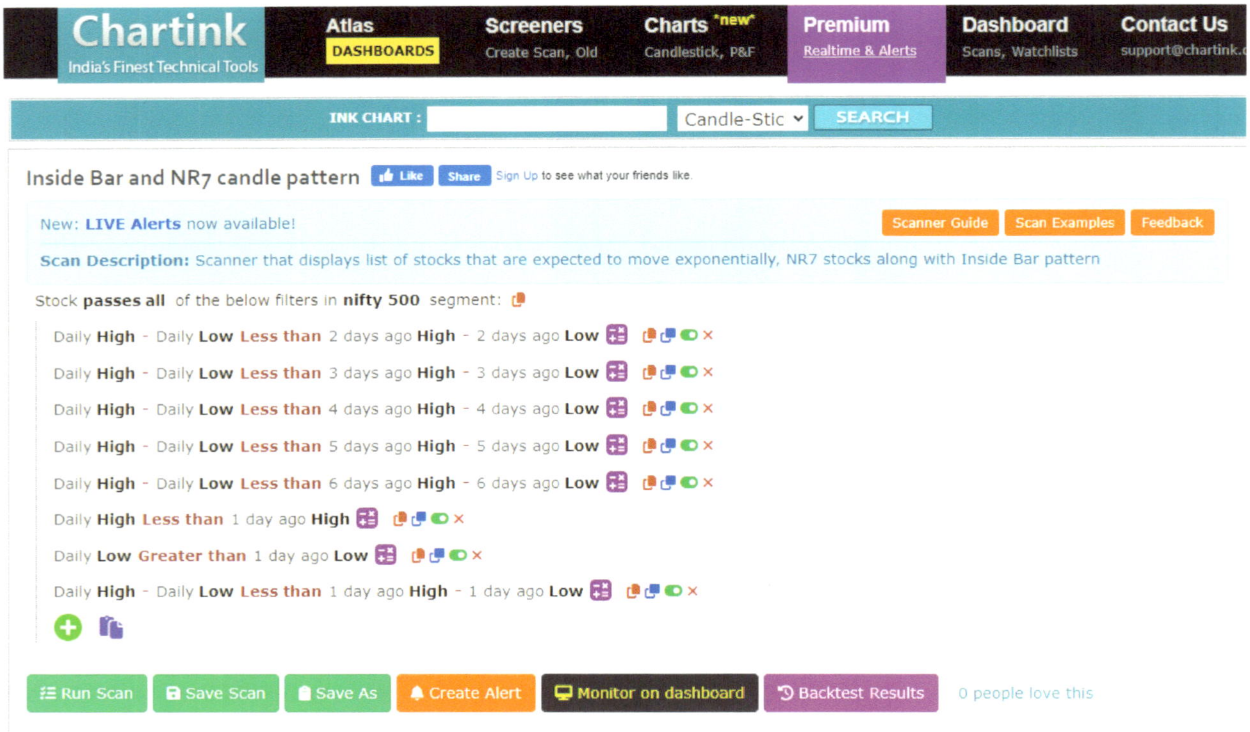

4. **Stocks having Engulfing pattern**

This is also called Outside Bar pattern which is also a powerful pattern depicting high probability of break-out of a stock which can be screened in advance.

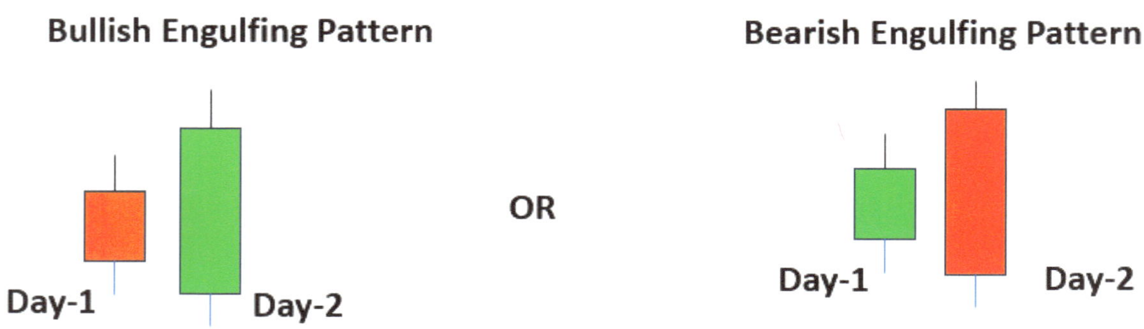

Stocks having this pattern need to be screened on a Daily timeframe. When high of the Day-2 candle of Bullish Engulfing pattern is broken on the 3rd day, then it is considered as a good break-out. Similarly, when low of the Day-2 candle of Bearish Engulfing pattern is broken on the 3rd day, then it is considered as a good break-down. You can go for the long or short trade respectively on the 3rd day following your chosen set-up.

Such pattern developing on support or resistance, like Bullish Engulfing pattern developed on the Support region or Bearish Engulfing pattern developed at the Resistance level enhances the probability of break-out to a greater extent. You can find out through your analysis and further screen the stocks for next day trading.

You can select stocks using Chartink screener at the end of the day to find out such stocks as follows.

Bullish Engulfing Pattern

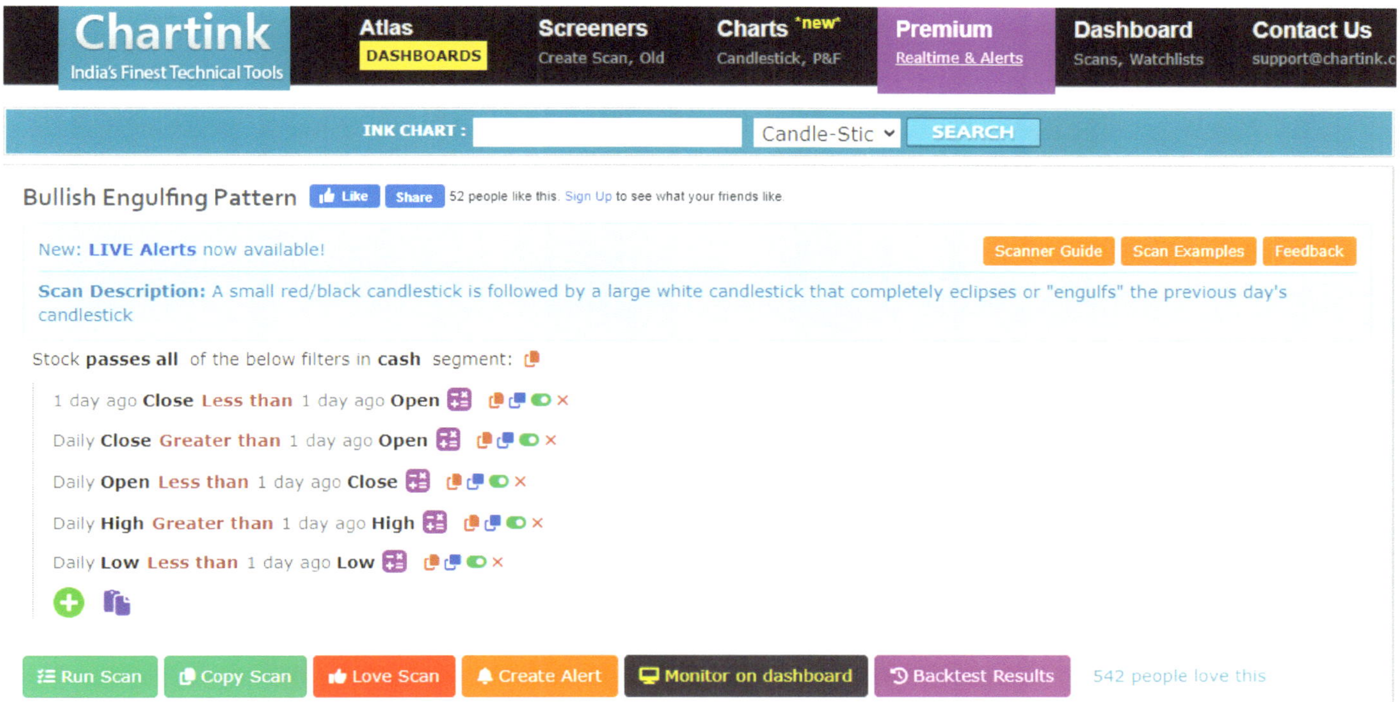

Bearish Engulfing Pattern

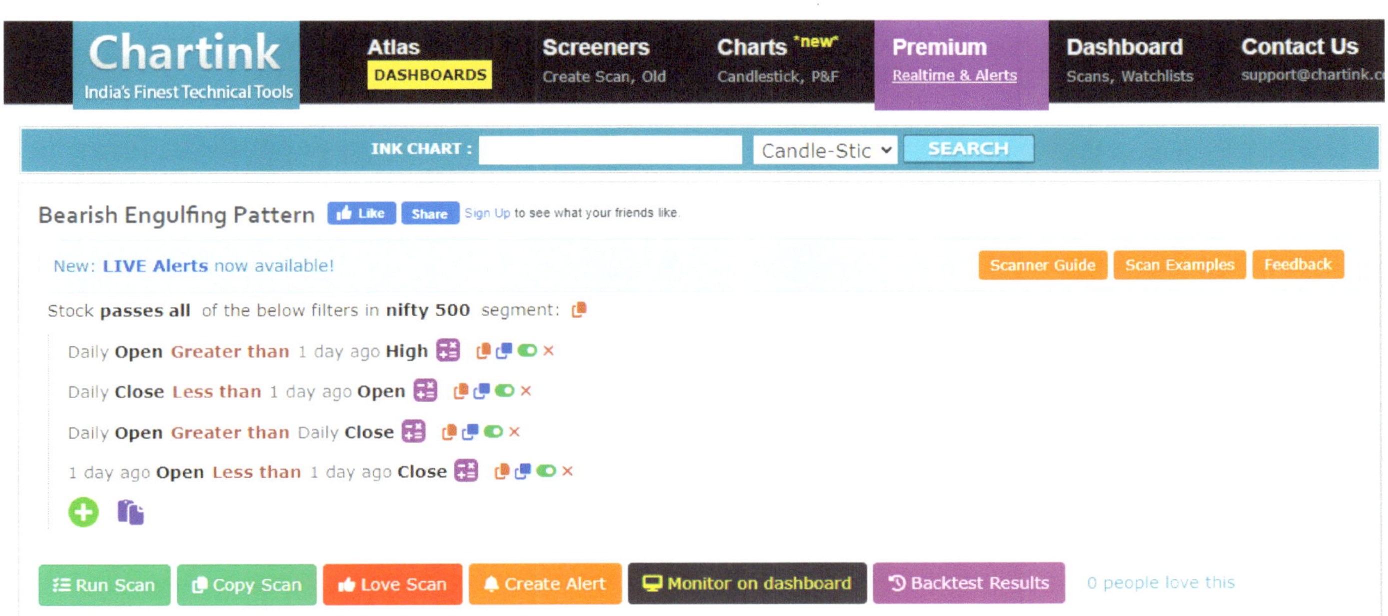

You can see the chart below of ICICI Bank on a daily timeframe.

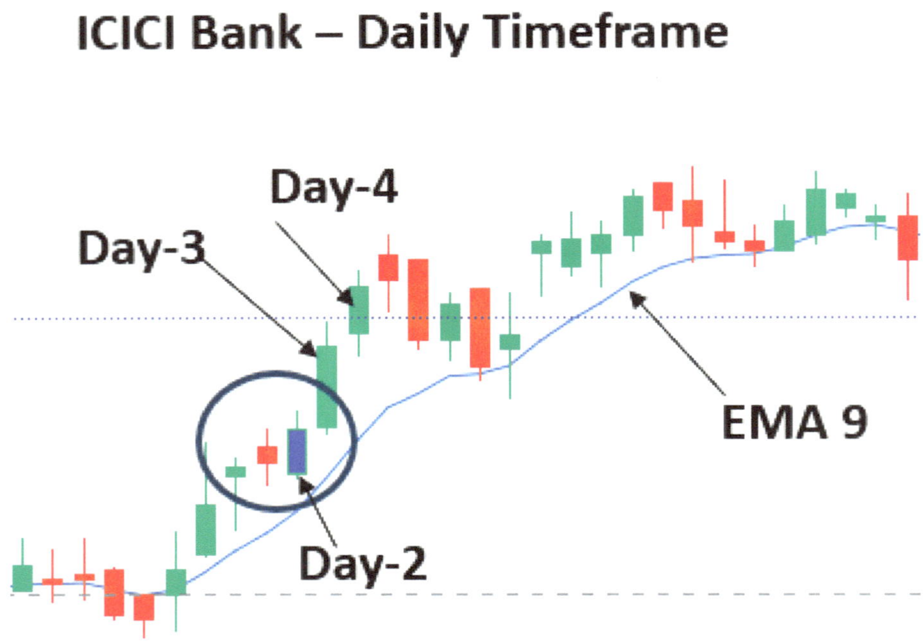

The purple candle is a Bullish Engulfing candle on Day-2. On the 3rd Day, you can see the breakout. The rally continued on Day-4 also. Moreover, you can observe, the pattern has developed above the EMA 9 which means there is up trend which very likely to continue. Therefore, such a situation enhances the probability of being on the up-trend.

You can apply engulfing indicator on TradingView charts, and easily find out the pattern.

5. Double-Inside Bar Stock Selection

This is also a very powerful screener which gives stocks which are very likely to be in momentum next day. This is a three-bar pattern.

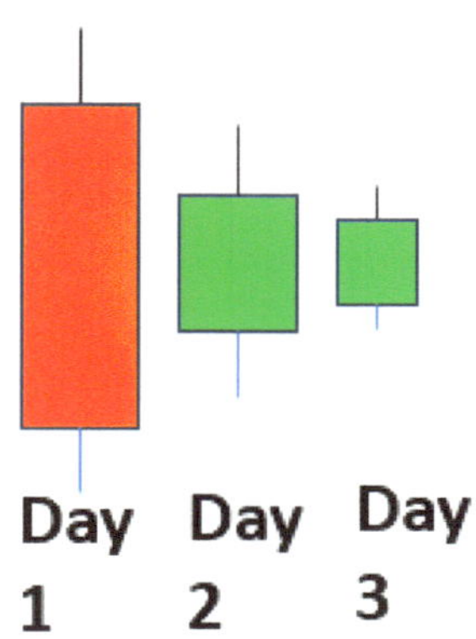

The colour of the candles is not important. There is consolidation for happening over last two days. This situation might give momentum either on upside or down side. It is important to draw trendline on a daily time frame along with support and resistance while doing analysis of the stocks. Then, switch over to lower timeframe on which you trade. Draw trendlines and support, resistance on the lower time frame. Use your set up while taking decisions when you get alert and confirmation.

Intraday trading involves buying and selling stocks within the same trading day, aiming to capitalize on such price movements. Here's how Beta is useful:

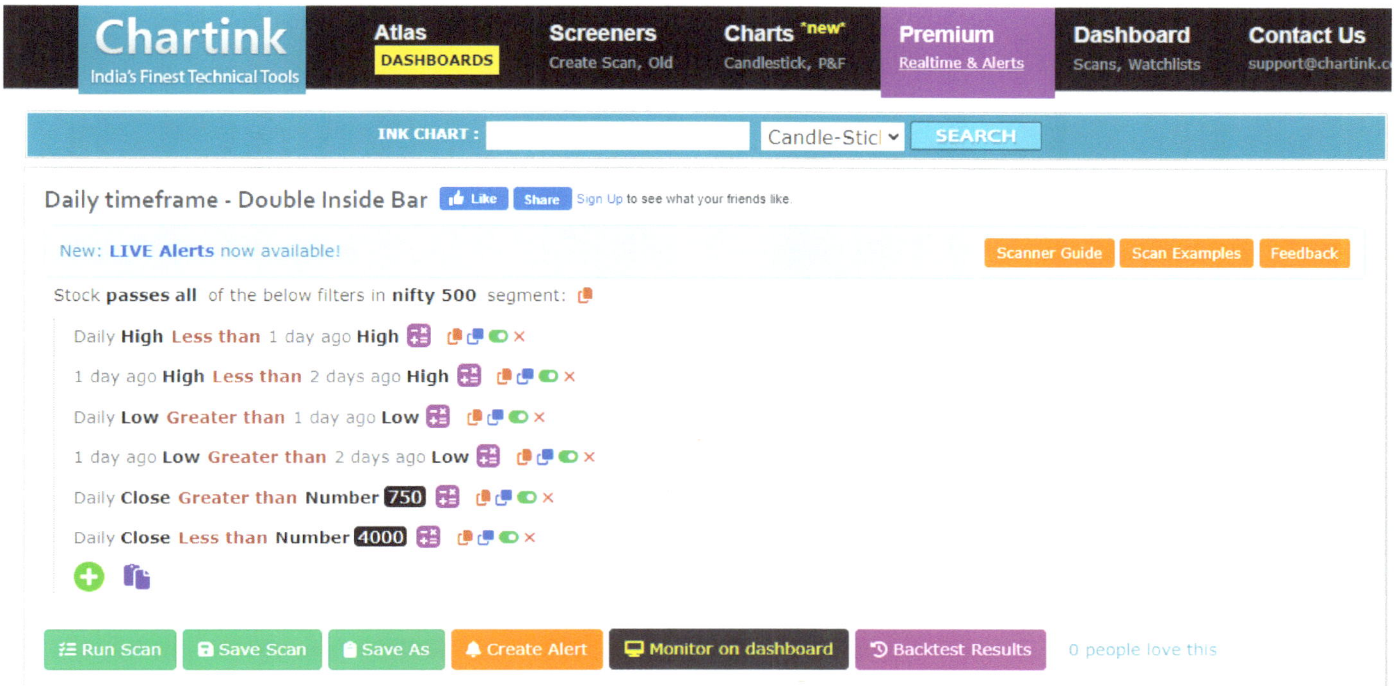

6. Stocks at the Break-out or Break-down of SuperTrend

This is a very good method of finding stocks on a Daily timeframe which are likely to give movement either on the up side or down side. At the end of the day, you have to find such stocks which have broken supertrend on the up side or down side. Also, the RSI has crossed over RSI Moving Average, and volume in the stock has been more than previous 20 days' average volume. Such stocks have very high probability of giving momentum. You have to make a watchlist of such stocks. You can draw line at the high of the candle in case supertrend shows "Buy", or you can draw line at the low of the candle in case supertrend shows "Sell". You can put alert on your TradingView chart on those lines of the selected stocks. This will help you to know when the price reaches at that level in those stocks, and you will not miss the opportunity for the trade.

The parameters are –

- Super trend (10,2) Close
- RSI 14, and RSI Moving Average 21.
- Volume great than Volume SMA 20.
- Stocks having the Price above Rs. 850.

Screener for Bullish Trade

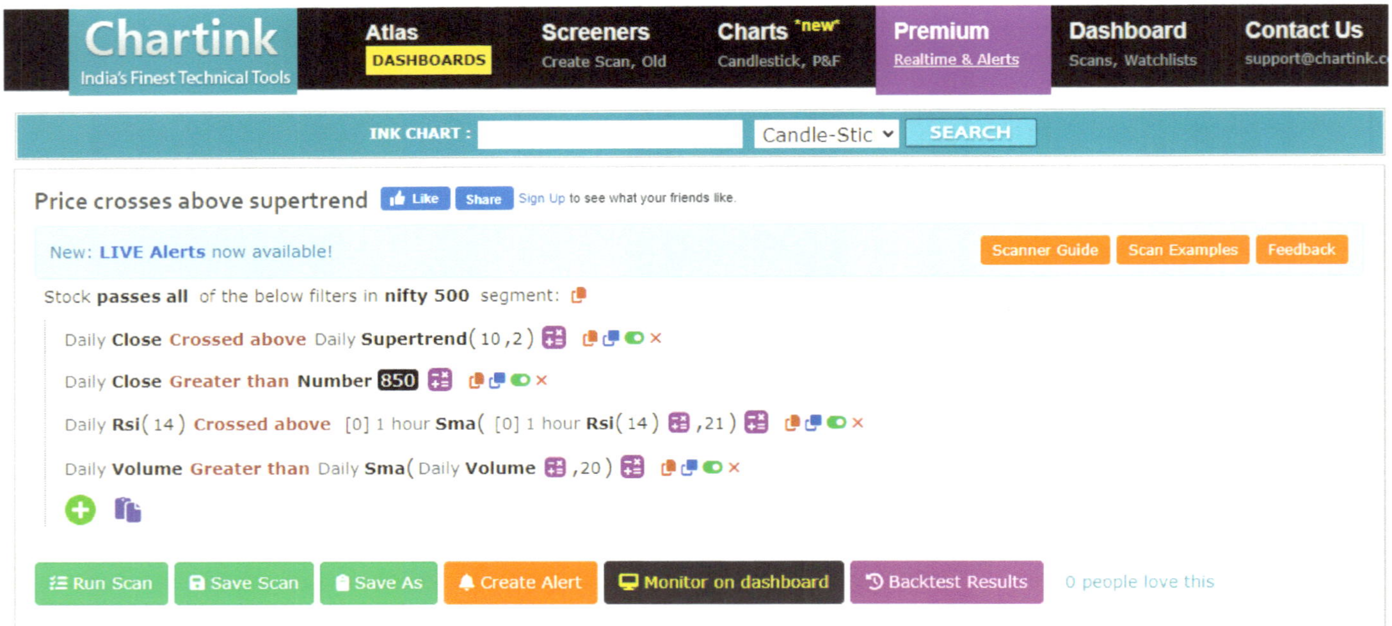

Screener for Bearish Trade

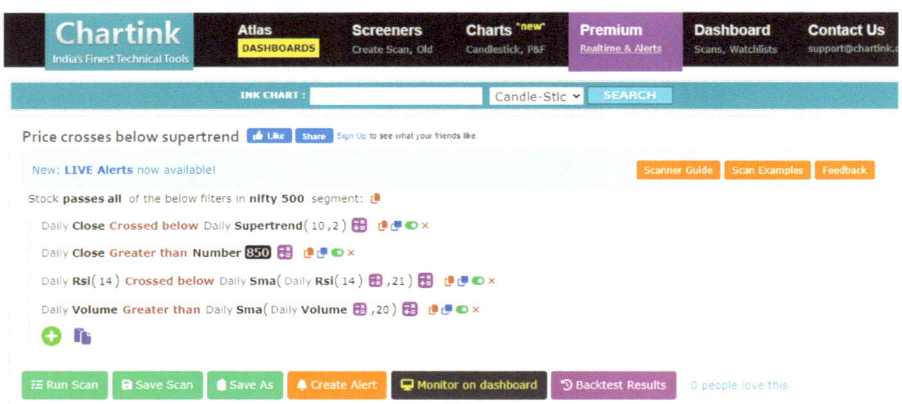

This is a very powerful screener which I use it for analysis and taking trades, giving a very good result.

7. Stocks with high *Beta* value

Beta (β) is a measure of a stock's volatility in relation to the overall market. It is a concept that measures the expected move in a stock relative to movements in the overall market. It quantifies the systematic risk of a stock compared to the market as a whole. Beta is interpreted as mentioned below.

Beta = 1: The stock's price moves with the market.
Beta > 1: The stock is more volatile than the market. It tends to amplify the market's movements.
Beta < 1: The stock is less volatile than the market. It tends to be more stable and less responsive to market changes.

If a stock's beta is 1.2, it is assumed to be 20% more volatile than the market. A beta greater than 1.0 suggests that the stock is more volatile than the broader market, and a beta less than 1.0 indicates a stock with lower volatility.

For example, if Beta of Reliance Industries is 1.3, it means that if Nifty index moves up by 1%, the price of Reliance will move up by 30%. Similarly, if the Nifty Index moves down by 1%, then Reliance will move down by 30%. Thus, it is compared with the market movement, and the market movement is reflected by Nifty Index. This indicates volatility of Reliance.

Intraday trading involves buying and selling stocks within the same trading day, aiming to capitalize on such price movements. Here's how Beta is useful:

Identifying Volatility: High Beta stocks ($\beta > 1$) are more volatile and are likely to experience significant price movements within a single day. This makes them ideal for intraday traders looking for quick gains from price fluctuations.

Risk Management: Understanding the Beta of a stock helps traders manage risk. High Beta stocks can be riskier but potentially more profitable, therefore, selection of stocks in advance helps to manage risk very easily as the stop loss is known which helps in determining quantities of trade in advance. Hence, there is no confusion while taking trade, but, gives more clarity and confidence when our trading setup is also decided in advance.

Strategic Selection: Intraday traders use Beta to select stocks that align with their trading strategy. For example, a trader might choose high Beta stocks to take advantage of large intraday swings or low Beta stocks for a more conservative approach.

The point to consider is that the Beta value of a stock varies depending on the source and the period of calculation. You can create a watchlist for a month, and revise it every month. This will help you to get such stocks with higher Beta value based on the data of the recent previous month. This type of fixed watchlist gives better depth of understanding in the price movement of selected stocks.

Steps to find out High Beta value Stocks

1. Go to "tickertape.in"
2. Go to "Stock Screener"
3. Go to "Stock Universe"
4. Select Nifty 100 or 500
5. Go to "Close Price"
6. Select the price range (you can select the range between Rs. 500 to Rs. 4000)
7. Go to "+Add filter" and Click
8. Go to "Technical Indicators" and Click
9. Select Beta box, it will be added in the filter on the left pane.
10. Select the Beat Value from 1.20 to 4
11. Again, Go to "+Add filter" and Click

12. Select % away from 52 week High and % away from 52 week Low (This will give a range of movement to the stocks. If stocks are near 52 week High and 52 week Low, they may not give momentum because they take time by consolidation for further movement). In the filter, you select 20, means stocks are away by 20% and more from 52-week high and low.
13. You will get around 30 stocks on the right pane.
14. You can add then individually on TradingView watchlist. (You will not be allowed to download as you require paid version).

This watchlist will be very useful for a period of month (20 days) to take good trades. You can follow your set-up on the lower timeframe by adding required alerts for the trades.

8. Finding Financial Results-awaited Stocks in advance.

This is another approach to find stocks which might give momentum. Preferably, such stocks should be from Nifty 200 as they always attract attention of big players for trading and investment. Result calendar is already prepared in advance.

Steps to find stocks

1. Google "Result Calendar Moneycontrol".
2. You will get a link on google page, click on it.
3. You will come to the page with title "Result Calendar"
4. You will get the list of stocks with dates on which results are going to be announced.
5. Prepare a watchlist of stocks which are in Nifty 200.
6. Go for trade in those stocks only on that particular date in your set-up.
7. You can set alert on Moneycontrol for tracking the announcement of result.

This will give an excellent opportunity for trade. If results are positive with very good growth in Sales and Net Profit, look for buying opportunities in your set up. If results are negative with noticeable decline, then look for short trades. Year -end result season starts from May to June, and Quarterly Result season starts from July onwards and continues through out the year. Almost round the year this goes on.

9. Finding Stocks at Ichimoku Cloud Lagging Span.

This exercise is done on a Daily time frame to find out stocks which are ready to be in momentum. Even, 5 or 15-minutes timeframe can also be used to find such stocks, provided you are using the set-up with the same timeframe – 5 or 15 minutes timeframe.

The Ichimoku Cloud was created by Japanese journalist Goichi Hosoda in the late 1960s. It was designed to provide a more complete view of the market at a glance, combining several indicators into one chart to help traders make more informed decisions. It provides insights into market trends, momentum, and support and resistance levels. It consists of multiple lines plotted on a price chart, forming a cloud that visually represents these elements. It has 5 components – Conversions line, Base line, Leading Span A, Leading Span B, and Lagging Span. However, all these put together on the chart, makes the chart very noisy and complex to understand. You can see the chart of Infosys below.

But, the one component – Lagging Span gives invaluable information which has tremendous predictive power of finding the momentum of the price of the stocks in advance. It is found that majority of the traders focus on components other than Lagging Span. We will understand the power of Lagging Span in the chart given below.

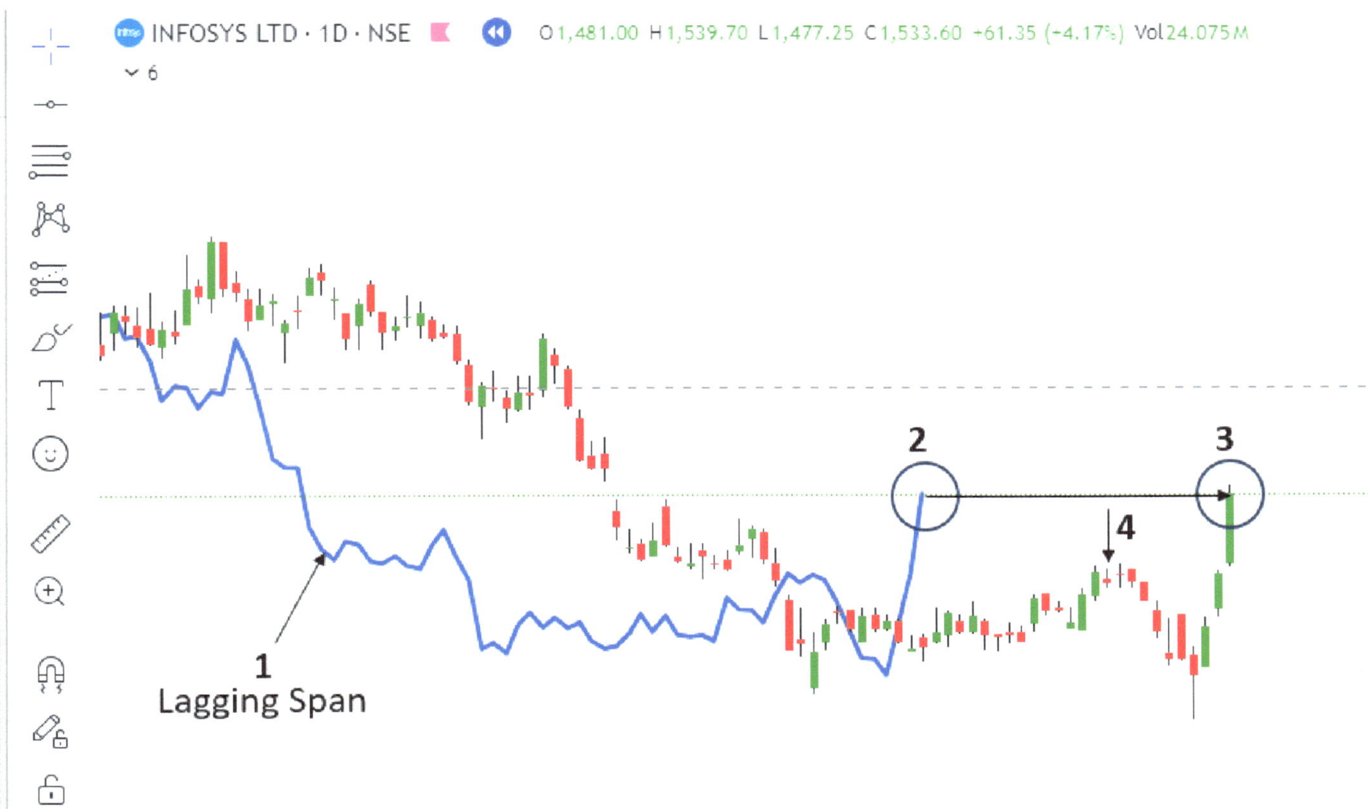

The above chart is of Infosys and on Daily timeframe. The blue coloured line is Lagging Span of Ichimoku cloud (Point no.1). At point no.2, the Blue colour line is showing closing price and it is behind 26 candles from the latest candle. That is why it is called a Lagging Span because it lags behind by 26 candles from the latest candle. At point no.3, it is the latest candle. Now, when the distance between Lagging Span and the latest candle is a virgin area, means Lagging Span does not touch any of the 25 subsequent candles, means closing price of the Lagging Span is above the high price of all subsequent 25 candles, and is equal to the closing price of 26th candle (latest candle), it indicates high momentum, and break-out, once the high of the latest candle is broken. You can see in the above chart that the Lagging Span is above all the subsequent 25 candles as seen at point no. 4. Now, let's see what happens next in the same chart given below.

You can see that once the high is broken, there is a break-out in the stock. Thus, Lagging Span has predictive power what is likely to happen under specified condition. The probability of break-out under the specified condition is very high (around 95%) as found in my observation and experimental research. Similarly, you can find the potential break-down.

The screener for such stocks is given below. The screener will shortlist many stocks, but you have to finally select those stocks which have fresh condition being occurred with Lagging Span. Many a times, you will find stocks which have already given the move, but, you have to ignore those stocks.

The screener is for bullish stocks with a potential break-out.

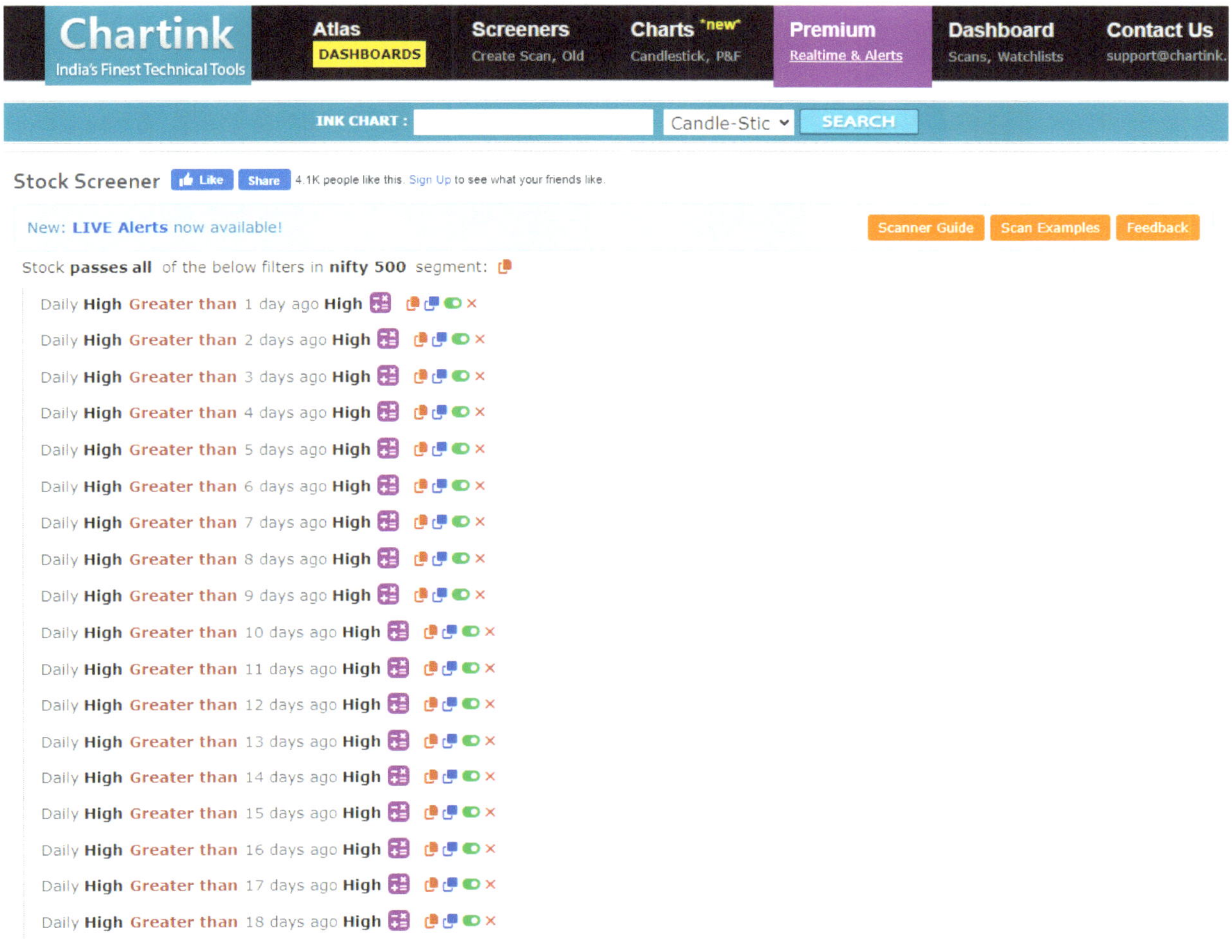

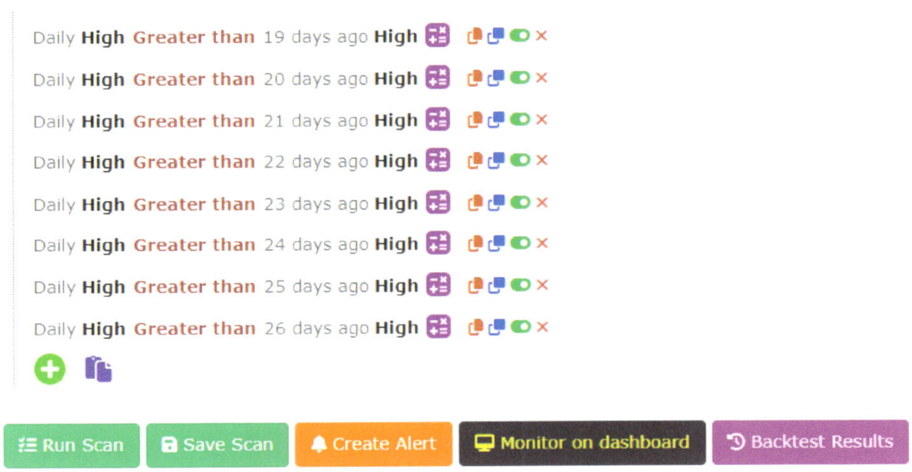

You can use this screener at the end of the day. Make a watchlist out of it by downloading the screened stocks. Analyze the stocks, and finally select stocks with fresh condition being met. You can keep the list for 3 to 4 days because such stocks give momentum for 3 to 4 days. Likewise, you can prepare a bearish screener, and select stocks for taking short trades.

Just before the commencement of the Trading Day (9.00 am to 9.15 am), and the Live Trade during the Day from 9.15 am to 2.30 pm.

10. Finding News-based Stocks at 8.00 am

This is another approach to stock selection. News always infuse momentum in the stocks. It can be on up side or down side. It depends on good news or bad news. There can be many sources to find such stocks in the morning as you get the latest happening news before the commencement of the market in the morning. I personally like to use Moneycontrol.com.

Steps to find stocks

1. Go to moneycontrol.com at 8.00 am. They come out with such News-based stocks at 8.00 am.
2. Click on "News"
3. Go to "Markets"
4. Go to "Stocks" and click.
5. You will get all the stocks which are in News and are likely to be impacted by the News. Such stocks will have good momentum.
6. Create a watchlist of such 5 stocks with "BUY" probability and 5 stocks with "Sell" probability which you can assess on the basis of good news or bad news.
7. When market opens, wait for 10 minutes, observe the market where it is going.
8. If market is in up trend, use "BUY" watchlist on 15 minutes timeframe. Enter the long trade on the break-out of High of first 15 minutes candle.
9. If market is in down trend, use "SELL" watchlist on 15 minutes timeframe. Enter the short trade on the break-down of Low of first 15 minutes candle.

Remember, such stocks are on higher probability of movement. It is not necessary that momentum will come, but, my personal research on this claims that there is a probability of 90% of movement in such stocks. When the stocks declare their financial results on the previous day after market hours, then they become News-based stocks, and such stocks have almost 95% probability of giving momentum.

11. Finding Stocks from News-channels AT 8.00 AM.

Finding momentum stocks involves identifying stocks that are experiencing an upward price movement and have the potential to continue growing. News channels play a significant role in this process by providing timely information and insights into market trends.

Many of the practitioners are of the view that traders should not use News channels as they give incorrect information. Their recommendations for stocks are deceptive and beneficial to a particular set of companies. I do not subscribe to this view as observed by me for a long period of time because no body can give any guarantee on a particular direction of the stocks. When any stocks are given recommendation of "Buy" or "Sell", our task is to build a view and not a bias in favour of the recommendation. You can prepare your own watchlist with "Buy" recommendation list and "Sell" recommendation list. Here, the purpose is to find such stocks which are going to be in momentum. Such recommendations create momentum, and by using our own set-up, we can take appropriate trading decisions for buy or sell. As an intraday trader, we must understand that we do not intend to be in the trade for the whole day.

Moreover, the discussions on such News channels are very intellectually-stimulating. You get to know so many things about economy, industry and market trend which help to generate good insights about the stock market which is beneficial in the long run. As a trader, you remain updated with global trends and our own market trends.

There are two good news channels which can be tracked for preparing a watchlist in the morning. CNBC Awaaz (Hindi) and Zee Business (Hindi).

You can start the channel at 8.00 am and watch the different show-segments. Experts give their recommendations. You prepare a watchlist. There will be few common stocks which may be focused more for trading. You can set alerts as per your set up, and when opportunity arises, you can trade. Here, we are looking forward to momentum, and there is a high probability to find momentum in such stocks.

12. Finding Stocks at pre-open market session

The market opens at 9.00 am, and you can place your orders between 9.00 am to 9.07 am. Thereafter, Opening Price is decided and at 9.08 am, the opening price is declared. Also, National Stock Exchange (NSE) makes available all the pre-open data to the public. The data give valuable information about the stocks which you can find and select for Intraday trading from 9.08 am to 9.15 am. You have around 5 minutes of time to find, select and keep them in the watchlist, and get ready at 9.15 am. As we have discussed earlier that we will not enter into the trade for first 5 minutes (if the trading set up is of 5 minutes duration), or first 15 minutes ((if the trading set up is of 15 minutes duration).

Steps to find stocks:

1. At 9.08 am, google "Pre-open NSE".
2. You will get the first link on Google. Click it and you will land up on the page on NSE web site.
3. Select "Securities in F&O" from the category.
4. You will get the list of stocks with pre-open market data.
5. Go to "Final Quantities" column.
6. Double click on it, and you will get data in a descending order.
7. Select first ten stocks with highest volume shown in the "Final Quantities" column.
8. Select stocks in the price range of Rs. 750 to Rs. 4000, and create your watchlist in TradingView.

13. Finding Stocks at 9.20 am on Sectoral Performance

Finding the movement of stocks around 9.20 am gives a good idea about the momentum in the stocks.

1. At 9.18 am, go to "Intradayscreener.com". You will be on Dashboard which gives excellent Market View.
2. Go to "Markets" in the upper bar, and click.
3. Go to "Sector Performance", and click.

4. Another Dashboard will appear with data which sectors are performing better with a visual bar chart.
5. Click on the best performing sector bar chart (green bar) or worst sector performing (red bar).
6. While you click on the bar, you will get list of such stocks.
7. However, sector will change as the time goes on. There may be one sector growing at 9.20, and the same sector may lag behind by 9.45 am, and another sector may rise.
8. Select the stocks for the trade which have risen between 1% to 2%, because such stocks will have potential to rise further. Those stocks which have risen by more than 2%, their potential for further rise may have been lost.
9. If overall market is in Red, select stocks from the worst performing sector, keep them in watchlist, and plan for short trade as per your set-up. If overall market is in Green, select stocks from the best performing sector, and go for long trade as per your set-up.

B. Finding Stocks during the live trading session

This is the most effective way of finding stocks. You do not require any preparation before the market starts. Here, you should be clear with your set-up, and accordingly you can find stocks using screener. TradingView has got a very good tool to find stocks during the live trading session. You can also use Chartink screener in the live market, but you have to pay subscription to get benefit of a screener in the live market. Please note that any screener will lag behind by 1 minute as they get data from NSE / BSE 1 minute late.

Steps to find stocks on different Trade set-ups in the live market

1. For Trade set-up 4, 5 and 6

You can use Stock Screener of TradingView platform and retrieve stocks on 3 or 5 minute timeframe for three set-ups as mentioned in the Chapter-10. This gives latest data every 1 minute on the screener. You can put on watchlist and open up the chart in your Trade set-up. If conditions are met, then go for the trade. Do not go for more than 2 trades, otherwise it will be difficult to monitor the position. Once you are completed with trade, then only go for another trades. Do not use more than 1 set up simultaneously.

- You can see various filters on the screener. Once you have completed the filters properly, then whole day the screener will fetch stocks for your set-up.

2. **For Trade set-up 1, and 2**

You can use Chartink screener as TradingView has no filter on Supertrend. Here also, every 1 minute you get list of stocks which meet with the conditions as shown below.

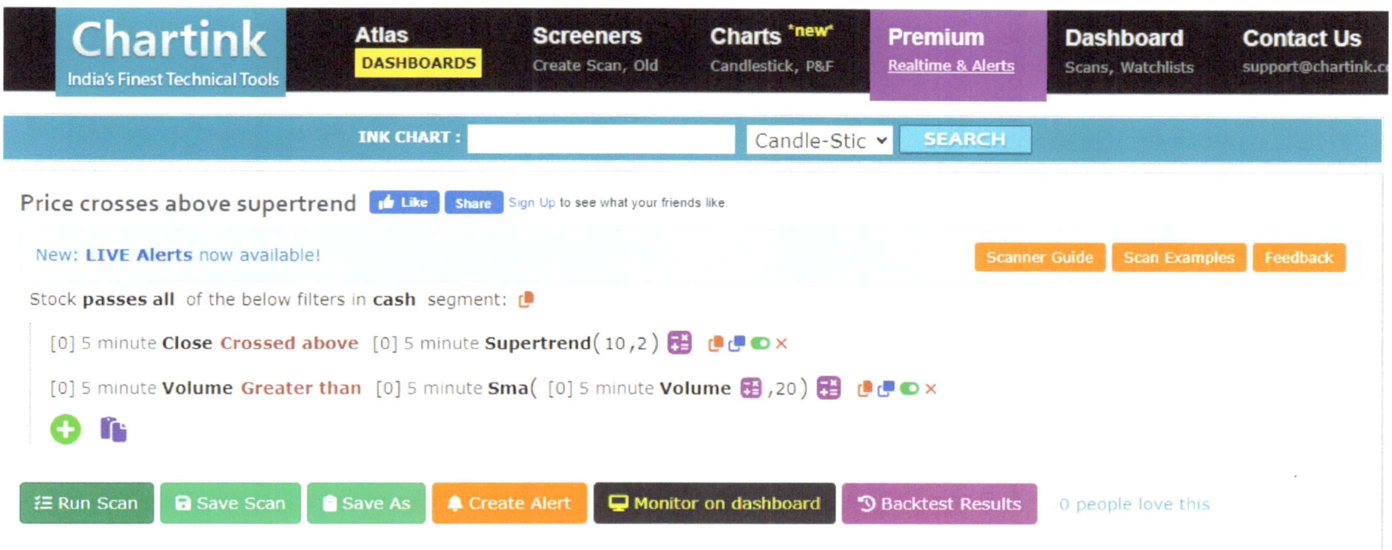

This screener is for taking Long trades. Here, along with Supertrend, one more filter on volume is added, as when there is break-out of supertrend, if the volume is more than the previous 20- period volumes, then such break-out has higher probability of sustaining the trend. However, you have to pay for the subscription in order to get stocks during the live trading session.

For short trades, the screener is given below.

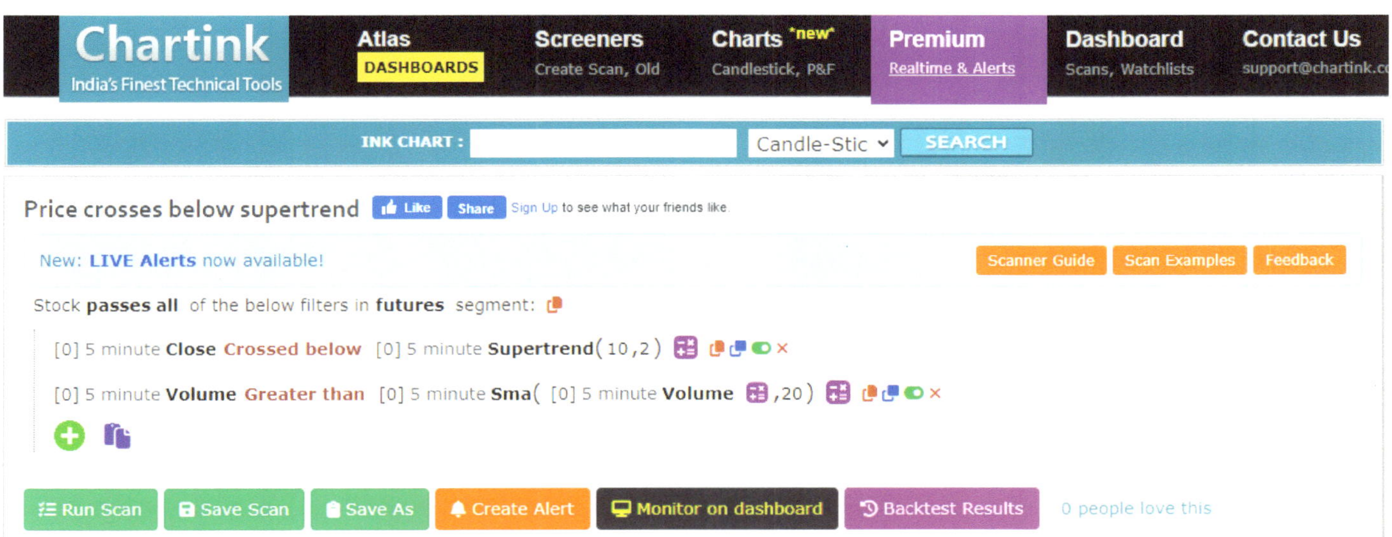

3. For Trade set-up 3

You can create a screener on TradingView platform for a crossover of VWAP and Simple Moving Average 10. Our set up has SMA 9, but you can use SMA 10 for finding stocks. When you are using set-up 3, then only you have to use this screener. This will help you to find such stocks in the live market which meet our set-up conditions. This is a bullish screener. You can make a bearish screener with a filter – VWAP crosses below SMA 9.

4. For Trade set-up 3 and 8

Here, you can select MACD as a filter to find stocks at TradingView platform.

Above is the bullish screener with different filters.

a. Symbol type is Common Stocks.
b. Volume level is 50K and more. Similarly, you can have filters for average volume.
c. Market capitalization is 10M and more.
d. MACD level crosses up MACD Signal. Here, MACD set up is (12,26). Though our set-up has MACD set up of (10,50). But, MACD (12,26) will help to find stocks earlier which will help you to get more time to observe and decide for the trade.

Similarly, you can have a screener for bearish stocks. When market is on the down trend, you can go for short trade only on that particular day.

5. For Trade set-up 10

Trade set-up 10 is the most lucrative set up among all. The combination of indicator makes it more relevant and accurate. As I have mentioned earlier, RSI is one of the most versatile indicators. It gives price action information from many angles. However, the least aspect of RSI used is cross-over of RSI and RSI Moving Average. I have observed that the cross-over gives timely signals for entry and exit with high accuracy. If you can make a screener with a pre-defined timeframe, then you get such stocks which are most relevant to your set-up no. 10. Chartink can give the screener both bullish and bearish stocks. However, for a live market stocks, you have subscribe to Chartink.

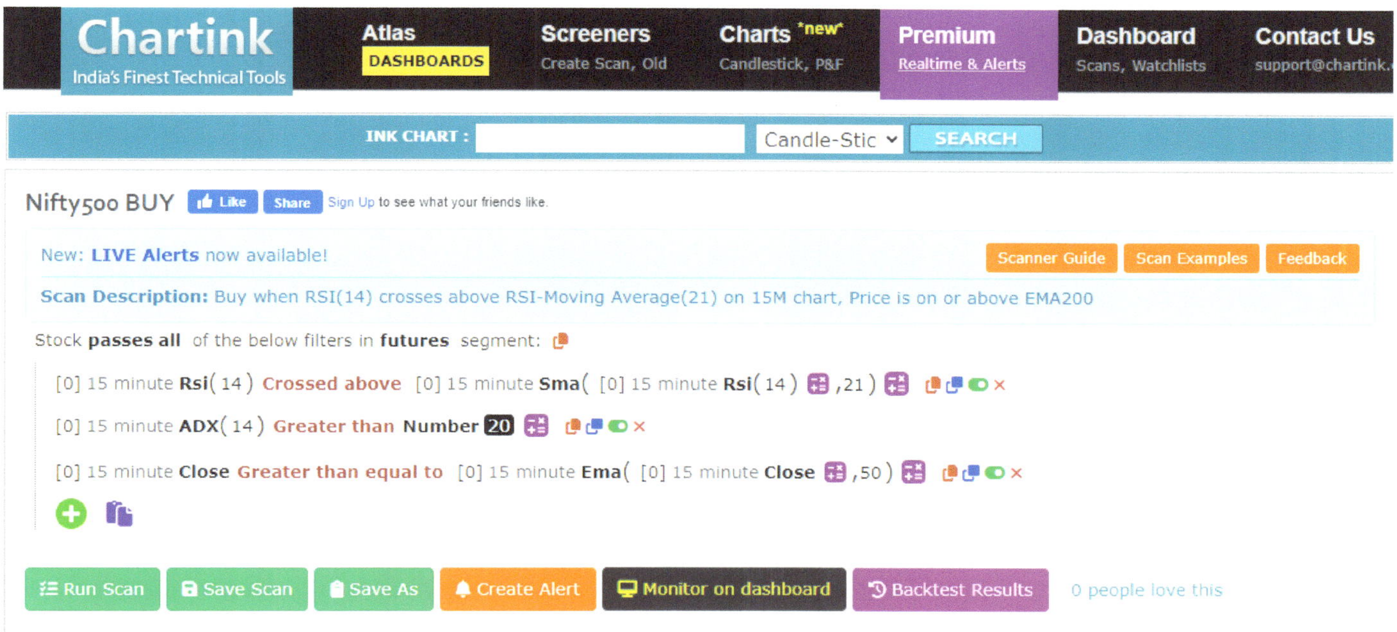

The above screener is to find bullish stocks in the live market on 15-minutes timeframe.
Filter 1 is about cross over of RSI and RSI Moving Average. Here, RSI (14) is considered, and RSI Moving Average 21 is considered. The default RSI Moving Average is 14. But, my observation and experimental research claims that RSI Moving Average 21 gives better results. Filter 2 is about ADX. We want stocks which have momentum. So, ADX greater than 20 is considered to find out momentum in the stocks. Filter 3 is about EMA 50. Stocks above EMA 50 are considered to be in bullish trend, hence, when all the three filters meet condition, we get such stocks which have higher probability of going up and giving momentum.
Similarly, you can make a bearish screener which you try out on your own on the basis of above screener.

6. Stock Selection at 9.20 AM, and Trade on 15-M Time frame

A. Steps to find stocks:

1. At 9.20 AM, when the market has started, google "Most Active Stocks NSE".
2. Click on link, you will land up on the page on NSE website.
3. Select 7 stocks "Most Active by Value" which have risen by more than 1% and less than 4%. Do not select stocks which have risen by more than 4%, as they may not give much rise further.
4. Prepare a watchlist on TradingView platform.
5. Check for Beta value of the selected 7 stocks. Retain stocks in the wtachlist with more than Beta value of 1 in the watchlist. You can get the value on your broker's platform when you click on the "Stock info".

B. Trade Set up:

1. Indicators: EMA 9 (Low), EMA 20 (High)
2. Timeframe: 15 Minutes.
3. Trade:
    a. First 15-M candle should not be a very big candle.
    b. Take a long trade, when there is a break-out of first 15-M candle crossing up EMA 20 (High).
    c. Take a short trade, when there is a break-down of first 15-M candle crossing down EMA 9 (Low).

CHAPTER – 10

Transaction Costs and Taxes in Intraday Trading

Understanding the costs and taxes associated with intraday trading is crucial for traders aiming to maximize their profits and maintain compliance with tax regulations. Intraday trading involves frequent buying and selling of securities within the same trading day, leading to multiple transaction costs such as brokerage fees, Securities Transaction Tax (STT), GST, and exchange fees. These costs can significantly impact overall profitability if not managed properly. Additionally, the gains from intraday trading are treated as speculative business income and taxed according to individual income tax slab rates, necessitating careful tax planning and compliance. Ignoring these financial aspects can result in reduced net gains and potential legal complications with tax authorities.

In addition to the direct costs mentioned, traders should also consider indirect costs such as opportunity costs and the potential impact of market liquidity on trade execution prices. High-frequency trading can lead to increased brokerage charges due to the volume of trades, and STT is levied at 0.025% on the sell side of intraday trades

Various Costs of an Intraday Trade

1. **Brokerage Fees**: Charges by the brokerage firm for executing trades.

Before you can trade or invest in shares, you need to have both a trading account and a demat account. These accounts facilitate the buying and selling of shares on the stock market. The brokerage firm that handles these transactions charges a fee for its services, known as the "brokerage." Brokerage charges are not standardized or regulated by any central authority, resulting in varying fees across different service providers. However, there is a regulatory upper limit on brokerage fees under the bye-laws of National Stock exchange and Bombay Stock Exchange, which is set at 2.5% of the transaction amount.

How Stock Brokers Levy Brokerage Charges in India

1. **Flat Fee for Every Trade**

A flat fee is charged for each trade, regardless of the trade value. If the percentage brokerage is less than the flat fee, the investor pays the lower amount.

For example:

Flat fee: INR 20

Percentage brokerage: 0.1%

For a traded value of INR 10,000, brokerage will be INR 10 (10,000 * 0.1%), which is lower than the flat fee of INR 20.

This method is popular among discount brokers.

Brokerage as a Percentage of the Traded Value

Stock brokers charge a percentage of the total trade value as brokerage. Higher trade values result in higher brokerage, and vice versa.

Monthly Trading Plans

Some brokers offer monthly trading plans allowing unlimited trades for a fixed monthly or yearly subscription fee, regardless of the trade value.

Zero Brokerage

Many discount brokers do not charge brokerage on delivery-based transactions. So, this is not applicable to Intraday Trading.

2. STT (Securities Transaction Tax): Levied on the transaction value of securities traded.

It is a tax by the Government on the value of transactions occurring out of the trades.

3. Exchange Transaction Charges: Fees charged by the stock exchanges (NSE/BSE) on trades executed.

These charges differ based on scrip, exchange, and broker's monthly turnover. However, they are low and do not incur significant costs in any trade.

4. GST (Goods and Services Tax): Applicable on brokerage and transaction charges.

This is a tax by the government as good as levied on almost all products and services in the country.

5. Stamp Duty: Levied by the state government on the value of shares traded.

These are the charges by the Government of India as per the Indian Stamp Act of 1899 for transacting in instruments on the stock exchanges and depositories.

6. SEBI Turnover Fees: Charged by SEBI on the total turnover of trades.

These are the fees charged by the Securities and Exchange Board of India (SEBI) to regulate the markets.

7. NSE IPFT Charges: Charges for Investor Protection Fund

NSE has created the Investor Protection Fund Trust (IPFT) to cover up for investors' claims when defaulters' assets are not enough. The fund also promotes investor education, awareness, and research. IPFT charges are levied on all trades executed on NSE and are levied separately but included under exchange transaction charges in the contract note.

Cost Structure at a Glance:

Brokerage	Zero Brokerage	0.03% or Rs. 20/executed order whichever is lower	0.03% or Rs. 20/executed order whichever is lower	Flat Rs. 20 per executed order
Charges	**Delivery**	**Intraday**	**Futures**	**Options**
STT/CTT	0.1% on Buy and Sell value	0.025% on Sell value	0.0125% on Sell value	0.0625% on Sell value (Premium)
Exchange Transaction Charges	NSE: 0.00325% BSE: 0.00375%	NSE: 0.00325% BSE: 0.00375%	NSE: 0.0019%	NSE: 0.05% (On premium) BSE: 0.00375%
Clearing Charges	0	0	0.0005%	0.009%
SEBI Turnover Fee	₹10/Crore	₹10/Crore	₹10/Crore	₹10/Crore
GST	18% on (Brokerage + Exchange Transaction charges + Clearing charges + SEBI Turnover Fee)	18% on (Brokerage + Exchange Transaction charges + Clearing charges + SEBI Turnover Fee)	18% on (Brokerage + Exchange Transaction charges + Clearing charges + SEBI Turnover Fee)	18% on (Brokerage + Exchange Transaction charges + Clearing charges + SEBI Turnover Fee)
Stamp Duty	0.015%	0.003%	0.002%	0.003%
NSE IPFT	₹10/Crore	₹10/Crore	₹10/Crore	₹50/Crore (On Premium)

Example:

During an Intraday trading, at 11.30 am, you buy 200 quantity of shares of SunTV at the rate of Rs. 850, and Sell the shares at Rs. 875 at 1.45 pm. The calculation of costs that you pay will be as follows. Out of your profit of Rs. 5000 (Rs. 25 per share*200 shares), you pay all the charges including brokerage Rs. 109.91, resulting into Net Profit of Rs. 4890.09 before Income-tax.

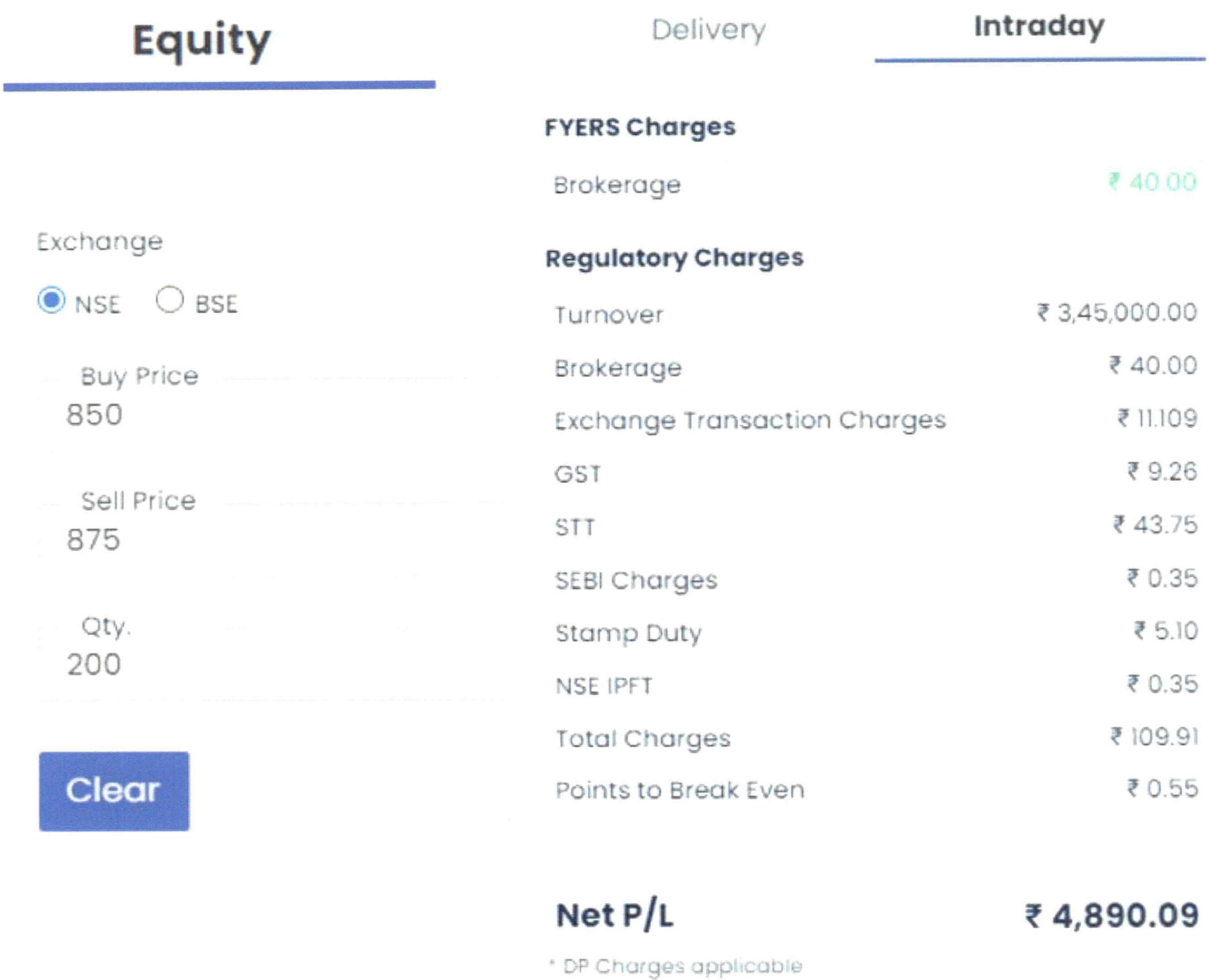

(Source : https://fyers.in/calculator/brokerage/)

Why Brokers Offer Zero Brokerage

Brokers offer zero brokerage for several strategic reasons:

1. **Customer Acquisition:** Zero brokerage is an attractive proposition for new customers, helping brokers to rapidly expand their user base.
2. **Increased Trading Volume:** By eliminating brokerage fees, brokers encourage higher trading volumes, which can lead to increased liquidity and market participation.
3. **Revenue from Other Sources:** Brokers can offset the loss of brokerage revenue by earning from other services such as margin funding, lending against securities, and premium subscriptions.

4. **One-Time Fees:** Some brokers charge a one-time fee for zero brokerage accounts, generating immediate revenue while providing long-term trading benefits to customers.
5. **Competitive Edge:** Offering zero brokerage helps brokers stand out in a competitive market, attracting clients away from traditional brokerage firms that charge higher fees.

However, Retail traders using zero brokerage firms may encounter several risks mentioned as follows.

1. **Reckless Trading:** Zero brokerage can encourage frequent trading, which might lead to impulsive and poorly thought-out decisions. Zero brokerage can lead to increased trading frequency and risky behaviors. For example, during the surge of retail trading in 2020, many investors experienced significant losses due to overtrading and lack of risk management.
2. **Hidden Costs:** Although brokerage is zero, there might be other fees such as charges on futures and options trades, account maintenance, or hidden fees for certain services. Some retail trading platforms have been criticized for obfuscating (clouding) brokerage costs and conflicts of interest. Reports have shown that while commissions might be zero, other fees and charges can add up, misleading investors about the true cost of trading. The Securities and Exchange Board of India (SEBI) has introduced a circular mandating uniform charges to address the issue of hidden costs and additional fees by brokers. This move aims to bring transparency and protect retail investors from misleading practices by standardizing the charges across the board.
3. **Quality of Service:** Discount brokers offering zero brokerage may compromise on customer service, trading tools, and research resources, affecting the trading experience.
4. **Order Execution:** There could be issues with the quality of order execution, as some brokers might prioritize certain types of trades or clients, leading to potential disadvantages in terms of price and speed. Concerns have been raised about the quality of order execution in zero brokerage models. Instances have been reported where brokers may route orders in ways that benefit them rather than the clients, potentially leading to less favorable trade executions for retail investors.
5. **Market Risks:** With increased trading activity, retail investors might expose themselves to greater market risks, especially if they lack adequate knowledge and risk management strategies.

Please note that zero brokerage is not offered to the traders in Intraday trading where delivery of shares is not involved. When you receive any such offer with zero brokerage in Intraday trading, then you have to be cautious as it is all likely to be a fraudulent offer.

Income Tax On Intraday Trading - How Profits From Intraday Trading Are Taxed

Identifying yourself as a trader or investor is the first step in filing your income tax return. You need to know that Investors benefit from lower tax rates on capital gains, while Traders have the advantage of claiming business expenses that reduce their income.

When you are an Intraday trader, understanding the difference between Capital Assets and Trading Assets is crucial in order to understand the tax implications.

A share can be called a 'Capital Asset' or 'Trading Asset or Stock-in-Trade' depending on whether you are identified as an investor or trader.

Investors are those who invest in stocks or other securities for the long term with the intention of holding them for a considerable period. They aim to earn returns through capital appreciation(income on sale of shares) and dividends. The income generated from the sale of shares is taxed as 'capital gains'. It is further classified as long-term and short-term capital gains based on how long the shares are held.

Traders are those who buy and sell stocks or other securities frequently with the intention of making a profit through short-term price movement. Their income from trading is treated as business income, and they are required to file their returns under the head "Profits and gains from business or profession." Their profits are taxed as per the applicable slab rates. In short, investors are taxed on their capital gains, while traders are taxed on their business income.

Based on this classification, your income will be divided into the following types:

C. From Capital Assets:

Long Term Capital Gain (LTCG) or Loss

Short Term Capital Gain (STCG) or Loss

D. From Trading Assets:

Speculative Business Income: Intraday transactions are speculative in nature, and hence, the income from these trades is called speculative business income. Income tax on intraday trading profit in India falls under this category.

Non-Speculative Business Income: All share transactions that are not speculative in nature fall under the category of non-speculative transactions. These include delivery-based equity trades, equity futures and options, commodity trades (both delivery and futures/options), and currency trades (both delivery and futures/options). Hence, the income from these transactions is called non-speculative business income.

Now, you are aware that shares bought and sold (long trades) or sold and bought (short trades) within a single trading day is known as intraday trading. The trader's purpose in intraday trading is not to own the equity shares, but they want to take advantage of the short-term price movements and make profits the very same day. These profits are taxable. There is no separate speculative income tax rate in India as it is taxed according to your income tax slab.

How will you pay ?

1. Profits and Gains from Intraday trading is taxed under the "Income Head: Profits and Gains from Business and Profession". Your income from intra-day trading will be considered as speculative business income. It is considered speculative because you are trading without intending to take the delivery (ownership) of the contract.
2. You have to file Income Tax Return (ITR). The Income-tax Act,1961 releases all the ITR forms and specifies the procedures to be followed. ITR is a form in which the taxpayers file information about their income earned and tax applicable, to the income tax department. The Income-tax Department has notified 7 forms to date. Every taxpayer should file his ITR on or before the

specified due date. The applicability of ITR forms varies depending on the sources of income of the taxpayer, the amount of the income earned and the category of the taxpayer like individuals, HUF, company, etc. For Intraday Traders, ITR-3 has to be filed.

3. ITR due date for intraday trading income is as follows.

   a. 31st July - if Tax Audit is not applicable (When you have made profits of at least 6% of Trading Turnover)
   b. 31st October - if Tax Audit is applicable (1. When you have incurred a loss or your profit which is lesser than 6% of Trading Turnover, Tax Audit is applicable, if your total income is more than ₹2.5 lakhs (basic exemption limit. 2. If you have made profits of at least 6% of Trading Turnover, and if you do not choose the Presumptive Taxation Scheme under Section 44AD, then tax audit is applicable. 3. Irrespective of the profit or loss, a tax audit is applicable if you have a turnover of more than ₹10 crores (Only if over 95% of transactions are digital, and Trading is 100% digital). Please note that turnover for Intraday Trading is equal to the absolute amounts of Profit/Losses.

CHAPTER – 11

NRIs' Opportunity for Intraday Trading in India

Non-Resident Indians (NRIs) have diverse opportunities to invest in the Indian stock market, but there are certain restrictions to be aware of. One significant limitation is that NRIs are not permitted to engage in intraday trading. Instead, they can participate in the market through delivery-based trading, which involves holding shares for a longer period rather than buying and selling them within the same trading day. This regulation ensures that NRIs focus on long-term investments in equity shares, mutual funds, and ETFs, rather than short-term speculative trades. Understanding these guidelines is crucial for NRIs looking to leverage the growth potential of the Indian stock market while adhering to the regulatory framework.

But, at the same time, it is important to note that when Intraday trading in Equity Cash segment (without delivery) is not permitted, but, Intraday trading in Future and Options segment is permitted. This is where NRIs can take the opportunity.

There are two lucrative opportunities for NRIs –

- Intraday and positional trading in Futures segment (Not in Options segment)
- Long-term investment in ETFs (Exchange Traded Funds)

Before, we discuss these opportunities, it is important to draw attention to the fact that how the timing factor can be leveraged for a profitable trade under these two alternatives.

Table A: When, in India, the market commences at 9.15 AM, the timings of different countries are ---

Country	**City/Region**	**Time**
USA	New York	11:45 PM (Previous Day)
UK	London	4:45 AM
Canada	Toronto	11:45 PM (Previous Day)
Australia	Sydney	1:45 PM
Africa	Nairobi	6:45 AM
Dubai	Dubai	7:45 AM
Oman	Muscat	7:45 AM

Table B: When, in India, the market is running at 3.00 PM, the timings of different countries are ---

(The closing time of the market is 3.30 pm)

Country	City/Region	Time
USA	New York	5:30 AM
UK	London	10:30 AM
Canada	Toronto	5:30 AM
Australia	Sydney	7:30 PM
Africa	Nairobi	12:30 PM
Dubai	Dubai	1:30 PM
Oman	Muscat	1:30 PM

1. Intraday and positional trading in Futures segment

Let me make it clear, that for NRIs, time is the important factor. Considering their fundamental constraint of time, it is advised to avoid Options segment, and not get lured by the trading opportunity available with a large quantity and small amount. Options involve decay in the premium due to time factor which limits the profit potential of the trade. Hence, trading in the futures segment is the best alternative for NRIs.

There are two types of Trading Styles emerging out of the timing situation. In the morning, when the market commences in India, the more suitable style or approach would be to trade on 1-minute timeframe assuming that you can spare maximum one hour.

15. Trading Strategies:

Trading Set-up – 15: Intraday

Time frame: 1 - Minute

a. Indicators: (1) EMA 9 (Low), EMA 20 (High)
(2) cm_ult_macd_mtf (12,48) by Chrismoody
b. Whenever the price goes above EMA 20, long trade is initiated. When the price goes down EMA9, short trade is initiated.
c. When the price moves between EMA 9 and EMA 20, the trade is to be avoided, as it shows sideways movement. This is a very simple method of taking trades on 1-minute timeframe.
d. The MACD indicator give information early about the trend. Once MACD gives buy information, get ready when the price moves up EMA 20, and when MACD gives information about Sell, get ready when price moves below EMA9.
e. Don't enter the trade when price remains in between two EMAs, even if, MACD gives signal, but wait for the price movement above EMA 20, or below EMA 9.
f. Place the stop loss at the previous swing low, if there is long trade, and the stop loss at previous swing high at the previous swing high.

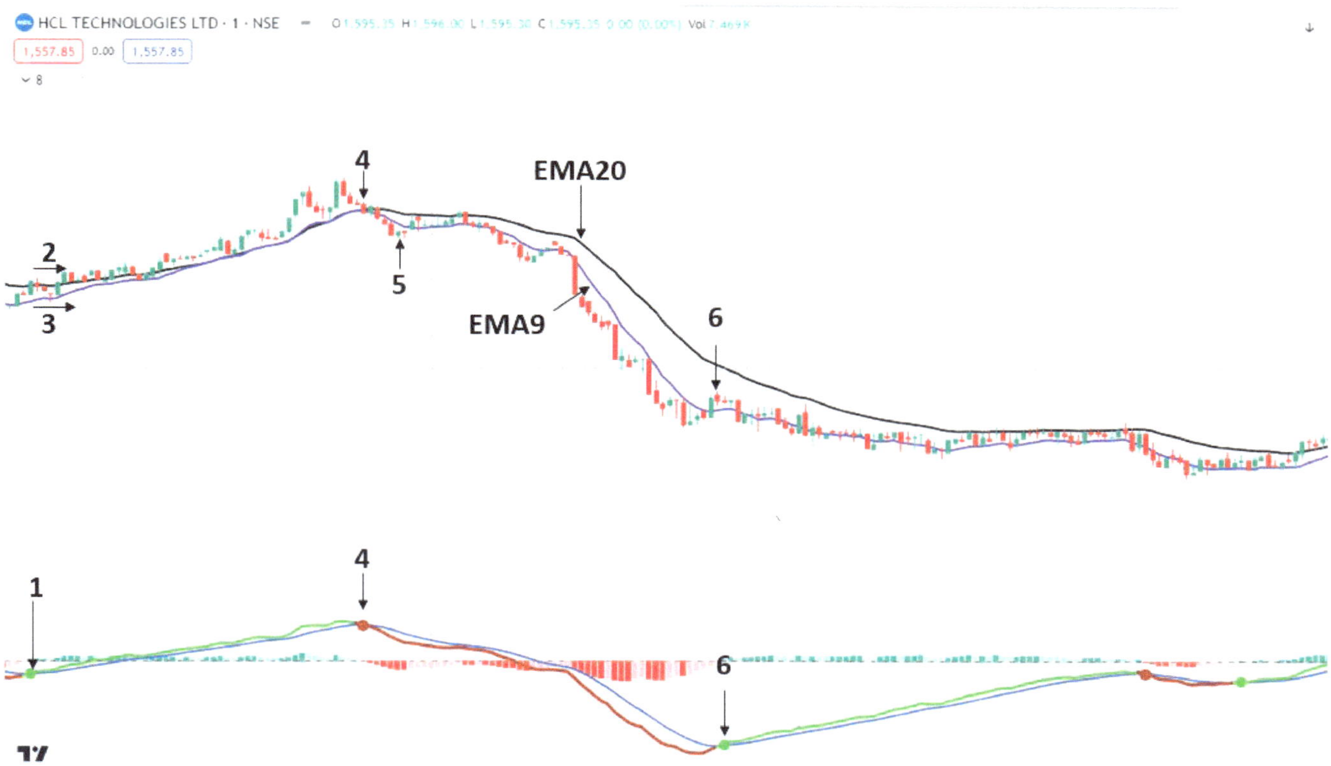

The above 1-minute chart shows that at point no.1, MACD gives buy signal. So, you enter the trade at high of the candle at point no.2, as it is above EMA20. At point no.3, you place the stop loss which is the latest previous swing low. At point no. 4, MACD gives signal to exit the trade and book the profit. So, at point no. 4 in the chart, you exit the trade. At the same time, at point no. 5, you initiate the short trade with a stop loss at previous swing high above point no. 4. At point no. 6, MACD gives exit signal, and you exit the trade at point no. 6 in the chart. If you practice this for a month, you will get a grip on this, and it will be a joyful experience for you.

I am giving you another chart for your analysis and exercise. Find out signals, trades with stop loss and exit.

You may note that you can also take EMA 9 (High) instead of EMA 20 (High). The only difference is that when price is above EMA 9 (Low) and EMA 20 (High) shows good momentum. You can refer to the previous chapter on Trading Strategies and Set up (Trade Set up 11) for EMA 9, Low and High set up.

16. Trading Set-up – 16: Positional (Swing)

Time frame: 75 - Minute

a. Indicators: (1) Colored EMA 9 (Close)
   (2) RSI (14,21)
b. Whenever RSI(14) crosses up RSI Moving Average (21), long trade is initiated. When RSI(14) crosses down RSI Moving Average (21), short trade is initiated.
c. The entry in the trade will be triggered when there is cross over of RSI and RSI Moving Average. The exit will be triggered when there is change of colour of Colored EMA9.
d. You will be able to remain in the trade for 2 to 3 days in any Futures stock. You can buy or sell any Futures stock.
e. The timing of the trade will be 3.00 PM (IST). You will be entering the trade during the last half an hour of the market.
f. Stock Selection Method –

   You will be going to Chartink.com at 3.00 pm, and run the screener to find out stocks which are in Futures segment. Select those stocks for entering the trade. The screener is as follows.

The screener below is for Buying the Futures stock. There are three parameters for screening the stock – (1) RSI and RSI-MA cross over, (2) ADX for ensuring momentum, (3) Volume more than the average volume for last 20 periods. This will help us to find those stocks which have higher probability of being in one direction for 2 to 3 days. You have to run the screener at 3.00 PM (IST).

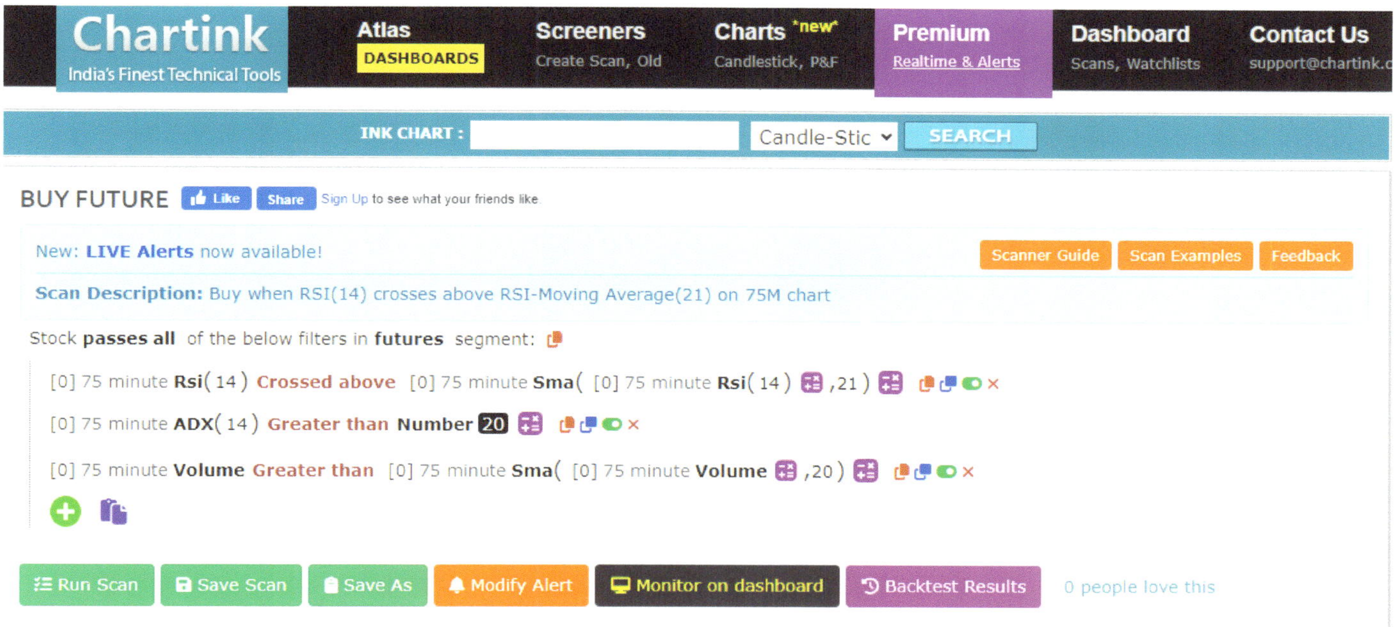

The screener for selling the stocks is given below.

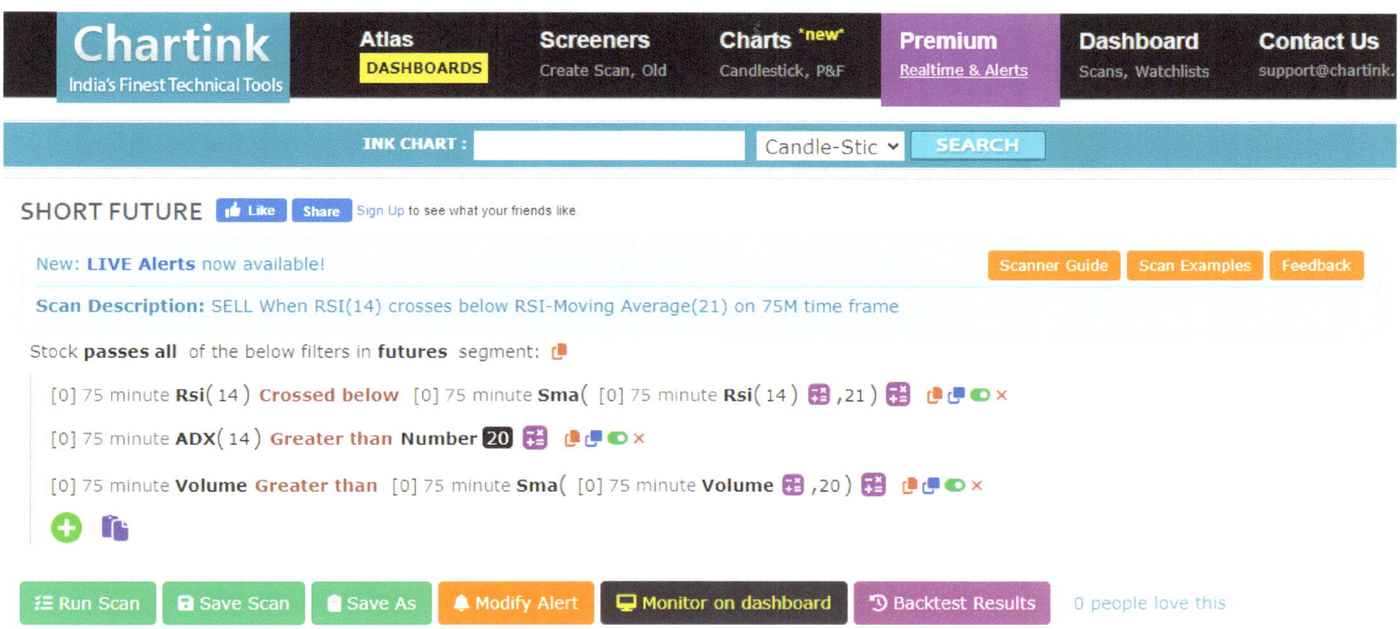

Let me give you a chart for better understanding of taking trades on selected stocks.

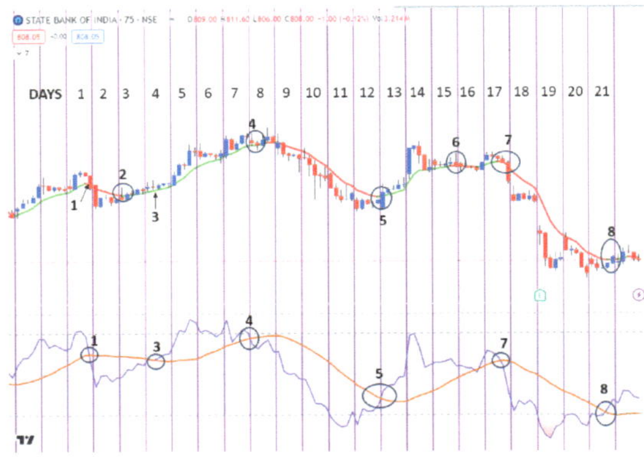

Above is the chart of State Bank of India of 75-minutes. You can see the price movement over 21 days. On Day-1, RSI is crossing down RSI-MA at point no. 1, so you can enter short trade as seen in the chart. On Day-3, you can exit the trade as EMA is getting red as seen at point no. 2. On Day-4, at point no. 3, RSI is crossing up, hence, it is a long trade. You can enter the trade as EMA is green. You can be in the trade till Day-8. At point no. 4, you can exit the trade as well as you can enter a fresh short trade as RSI is crossing down RSI MA. You can hold the trade till Day-12. Again, you can exit and enter the fresh long trade at point no. 5. You can exit at point no. 6 as EMA is getting red. You can enter the fresh short trade at point no. 7 on day-17, and remain in the trade till Day-21 (point no. 8).

- **Long-term investment in ETFs (Exchange Traded Funds)**

1. **What is an ETF?**

An Exchange Traded Fund (ETF) is a type of investment fund that is traded on stock exchanges, similar to stocks. ETFs typically track an index, commodity, bonds, or a basket of assets. They combine the diversification benefits of mutual funds with the trading flexibility of stocks.

2. **ETFs in the Indian Context**

In India, ETFs have gained popularity as an efficient and cost-effective way to invest in various asset classes. They are regulated by the Securities and Exchange Board of India (SEBI). Indian ETFs often track major indices like the Nifty 50 or Sensex, and some ETFs focus on sectors, commodities like gold, or international indices. As of now, there are over 100 ETFs listed on Indian stock exchanges, covering various indices, sectors, and commodities.

When you invest in an ETF, you essentially own a share of the fund's portfolio. This structure allows you to gain exposure to a wide range of assets without having to buy each one individually. For example, a Nifty 50 ETF will replicate the performance of the Nifty 50 index, which comprises 50 of the largest and most liquid companies listed on the National Stock Exchange (NSE) of India. The best part of it is that it never becomes zero value. When a particular stock is not performing, then it is taken out and replaced with the best performing stock.

3. **How ETFs Differ from Mutual Funds**

Trading: ETFs are traded like stocks on an exchange throughout the day at market prices, while mutual funds are bought or sold at the closing NAV (Net Asset Value) of the day [4].

Cost: ETFs generally have lower expense ratios than mutual funds because they are passively managed [1].

Flexibility: Investors can buy or sell ETFs any time during trading hours, whereas mutual funds can only be traded at the end of the trading day [6].

Trading in ETFs offers several benefits over mutual funds for retail investors:

1. **Liquidity:** ETFs trade on stock exchanges like individual stocks, allowing investors to buy or sell throughout the trading day at market prices. Mutual funds, on the other hand, can only be traded at the end of the trading day at the NAV (Net Asset Value) [5].
2. **Lower Costs:** ETFs generally have lower expense ratios compared to mutual funds, as most ETFs are passively managed, reducing management fees. This makes them more cost-effective for long-term investors [5].
3. **Tax Efficiency:** ETFs are more tax-efficient due to their structure. They tend to realize fewer capital gains, which can result in lower tax liability for investors compared to actively managed mutual funds [3].
4. **Transparency:** ETFs typically disclose their holdings daily, giving investors a clear view of the assets within the fund. Mutual funds usually provide this information less frequently [4].

Let me introduce you to some of the best ETFs in terms of Return, Expense ratio, etc.

1. NiftyBeEs:

Nifty BeES stands for 'Benchmark Exchange Traded Scheme'. It was introduced by an Asset Management Company called 'BENCHMARK' on 8th January 2022 and is currently managed by Nippon India Mutual Fund. t is an Exchange Traded Fund (ETF) that tracks the S&P CNX Nifty index to replicate its returns. Like other ETFs, Nifty BeES is listed and traded on the stock exchange.

The Nifty BeES was launched in 1992 as the first ETF in India. The ETF is listed on the National Stock Exchange (NSE).

Each unit of the Nifty BeES fund is equal to 1/10th of the S&P CNX Nifty Index or commonly called Nifty 50 (an index that tracks the top 50 companies from across sectors). The face value of each unit is Rs.10, but depending on the trading volume and demand and supply, the per-unit market price fluctuates.

2. Mid-Cap ETF:

NIFTY Midcap 150 index consists of 150 companies (ranked 101-250) based on the full market cap from the NIFTY 500 Index. Full market cap is the multiplication of a company's stock price with all its shares (active shares readily available in the market and inactive shares such as those held by promoters or the government).

Simplifying further, the 100 largest companies (in terms of full market cap) in the NIFTY 500 index comprise the NIFTY 100 index. And the companies ranked 101 to 250 based on full market cap comprise the NIFTY Midcap 150 index.

Now, the NIFTY Midcap 150 index is constructed in a manner that the 150 companies that comprise the index belong to different sectors and have different weights.

3. Small- Cap ETF:

Small-Cap is an indicative term for the market capitalisation of a company. A company with a market capitalisation of less than INR 500 Cr is a small-cap company, and stocks of such a company are called small-cap stocks. An Exchange Traded Fund or ETF is a basket of securities that are traded on stock markets. Therefore, Small-Cap ETFs are funds invested in the basket of securities of small-cap funds.

Small-Cap ETFs invest in companies with massive growth potential. As an investor, you are fundamentally investing in multiple companies with ETFs. Therefore, with ETFs, you can expect to earn higher returns with lower investment costs.

4. Momentum ETF:

A Momentum ETF is a type of exchange-traded fund that invests in stocks demonstrating strong price momentum. This strategy selects companies whose stock prices have been rising consistently and significantly, with the idea that they will continue to perform well in the near term.

The Nifty 200 Momentum 30 Index is commonly tracked by Momentum ETFs. This index comprises 30 high-momentum stocks selected from the Nifty 200, which includes large and mid-cap stocks. The objective of these ETFs is to replicate the performance of this index as closely as possible.

For example, the Motilal Oswal Nifty 200 Momentum 30 ETF and the ICICI Prudential Nifty 200 Momentum 30 ETF are popular options available in the Indian market. These funds aim to provide returns that correspond to the total returns of the securities represented by the Nifty 200 Momentum 30 Index.

5. **Sectoral ETF:**

A Sectoral ETF is an exchange-traded fund that focuses on a specific sector of the economy, such as technology, healthcare, or finance. These ETFs invest in a diversified portfolio of stocks within that particular sector, allowing investors to gain exposure to the entire sector rather than picking individual stocks.

Some of the best Sectoral ETFs in India for 2024 include:

- ICICI Prudential Nifty Commodities ETF - Focuses on commodities-related companies.
- Tata Nifty India Digital ETF - Invests in digital and technology companies.
- ICICI Prudential Nifty FMCG ETF - Concentrates on the fast-moving consumer goods sector.
- Nippon India Nifty Pharma ETF - Targets the pharmaceutical sector.
- These ETFs allow investors to take advantage of growth opportunities within specific sectors that they believe will outperform the broader market.

6. Gold ETFs:

A Gold ETF is a type of exchange-traded fund that invests primarily in gold bullion. These funds are listed on stock exchanges and are traded like stocks. Each unit of a Gold ETF represents a certain amount of gold, and its value is directly linked to the price of gold in the market. Investors can buy and sell these units, allowing them to gain exposure to gold without the need to physically own the metal.

Some of the best Gold ETFs in India for 2024 include:

- AXIS Gold ETF.
- Nippon India ETF Gold BeES.
- ICICI Prudential Gold ETF.
- HDFC Gold Exchange Traded Fund.

These ETFs are popular for those looking to invest in gold without dealing with storage and security concerns associated with physical gold.

7. Silver ETFs:

- A Silver ETF is a type of exchange-traded fund that primarily invests in physical silver or silver-related instruments. These ETFs are designed to track the price of silver in the market, allowing investors to gain exposure to silver without physically owning the metal. Silver ETFs are traded on stock exchanges, similar to stocks, providing liquidity and ease of access to investors.

Some of the best Silver ETFs in India for 2024 include:

- Nippon India Silver ETF - Provides an average return of 16.46% over the past year.
- ICICI Prudential Silver ETF - Delivered a 21.72% return in 2024, making it one of the top-performing silver ETFs.
- Aditya Birla Sun Life Silver ETF - Another popular choice among investors, it is one of the three primary silver ETFs available in the Indian market.
- These ETFs offer a convenient way to invest in silver, especially for those looking to diversify their portfolios with commodities.

Strategy to Invest in ETFs

1. Make a portfolio of 7 ETFs mentioned above. Create a watchlist on TradingView platform.
2. On 75-Minutes chart, when the Supertrend gives "Sell" signal, Buy the ETF. It may sound weird, but here, you have to apply the concept "Buy on Dip, Sell on Rise". Keep on buying till Supertrend is in Sell mode. The moment Supertrend becomes green and gives "Buy" signal, stop investing. You can see the following chart.

The above chart is of Nifty BEES on 75-minutes timeframe. Whenever the supertrend is in red, giving Sell signal, keep on buying on Red candles. Don't buy on Green candles even if, it falls in Buy Zone. Stop buying when Supertrend turns green, and gives "buy" signal. Don't buy on Red candle, even if, Supertrend is green.

3. At 3.00 pm (IST), you can open your watchlist, and analyze seven ETFs. To begin with, you can earmark some funds to invest equally to all seven ETFs. You can complete the allocation over a month or so in all the seven ETFs, provided you get buy opportunities, otherwise wait and have patience.

4. Once you are done with allocation, you hold the portfolio for a longer time. Whenever there is buy opportunity, you keep on investing. You can create a SIP (Systematic Investment Plan). This can be your emergency fund or you can gift to your grand children.
5. Another approach to investment is whenever, on a particular day, there is decline by more than 1% in a particular ETF out of the seven ETFs, you invest. Keep on investing under the situation. Over the years, you will build a very handsome portfolio, which will be better than any Mutual Fund portfolio.

Taxation of ETFs:

The Union Budget 2024-2025 introduced notable changes to the taxation of Exchange-Traded Funds (ETFs) in India, particularly regarding capital gains and tax exemptions for certain funds.

Key Tax Changes for ETFs:

Capital Gains Tax Rates:

Short-Term Capital Gains (STCG): Gains from the sale of ETFs held for less than 24 months will be taxed at 20%.

Long-Term Capital Gains (LTCG): Gains from ETFs held for more than 24 months will be taxed at 12.5%, without the benefit of indexation. This aligns ETFs with the treatment of other long-term investments.

Tax Exemptions for ETFs in IFSC:

ETFs set up in the International Financial Services Centre (IFSC) Gift City will enjoy tax exemptions similar to those available to Category III Alternative Investment Funds (AIFs). This includes a concessional tax rate of 10% on interest and dividend income, along with capital gains tax exemptions on various securities (excluding shares in Indian companies). This change aims to promote investment in the IFSC and enhance its attractiveness as a financial hub.

Regulatory aspects of Trading – NRIs must know:

Briefly, regulator aspects have been given below in an easy-to-read format which will help the NRIs to understand how to initiate the trading in stock market in India.

1. A person who stays in India for less than 182 days during the upcoming fiscal year is considered a non-residential Indian.
2. A person who has left the country in search of job is also referred to as an NRI. An NRI is a person who travels abroad for work-related reasons.
3. **NRE Bank Account:** Designed for NRIs earning income in foreign currency but intending to convert and remit it in Indian Rupees, the NRE account facilitates such transactions. Funds from the NRE account can be utilized for investments in Indian companies. Moreover, all deposits or fund balances from the NRE account are fully repatriable, allowing NRIs to transfer them abroad without restrictions.

4. **NRO Bank Account:** NRIs seeking to manage income earned within India can opt for an NRO savings bank account. Since NRIs maintain Indian citizenship, any income received in Indian currency, such as rent, pension, business income, or dividends, should be deposited into an NRO account. Unlike NRE accounts, the balance and interest earned in NRO accounts are not entirely repatriable. NRIs can repatriate a maximum of USD 1 million per financial year from their NRO account.
5. After opening an NRI bank account, NRIs can opt to invest in India through either the Portfolio Investment Scheme (PIS) or non-PIS mode. PIS is an RBI scheme enabling NRIs to invest in listed Indian companies on the Bombay Stock Exchange (BSE) and National Stock Exchange (NSE).
6. NRIs also have the flexibility to invest in India using a non-PIS NRO trading account, making PIS optional, and allowing trading without Portfolio Management Services (PMS).
7. **NRI Trading Account:** The trading account functions similarly for residents and non-residents, serving as a platform to place and execute buy and sell orders. Through an NRI trading account, NRIs can engage in trading activities such as buying and selling stocks listed on the BSE and NSE, trading in Futures and Options (F&O) contracts, or investing in mutual funds. NRIs have the option to link either an NRE or NRO bank account to their trading account, enabling them to invest on either a repatriation or non-repatriation basis.
8. **NRI Demat Account:** An NRI Demat Account is crucial for receiving delivery of shares and securities in dematerialized form. This account ensures the safekeeping of all equity and mutual fund investments held by NRIs, providing convenience and security.

9. NRI trading rules:

a. NRIs are allowed to invest up to 5% of the paid-up capital of listed Indian company in recognized Stock exchange on repatriation or non-repatriation basis
b. NRIs are allowed to invest up to 5% of the paid-up value of each series of debentures of listed Indian companies on repatriation or non-repatriation basis.
c. Investments by all NRIs clubbed together cannot exceed 10% of paid-up capital of the Indian listed company or paid-up value of each series of debentures of the company.
d. The above aggregate ceiling can be raised to 24% if the Indian company passes a special resolution to that effect.
e. To trade in the derivatives market, NRIs need a custodial participant code. NRI investments should be on a non-repatriation basis and Rupee funds held in India should be used.

CHAPTER – 12

It's All About Mind in Intraday Trading – "Happy Mind"

Psychology plays a critical role in trading, as it influences how traders react to market events, manage risk, and make decisions under pressure. Emotions like fear and greed can lead to impulsive actions, causing traders to deviate from their strategies, resulting in significant losses.

Consider a trader who meticulously develops a strategy and plans to stick to it. However, when the market becomes volatile, fear of losing money may cause the trader to exit a position prematurely, missing out on potential gains. Conversely, greed might drive the trader to hold onto a winning trade too long, only to see profits diminish as the market reverses.

A famous example from trading history involves Jesse Livermore, a legendary trader known for making and losing fortunes. Livermore once remarked that his biggest losses came not from bad market analysis but from failing to control his emotions. He emphasized that mastering one's emotions is as crucial as mastering the market itself.

Psychology isn't just about avoiding losses; it's about maintaining discipline, sticking to a well-thought-out plan, and being able to walk away when necessary. This mental resilience often distinguishes successful traders from unsuccessful ones.

A "happy mind" significantly enhances trading performance by improving decision-making, focus, and resilience. When a trader is in a positive mental state, they are less likely to be swayed by fear or greed, which are the primary emotions that lead to poor trading decisions. A content and balanced mind fosters clarity, allowing traders to stick to their strategies and make objective decisions, even under pressure.

Imagine a trader who begins the day with a relaxed and positive mindset, perhaps after a morning routine that includes exercise and meditation. As they enter the market, they encounter a sudden downturn. Instead of panicking, the trader calmly assesses the situation, decides to hold their position based on sound analysis, and eventually benefits as the market recovers. This is a stark contrast to a trader who might be stressed or anxious, who could make impulsive decisions, leading to losses.

Paul Tudor Jones, a renowned hedge fund manager, once emphasized the importance of mental health in trading. He shared how maintaining a happy and balanced life outside trading, such as through exercise and spending time with family, positively influenced his ability to stay focused and disciplined in the market. His story illustrates that a happy mind not only improves trading performance but also helps in sustaining long-term success in the volatile world of trading.

Common Psychological Pitfalls in Intraday Trading:

Intraday trading demands quick decision-making, which makes traders susceptible to various psychological pitfalls. These mental traps can lead to poor trading decisions and significant losses.

1. **Overconfidence:** Traders who have experienced success might develop an inflated sense of their abilities. This overconfidence can lead to taking excessive risks without proper analysis, resulting in losses when the market behaves unexpectedly.
2. **Fear of Missing Out (FOMO):** The anxiety of missing a profitable trade often drives traders to enter trades without a solid strategy, chasing prices as they rise or fall rapidly. This can result in buying high and selling low, a recipe for losses.
3. **Loss Aversion:** Traders often hold onto losing positions for too long, hoping for a reversal. This behaviour is driven by the fear of realizing a loss, which can lead to even greater losses as the position deteriorates further.
4. **Confirmation Bias:** Traders may seek out information that confirms their pre-existing beliefs about a trade while ignoring contrary evidence. This bias can lead to overconfidence in a trade that is not as solid as it seems.
5. **Revenge Trading:** After a loss, some traders might try to quickly recoup their losses by making impulsive trades without proper analysis. This behaviour often leads to further losses and emotional distress.

Once you recognize these psychological pitfalls and managing them effectively, then the probability of success enhances in intraday trading.

Hence, building awareness of mental patterns in intraday trading is crucial for avoiding impulsive decisions and emotional biases that can lead to losses.

Steps to Build Awareness:

1. **Identify Triggers:** Recognize situations or market conditions that provoke strong emotions like fear or greed. For instance, a sudden market drop might trigger panic, leading to hasty decisions.
2. **Reflect on Past Trades:** Regularly review your trading history to identify patterns. Ask yourself why you made certain decisions and whether they were driven by emotions rather than logic.
3. **Develop a Trading Plan:** A well-defined plan helps you stay disciplined. It should include clear entry and exit strategies, risk management, and predefined limits to prevent emotional trading. Follow any trade set-up you are comfortable with consistently.
4. **Mindfulness and Journaling:** Practice mindfulness to stay present during trading. Journaling your trades with thoughts and feelings before and after trades can reveal emotional patterns that influence your decisions.

For Example, Kunal Shah, a day trader who often exits trades too early out of fear of losing profits. Through journaling, he realizes that his fear stems from past losses. By becoming aware of this pattern, Kunal starts setting stricter exit rules in his trading plan. This awareness reduces his anxiety, allowing him to follow his plan more consistently and improve his overall performance. Thus, awareness of mental patterns can lead to more disciplined and successful trading.

Neuroscience Behind Positive Thinking:

Positive thinking is more than just a mindset—it's a process that actively influences brain function. Neuroscientific research reveals that positive thinking enhances neural pathways associated with decision-making, creativity, and emotional regulation. Positive thoughts stimulate the release of neurotransmitters like dopamine and serotonin, which improve mood and cognitive function. This heightened mental state can lead to better problem-solving abilities and more rational decision-making, especially in high-pressure environments like intraday trading.

In intraday trading, where decisions need to be made rapidly and under stress, maintaining a positive outlook can help traders stay calm and focused. For example, if a trader enters the market with optimism, their brain is primed to view setbacks as opportunities to learn rather than as threats. This mindset reduces anxiety and helps them adhere to their trading strategy rather than making impulsive decisions out of fear.

When an intraday trader experiences a series of losses, instead of dwelling on the negatives, he adopts a positive mindset by focusing on what he can learn from each trade. This approach reduces his stress and prevents him from making rash decisions to recover losses quickly. As a result, his decision-making improves, and starts to see more consistent gains over time. So, building a "Learning Attitude" opens up new ways of trading methods which bring profits consistently.

Interestingly, Neuro-finance researchers have found that brain scan images of traders about to make a trade are indistinguishable from those of drug addicts about to take a hit. They found a snowball effect and an increased desire to continue, regardless of the outcome of their behaviour. Unfortunately, when faced with losses, traders assume more risk rather than less, often leading to the death of their accounts. Taking trades in such situation is not positive thinking. As a trader, you must get deeper into the aspects before taking further trades where the mistake is occurring. This could be a FOMO, or it could be lack of concentration and failing to understand price movement, or interpreting indicator wrongly. To avoid such situations, my strong recommendation, at this point, is practice, practice, practice. Select one Trade Set-up after experimenting with many set-ups, find which one suits to your personality, practice on that set-up continuously (without break) during live trading sessions for 60 days, enhance your concentration power and mental peace by regular mediation, you are guaranteed for the success.

Without knowing the neuroscience, Warren Buffett clearly understood the problem, as seen in his statement, "Once you have ordinary intelligence, what you need is the temperament to control the urges that get other people into trouble in investing. The great traders control their emotions and constantly follow their rules."

Techniques to maintain mental balance during volatile markets in Intraday trading:

1. **Risk Management:**

Managing risk is crucial in volatile markets. For instance, setting a stop-loss can prevent emotional decision-making when the market moves against you. A trader named Raj once ignored his stop-loss, leading to a significant loss. After this incident, he always set a strict stop-loss, which helped him maintain mental balance during future volatile trades.

2. **Taking Breaks:**

After executing a trade, with proper stop loss, stepping away from the screen can prevent overtrading and reduce stress. However, this practice can be followed when you are on a set up with higher time frame. For example, after taking trade, go for some snacks and coffee, or lunch, have a chitchat with family members, read newspapers, etc. Such activities make you stress-free and relaxed, and help you in taking good trades further.

3. **Financial Preparedness:**

Having a financial cushion allows traders to face downturns without panic. For example, during a sudden market drop, a well-prepared trader is less likely to make impulsive decisions out of fear, knowing they have reserves to weather the storm. Therefore, allocate your funds in a way that helps in future trades.

4. **Patience:**

Waiting for the right opportunity rather than chasing the market can prevent emotional exhaustion. An experienced trader once missed several small opportunities but waited for a big move, which paid off and reinforced the value of patience. If you don't get a trade as per your set up, don't get disappointed. Always remember, "no trade is a good trade". There are going to be immense opportunities in the coming days. For an Intraday trader, whether market moves up or moves down, profitable trading opportunities do exist.

Daily Routine for an Intraday Trader:

1. Morning Mindfulness Meditation:

Start the day with 15 minutes of mindfulness meditation. Focus on your breath, observing it without judgment. Feel that you are merged with the energy (God). You may choose a deity as per your religious beliefs. That helps to create one-ness with energy (God). That will make your mind calm, peaceful and relaxed. You can increase the duration of meditation after a month or so. This practice helps in developing a calm mind, reducing stress, and increasing focus, which are critical for making clear trading decisions.

2. Visualization for Trading Success:

This is a very important step for an Intraday trader. While following the step-1 above, spend 10 minutes more on visualizing successful trades. Picture yourself executing trades as per your chosen trade set up. Visualize the chart on your trade set up (don't bring name of the company), visualize price movement, visualize taking trades as per the set up, visualize making profit, strongly feel the joy of making profit. Do this exercise with precision and calmness as if it is happening in reality. Initially, it may not work as per your visualization, but, don't discard the practice, don't create pessimistic and negative thoughts about its efficacy. If you stay over with a positive mind – set, no wonder, after a practice over a period of time, you will see what was happening in your visualization, is happening in reality. It will become a very joyful and stress-free trading. This technique helps in building confidence and creating a positive mindset, reducing the fear of losses.

3. Progressive Muscle Relaxation (PMR):

Use PMR during trading breaks. Tense and then slowly relax different muscle groups in your body. This exercise helps release physical tension caused by market volatility, allowing you to return to trading with a relaxed state of mind.

4. Midday Breathing Exercises:

During market hours, take a few minutes for deep breathing exercises. Inhale deeply, hold for a few seconds, and exhale slowly. This helps in regaining focus and managing emotions during the intense moments of trading.

5. Evening Gratitude Meditation:

End the trading day with a gratitude meditation. After you are done with your trading, relax by washing face, and pouring water on your feet. This will remove physical stress. Sit for 10-minute meditation. Reflect on what went well, even if the day was challenging. Thank and express your gratitude to the energy (God) for a wonderful day. This practice reinforces a positive mindset, helping you to build resilience over time.

Developing Trading Strategies Matching our Psychological Strengths:

Developing trading strategies that align with our psychological strengths involves understanding your mental tendencies, strengths, and weaknesses.

1. **Self-Assessment:** Begin by identifying your psychological strengths, such as patience, decisiveness, or emotional control. Determine your risk tolerance, whether you're more comfortable with aggressive or conservative strategies.
2. **Match Strategy to Personality:** If you're patient and disciplined, trend-following strategies might suit you. If you prefer quick decisions and high energy, scalping could be a better fit. The goal is to pick a strategy that you can consistently execute without emotional interference.
3. **Back-test and Refine:** Test your chosen strategies in a simulated environment. This helps identify whether the strategy aligns with your psychological profile, and allows for refinement before real-world application.
4. **Develop Mental Toughness:** Building resilience and mental toughness is essential to stick to your strategy during challenging market conditions. This involves regular mental conditioning exercises, such as mindfulness and stress management as mentioned above.
5. **Continuous Evaluation:** Regularly review your performance and psychological responses. Adjust your strategies as needed to maintain alignment with your mental strengths and market conditions.

Real-life Examples of successful traders who prioritized mindset:

1. **Paul Tudor Jones (USA):** A legendary trader known for his macro trading strategies, Paul Tudor Jones emphasizes the importance of a disciplined mindset, which has been key to his success. He is particularly known for predicting and profiting from the 1987 market crash.
2. **Rakesh Jhunjhunwala (India):** Known as India's Warren Buffett, Rakesh Jhunjhunwala believed that patience and a positive mindset were crucial to successful investing. His long-term perspective and mental toughness played a significant role in his rise to prominence in the Indian stock market.
3. **Yasuo Hamanaka (Japan):** Although he faced significant losses, Yasuo Hamanaka, known as "Mr. Copper," was once one of Japan's most successful traders. His success earlier in his career was attributed to his disciplined approach and deep understanding of market psychology.
4. **Nick Leeson (UK):** Despite his downfall, Nick Leeson initially succeeded as a trader at Barings Bank due to his strong mindset and aggressive trading strategies. His story serves as both a lesson in the importance of mindset and the risks of overconfidence.
5. **Rayner Teo (Singapore)**: Rayner Teo started his trading journey with a significant loss, losing 50% of his account on his first day of trading. This setback led him to realize the importance of mindset in trading. By committing to continuous learning and developing a disciplined approach, Rayner transformed his performance and eventually became a successful trader.

During my exploration of various trading techniques, I had the privilege of discovering an exceptional program led by Shri Raja Bhaiya Gandhi, known affectionately as Guruji by his followers. Based in Bhopal, Guruji has dedicated his life to a profound mission—he aspires to create 100 billionaires through stock trading. His unique approach to achieving this is centered around Mind Training for stock traders, a transformative program that he shares through his popular YouTube channel, *Trading Astrology*.

What sets this program apart is its deep focus on chakra development as a way to strengthen and sharpen the mind specifically for trading. Guruji's one-day intensive training sessions are designed to create a powerful mindset that can withstand the pressures of the stock market. With patience, concentration, and calmness as essential virtues for successful trading, this training offers practical tools to cultivate these traits.

For those who commit to the practice of the techniques taught in just one day for six months continuously, the benefits can be life-changing. Over time, these teachings nurture the mental resilience, clarity, and emotional balance that are critical for thriving in the fast-paced world of stock trading.

Lastly, what is most important in the skills development is practice, practice and practice. Once the set-up is chosen, it should be practiced 60 days uninterrupted.

In the realm of stock trading, much like in life, mastery lies not in a scattershot approach but in the disciplined repetition of a single, well-honed skill. The quote by Bruce Lee, "*I fear not the man who has practiced 10,000 kicks once, but I fear the man who has practiced one kick 10,000 times*," speaks deeply to the essence of focus, dedication, and persistence.

Consider this in the context of intraday trading. The trader who chases countless strategies, experimenting with every new trend or market signal, may experience flashes of success, but their understanding remains shallow, their edge unrefined. In contrast, the trader who relentlessly practices one method—be it price action analysis, technical indicators, or trend-following—over and over again, masters not only the strategy itself but also the nuances of market behaviour. They develop an intuitive understanding that no book or one-time attempt can ever teach. It is through repetition that they become attuned to the market's rhythm, much like a seasoned warrior becomes one with their weapon.

This philosophy is echoed in the ancient Indian Vedas, particularly in the concept of ***Abhyasa***—the practice of continuous repetition to attain perfection. The Bhagavad Gita speaks of "*Abhyasa Yoga*," the yoga of constant practice. Just as an archer in ancient India would practice hitting the bullseye repeatedly until their focus became unwavering and their precision flawless, the disciplined trader learns to respond to the market's movements with calm, confidence, and skill.

Take, for example, the principle of ***Shraddha*** (faith) and ***Saburi*** (patience) from the teachings of Shri Sai Baba, which are rooted in the Vedas. The dedicated trader must have faith in their strategy and patience to endure losses and setbacks, understanding that true mastery comes only with time and persistence. The initial failures, much like the misfires of an archer, are not indicative of defeat but of the learning curve every master must walk. Through repeated effort and belief in their method, the trader aligns themselves with the natural flow of the market, akin to the ***Sadhaka*** (a spiritual seeker) aligning with universal truths.

Thus, the feared trader is not the one who dabbles in many techniques, but the one who has perfected one strategy with the discipline of *Abhyasa* and the unwavering focus drawn from *Shraddha* and *Saburi*. This trader embodies the wisdom of the Vedas, the essence of persistence, and the deep emotional strength that arises from deep dedication—a force far more powerful than mere technical knowledge.

References

I extend my heartfelt gratitude to the brilliant authors, insightful writers, and influential voices who have woven a vast tapestry of knowledge as applied skills in the realm of stock market trading. Your collective knowledgeable experience has been invaluable in guiding me through the creation of this book. Together, you represent an unparalleled University of thought, inspiration, and expertise.

1. BOOKS:

Sr No.	Authors	Name of the Book	Publisher	Year
1	Akira Tsuchiya	Ichimoku Kinko Hyo Strategies	Nikkei Publishing	2015
2	Al Brooks	Reading Price Charts Bar by Bar	Wiley Trading	2009
3	Alexander Elder	Come Into My Trading Room	John Wiley & Sons	2002
4	Andrew Aziz	How to Day Trade for a Living	AMS Publishing Group	2016
5	Aniruddha Deshpande	Intraday Trading Using Market Profile	Buzzingstock Publishing House	2020
7	Ashwani Gujral	How to Make Money in Intraday Trading	Vision Books	2018
8	Brett N. Steenbarger	The Psychology of Trading	Wiley	2002
9	Goichi Hosoda	Ichimoku Kinko Hyo	Tenkai Publishing	1969
10	Hideki Matsunaga	Price Action Techniques of Japanese Traders	Jitsugyo No Nihonsha	2001
11	Hidenobu Sasaki	Candlestick Charting Explained	Tōkyō Keizai Shinpōsha	1993
12	Indrazith Shantharaj	The Subtle Art of Intraday Trading	Notion Press	2021
13	Jack D. Schwager	Market Wizards: Interviews with Top Traders	HarperBusiness	1989
14	John F. Carter	Mastering the Trade	McGraw-Hill Education	2018
15	Josh DiPetrio	The Truth About Day Trading Stocks	Wiley	2009
16	Kathy Lien	Day Trading the Currency Market	Wiley	2005
17	Katsuhiro Hosono	Trading Systems with Ichimoku Clouds	Nikkei Publishing	2007
18	Larry Williams	Long-Term Secrets to Short-Term Trading	Wiley	1999
19	Mark Douglas	Trading in the Zone	New York Institute of Finance	2000
20	Markus Heitkoetter	The Complete Guide to Day Trading	Rockwell Trading Services LLC	2008

21	Seiki Shimizu	The Japanese Chart of Charts	New York Institute of Finance	1986
22	Steve Nison	Japanese Candlestick Charting Techniques	Prentice Hall Press	1991
23	Toni Turner	A Beginner's Guide to Day Trading Online	Adams Media	2007
24	William J. O'Neil	How to Make Money in Stocks	McGraw-Hill	1988
25	Yukio Ishizuka	Lifetrack: Applications of Market Psychology	Jibun Shoten	2002
26	Yutaka Katsura	Technical Analysis of Stocks and Commodities	Gendai Shuppansha	1982
27	Yvan Byeajee	Intraday Trading for Profit	Independently Published	2017

Article Links

1 https://www.babypips.com/trading/impact-of-stress-on-trader-performance-2024-01-15
2 https://www.warriortrading.com/4-important-tips-dealing-trading-stress/
3 https://www.protradingschool.com/how-do-you-handle-trading-stress/
4 https://economictimes.indiatimes.com/nri/invest/how-to-file-income-tax-returns-a-step-by-step-guide-for-nris/step-8-verification-of-itr/slideshow/108344508.cms
5 https://economictimes.indiatimes.com/nri/invest/nri-trading-in-india-everything-you-need-to-know-about-accounts-rules-amp-eligibility/who-is-an-nri/slideshow/108942082.cms?from=mdr
6 https://cleartax.in/s/income-tax-on-intraday-trading
7 https://www.incometax.gov.in/iec/foportal/help/individual-business-profession
8 https://policyreview.info/articles/analysis/obfuscated-brokerage-retail-trading-platforms
9 https://www.forbes.com/advisor/in/investing/brokerage-charges-in-stock-market/
10 https://economictimes.indiatimes.com/wealth/invest/stock-market-trading-know-all-about-charges-fees-and-taxes/investing-in-the-stock-market-charges-you-must-know/slideshow/107464889.cms?from=mdr
11 https://corporatefinanceinstitute.com/resources/career-map/sell-side/capital-markets/ichimoku-cloud/
12 https://www.investopedia.com/trading/introduction-to-momentum-trading/
13 https://www.investopedia.com/terms/1/80-20-rule.asp
14 https://www.investopedia.com/day-trading/pick-stocks-intraday-trading/
15 https://tradingstrategyguides.com/order-flow-trading-strategy/
16 https://citytradersimperium.com/order-flow-trading-analysis/
17 https://www.inderscienceonline.com/doi/pdf/10.1504/IJEBR.2021.116353
18 https://rajeevprakash.com/financial-astrology-a-new-approach-to-market-forecasting/
19 https://www.investopedia.com/articles/trading/08/trading-breakouts.asp
20 https://www.kotaksecurities.com/share-market/what-is-breakout-trading/#:~:text=A%20breakout%20occurs%20when%20trading,breaks%20above%20a%20resistance%20level.
21 https://select.finology.in/articles/broker/factors-to-consider-when-choosing-a-stock-broker
22 https://blog.cubed.run/how-i-can-deploy-virtually-any-trading-strategy-without-any-code-395488640777?gi=b1b378e12ba5
23 https://www.bajajfinserv.in/intraday-trading
24 https://utradealgos.com/blog/why-algorithmic-trading-is-transforming-the-financial-markets/#:~:text=Transforming%20Financial%20Markets-,Speed%20and%20Efficiency,timely%20responses%20to%20market%20changes.
25 https://www.linkedin.com/pulse/algo-trading-game-changer-modern-finance-gyizer-x0gtf/
26 https://hmarkets.com/learn-to-trade/learning-hub/bollinger-bands/#:~:text=The%20Bollinger%20Bands%20consist%20of,band%2C%20it%20is%20considered%20oversold.
27 https://blog.elearnmarkets.com/difference-volume-traded-and-delivery/

Video Channels

1 A & A Trading Blog

@aatradingblog•106K subscribers

2 Aapka Investments

@aapkainvestments1596•20.8K subscribers

3 Abhishek Kar

@AbhishekKar•1.57M subscribers

4 AFTechTrades

@Aftechtrades•5.97K subscribers

5 AI Signals

@AI-Signals•3.73K subscribers

6 ajay raipuriya

@ajayraipuriya•134K subscribers

7 AlgoTrade Pro

@algotradepro•12.8K subscribers

8 ALL ABOUT TRADING

@allabouttradingankitdwived3648•128K subscribers

9 Analyse with Rajesh

@analyse_with_rajesh•61K subscribers

10 ApkaTradingPartner

@ApkaTradingPartner•945 subscribers

11 Art of Option Learning

@btcmagazinebroadcast•1.48M subscribers

12 Ashok Devanampriya

@precisionpriceactiontrader•47.6K subscribers

12 AS Pandit: Money,Life & Fitness

@AS.Pandit•141K subscribers

13 Ashutosh Kumar

@ashutosh_kumarYt•74.8K subscribers

14 Ashwini Kumar Bansal

@AshwiniKumarBansal•38.9K subscribers

15 Asset Yogi

@AssetYogi•3.84M subscribers

16 Atul Patel - Stocks Trader

@SwingTraderAtul•332K subscribers

17 Averageman Trader

@AveragemanTrader•22.5K subscribers

18 Beast Trading Club

@beasttradingclub•55.3K subscribers

19 Being Trader

@BeingTraderOfficial•100K subscribers

20 Bharat Jhunjhunwala

@jhunjhunwala_b•829K subscribers

21 Booming Bulls

@BoomingBulls•2.26M subscribers

22 Bullishfund

@Bullishfund•2.77K subscribers

23 CA Akshatha Udupa

@caakshathaudupaa•135K subscribers

24 CA Sumit Sharma

@CASumitSharma•218K subscribers

25 Chart Trade

@CHARTTRADE•37.5K subscribers

26 CPR TRADING

@cprtrading•17.7K subscribers

27 Critical Trading

@CriticalTrading•39.3K subscribers

28 Crude Bull

@CrudeBull•44.5K subscribers

29 Data Trader

@DataTraders•442K subscribers

30 Definedge

@Definedge•51K subscribers

31 Dhan

@DhanHQ•150K subscribers

32 Dr. Mukul Agrawal

@MukulAgrawal•1.66M subscribers

33 drravirkumar

@DrRaviRKumar•73.1K subscribers

34 Earn2Trade

@Earn2Trade•13.6K subscribers

35 Earning Funda

@earningfundaofficial•29.6K subscribers

36 EQUITY STAR

@EQUITYSTAR•43.4K subscribers

37 Equity2Commodity

@Equity2commodity•511K subscribers

38 exTRADING

@exTRADING•38.4K subscribers

39 FBN Trading

@FBNtradingOfficial•1.3K subscribers

40 Fearless Trader Shivam

@FearlessTraderShivam•382K subscribers

41 Financial Astrology

@FinancialAstrology•4.53K subscribers

42 Financial Frontline

@financial.frontline•26.2K subscribers

43 FinYugs

@finyugs•10.4K subscribers

44 FXSMART

@FXSMARTT•17.3K subscribers

45 Gediya Nitin

@Gediyanitin_878•2.84K subscribers

46 Ghanshyam Verma

@GhanshyamVermaTrading•7.2K subscribers

47 GUI Trading

@guitrading•14.9K subscribers

48 Harshubh

@Astroisking•157K subscribers

49 Help Of Stock Market

@VIJAYHOSM•388K subscribers

50 howtoSTATA

@howtoSTATA•27.1K subscribers

51 IITian Trader

@iitiantrader•1.05M subscribers

52 Indrazith Shantharaj

@indrazith1•23.5K subscribers

53 InvestarIndia

@investarindia•27.3K subscribers

54 Investing Daddy

@ltpcalculator•790K subscribers

55 Investobull

@investobull-•214K subscribers

56 Investographer

@Investographer•914K subscribers

57 Investonomics By Saurabh

@IBSaurabh•263K subscribers

58 Jayesh Thakkar (SEBI Registered Research Analyst)

@intradaygeeks•20.5K subscribers

61 Learn with Mukul Agrawal

@learnwithmukulagrawal•124K subscribers

62 Learning with Earning

@TradewithAjay3•862 subscribers

63 Learnn with KK

@learnnwithkk77•19K subscribers

64 LETS LEARN TRADING

@drkjsingh•6.15K subscribers

65 LIFT SKILL

@arvindutareja•38.2K subscribers

66 Logical Trader

@logicaltrader•26.8K subscribers

67 Magic Indicator Strategies

@magicindicatorstrategies•119K subscribers

68 Magical Trading

@MagicalTrading•115K subscribers

69 Mahesh Chander Kaushik

@Maheshchanderkaushik•503K subscribers

70 Malkansview

@Malkansview1•945K subscribers

71 Market Accurate

@MarketAccurate•19.6K subscribers

72 Market Analysis with Sarjeet Rathi

@sarjeetrathiofficial•26.2K subscribers

73 MARKET FUNDA

@marketfundaa•16.3K subscribers

74 Market Trader

@Marketrader1•166K subscribers

75 MCX Khiladi

@MCXKhiladiOfficial•24.6K subscribers

76 Metaverse Trading Academy

@metaversetradingacademy•22.7K subscribers

77 MH FinServ

@MHFinServ•350 subscribers

78 Mind Math Money

@MindMathMoney•155K subscribers

79 Momentrade

@Momentrade•3.57K subscribers

80 Moti Rakam

@MotiRakam•27K subscribers

81 MrPersonalTrader

@MrPersonalTrader•5.14K subscribers

83 Nataraj Malavade

@natarajmalavade•22.2K subscribers

84 Neerav Vadera - G7FX

@nvforex•46.5K subscribers

85 Options 2.0

@Options2.0•21.4K subscribers

86 ParaTrade

@ParaTrade•5.84K subscribers

87 PhyZan

@phyzan•29.3K subscribers

88 PineTrades

@pinetrades•81.6K subscribers

89 Power of Trading

@PowerofTradingStrategies•301K subscribers

90 Prateek Singh – LearnApp

@PrateekSinghLearnApp•353K subscribers

91 Praveen Pathiyil

@PraveenPathiyil•23K subscribers

92 Prime Technical

@primetechnical8728•5.56K subscribers

93 Profit G

@Profitg12•11K subscribers

94 Prosecurities Himanshu Miglani

@ProSecuritieshimanshumiglani•293K subscribers

95 Pushkar Raj Thakur: Stock Market Educator ⊠

@PushkarRajThakurOfficial•12.7M subscribers

96 R K Arora - Finance & Happiness

@RKArora•15.1K subscribers

97 RAFA Ji

@rafaji•4.37K subscribers

98 Rayner Teo

@tradingwithrayner•1.96M subscribers

99 Retail Scalper

@retailscalper1120•737 subscribers

100 Rinkal Lodhi

@RinkalLodhi•4.45K subscribers

101 Rishi Money

@RishiMoney•231K subscribers

102 Sachin Trades

@sachintrades•3.84K subscribers

103 Sagar Sinha

@SagarSinhaMotivation•2.88M subscribers

104 Secrets of Trading

@Tradingsecretes.•10.5K subscribers

105 SIDDHARTH BHANUSHALI

@SIDDHARTHBHANUSHALI•1.19M subscribers

106 Silent Trader

@SilentTrader24•24.5K subscribers

107 SNS Gyan

@snsgyan•20.4K subscribers

108 Soheil PKO

@SoheilPKO•133K subscribers

109 Solvy Help

@solvyhelp•2.46K subscribers

110 Soumya Das

@soumyadas7399•2.91K subscribers

111 Startegy Land

@StartegyLand•2.73K subscribers

112 Stock 4 Retail

@Stock4Retail•805K subscribers

113 STOCK247

@STOCK247bypoojasingh•277K subscribers

114 Stock Accurate

@StockAccurate•70.7K subscribers

115 Stock Burner

@stockburnerofficial•785K subscribers

116 STOCK IDEAS

@stockideas1201•4.78K subscribers

117 Stock Market OK

@StockMarketOK•49.4K subscribers

118 Stock Market Training - T4W

@StockMarketTrainingT4W•10.2K subscribers

119 Stock Market University

@StockMarketUniversity•88.1K subscribers

120 Stock Market Unlimited

@stockmarketunlimited•35.3K subscribers

121 Stock Market का Commando

@stockmarketcommando•1.9M subscribers

122 Stock Pro

@Stockpro•331K subscribers

123 Stocks How

@stocks_how•18.6K subscribers

124 Stocks Rin

@StocksRin•55K subscribers

125 STOCKS TV.

@stockstv•762 subscribers

126 StocksTechnoFunda

@stockstechnofunda•12K subscribers

127 Stop loss Hunter

@StoplossHunter•3.25K subscribers

128 swing trader

@swingtrader1243•4.49K subscribers

129 Swing Trading Boom

@swingtradingboom9436•19.3K subscribers

130 Switch Stats

@switchstats•94K subscribers

131 T-दक्ष Trading

@TheHarshDalal•69.1K subscribers

132 The big bull bank nifty

@bankniftyfreecall80•22.7K subscribers

133 The Chartistt

@TheChartistt•244K subscribers

134 The IITian Trader

@theiitiantrader_official•162K subscribers

135 The Live Trade Bull

@TheLiveTradeBull•484 subscribers

136 THE MARKETVERSE

@themarketverse•15.9K subscribers

137 The Trade Trekker

@TheTradeTrekker•9.16K subscribers

138 The Trading Geek

@TheTradingGeeks•29.7K subscribers

139 The Trading Legacy

@TheTradingLegacy7084•26K subscribers

140 Trade Hunter

@tradehunter458•103K subscribers

141 Trade karo India

@TradekaroIndia•6.35K subscribers

142 Trade Swings

@TradeSwings•328K subscribers

143 Trade With Dr Devendra

@TradeWithDrDevendra•113K subscribers

144 Trade with Sanchit

@tradewithsanchit•53.8K subscribers

145 Trader Sakshi

@TraderSakshi•114K subscribers

146 Trader Shivay

@tradershivay•3.67K subscribers

147 Traders Monopoly

@TradersMonopoly•30.4K subscribers

148 TRADING

@TRADING1026•18.7K subscribers

149 Trades By Mo

@tradesbymo•18.8K subscribers

150 Trading Arena

@TradersArena•30.2K subscribers

151 Trading Astrolo G

@tradingastrolog•21.6K subscribers

152 TRADING CAFE INDIA

@TRADINGCAFEINDIA•119K subscribers

153 Trading Chanakya

@TradingChanakya•465K subscribers

154 Trading Geeks

@TradingGeeks•119K subscribers

155 Trading India

@tradingindia•40.7K subscribers

156 Trading Pathshla

@tradingpathshla5153•1.07K subscribers

157 TRADING RUSH

@TRADINGRUSH•333K subscribers

158 Trading source

@tradingsourcebyAshish•6.06K subscribers

159 Trading Techstreet

@TradingTechstreet•748K subscribers

160 Trading With Rohan

@TradingWithRohan•19.5K subscribers

161 Trading With Vivek

@TradingWithVivek•564K subscribers

162 TREND TRADER KARAN

@TRENDTRADERKARAN•301K subscribers

163 UD Trend

@UDTrend•73.3K subscribers

164 Uday Mandal

@uday_mandal•18.1K subscribers

165 Vibhor Varshney

@VibhorVarshney•253K subscribers

166 Vihan Capital

@VihanCapitals•579 subscribers

167 Vivek Bajaj

@VivekBajaj•900K subscribers

168 VRDNation

@VRDNation•282K subscribers

169 Wealth SaGa

@wealthsagaofficial•965K subscribers

170 WealthKosh

@wealthkosh9511•7.83K subscribers

171 जीतने 🎯 की कला

@jeetnekikala•167K subscribers

Afterword

As I close this journey of writing, I am filled with a deep sense of reflection and gratitude. The path that led me here was not always clear, but it was one defined by profound transformations—both in the world around us and within ourselves. The year 2020 was a watershed moment, a time when the world as we knew it was turned upside down. Yet, amidst the chaos and uncertainty, one thing became abundantly clear: the resilience of the human spirit.

This book is more than a guide to stock trading; it is a celebration of our ability to adapt, to learn, and to grow in the face of adversity. It is about the courage to embrace change, to equip ourselves with practical skills, and to dare to step into the unknown. It is a reminder that life is a journey, not just of survival, but of thriving—even when the odds are stacked against us.

In the end, it is not the knowledge we accumulate that shapes our destiny, but the skills we master and the actions we take. Socrates wisely said, "The only good is knowledge and the only evil is ignorance." But in our modern world, this truth has evolved. Today, the only good is knowledge that is applied, and the only evil is potential that remains untapped. This book is a testament to that belief. It is a call to action, urging you not just to learn but to apply what you learn, to turn your knowledge into power, and to unlock the limitless potential within yourself.

As you turn these pages, may you find the inspiration to continue your own journey, to never stop learning, and to always seek growth. May this book serve as a beacon of hope and a source of strength as you navigate the challenges and opportunities that lie ahead. Remember, your journey is yours alone, and it is only just beginning. May you walk it with courage, wisdom, and determination.

If you have generated more interest and need more help to master the skill of stock trading, I am ready to be your "Driving Coach". You can get more details, and updates on www.skillchampions.in.

Nikhil Zaveri

About the Author

CA (Dr.) Nikhil Zaveri is a well-acclaimed academician, with an impressive tenure as the former Vice-Chancellor (Provost) of GSFC University, Vadodara. A Gold Medalist in M.Com, a Chartered Accountant, and a Ph.D., he is also an alumnus of the prestigious Indian Institute of Management, Ahmedabad. Dr. Zaveri's visionary leadership at Charutar Vidya Mandal's SEMCOM for over 20 years transformed the institution into a powerhouse of management education, with groundbreaking initiatives like India's pioneering postgraduate program in E-Commerce and E-Business. His relentless pursuit of academic excellence led SEMCOM to earn consecutive two-times 'A' grade accreditation from NAAC under his stewardship.

Recognized among the top 15 business professors globally on the basis of students' choice by *The Economist* magazine, Dr. Zaveri has also served as Dean of the Faculty of Management at Sardar Patel University and as a long-standing member of its Syndicate (Board). He was also honoured with Fellowship by the Indian Institute of Materials Management, New Delhi. With over three decades of experience, he has authored numerous articles and research papers and designed Management Development Programs for top-tier professionals and officials. He has been a renowned speaker on Management on public platforms of several institutions and business organzations. Notably, he was honored by the then Chief Minister of Gujarat, Shri Narendra Modi, for his contributions to educational excellence. He is the certified Independent Director.

A revered mentor in the academic world, Dr. Zaveri has inspired many young educators to excel in their teaching and foster meaningful student relationships. Currently, he is pioneering work in the science of happiness, offering guidance as a Happiness Coach to individuals and corporations alike. His online academy, skillchampions.in, is a significant part of the *"Atma Nirbhar Bharat"* initiative, focusing on developing stock trading skills among aspiring professionals as well as homemakers.

www.ingramcontent.com/pod-product-compliance
Ingram Content Group UK Ltd.
Pitfield, Milton Keynes, MK11 3LW, UK
UKHW060016051026
15591UKWH00002B/231
9798895563908